C000294519

A GUIDE TO THE REVELATION

TEF Study Guides

This series was first sponsored and subsidized by the Theological Education Fund of the WCC in response to requests from Africa, Asia, the Caribbean, and the Pacific. The books are prepared by and in consultation with theological teachers in those areas. Special attention is given to problems of interpretation and application arising there as well as in the west, and to the particular needs of students using English as a second language.

General Editors: Daphne Terry and Nicholas Beddow

ALREADY PUBLISHED

IN PREPARATION

TEF Study Guide 20

A GUIDE TO
THE REVELATION

David H. van Daalen

First published in 1986
SPCK
Holy Trinity Church
Marylebone Road
London NW1 4DU

© David H. van Daalen 1986

Unless otherwise stated the Scripture quotations in this publication are from the Revised Standard Version of the Bible
(Ecumenical Edition), copyrighted 1973 by the Division of
Christian Education of the National Council of the Churches
of Christ in the USA.

The photographs are reproduced by courtesy of USPG
(p. 4); National Tourist Organization of Greece (p. 23); Lee/
Dennis, Methodist Information (p. 35); Barnabys Picture
Library (pp. 43, 57, 196); CMS (pp. 85, 149); Third World
Photographs by Sean Sprague (pp. 117, 132, 168a); and
Camera Press Ltd.

British Library Cataloguing in Publication Data

Van Daalen, David H.
    A guide to the Revelation.—(TEF study guide; 20)
    1. Bible.N.T. Revelation—Commentaries
    I. Title   II. Society for Promoting Christian
    Knowledge   III. Series
    228'.07   BS2825.3

Printed in Great Britain by
the University Press, Cambridge

ISBN 0 281 04193 8 (net edition)
ISBN 0 281 04194 6 (non-net edition for Africa, Asia, S. Pacific, and Caribbean)

Contents

Preface

A book such as this Study Guide could not be the work of one man only. I must acknowledge my debt to many commentators and others who have written on the Revelation. Mentioning G. B. Caird, R. H. Charles, E. Lohmeyer, E. Lohse, K. H. Miskotte, J. Sweet, and J. de Zwaan, I am aware that I am leaving many names out. I further wish to thank the members of the Harrington URC Bible Study Group, with whom I worked through the Revelation during one winter session, and Professor James D. G. Dunn, Dr Zolile Mbali, Dr Andrew Wingate and Dr Sonny Yegadon, who read the manuscript and gave many helpful comments and suggestions. Last but not least, I wish to express my gratitude to the Editors, the Rev. Nicholas Beddow, and Miss Daphne Terry who prepared the manuscript for publication and found the illustrations, and without whose labour this Study Guide could not have been completed.

David H. van Daalen

Using This Guide

The plan of this Guide follows much the same pattern as that of other biblical Guides in the series.

In his *Introduction* the author sets the scene for our study of the Revelation by providing a brief survey of its historical and literary background, of John's purpose in writing it and its meaning for his first readers, and of its relevance for Christians today. In the light of understanding gained from close study of the book, the *Postscript* points to the remarkable similarities, as well as differences, between John's time and our own; and reminds us, as John reminded the first century Christians, of the challenges, dangers, and opportunities confronting the Church, whose task must always be to try and ensure that the will of God in Christ is done in the world.

Study of the Revelation itself has been divided into short sections according to natural breaks in the text. But before beginning their work readers may find it helpful to consider how they can make the best use of this Guide.

Each section consists of:

1. A *Summary* of the passage, indicating very briefly the subject matter it contains. Of course the summary is not intended as a substitute for the words of the Bible itself, which need to be read very carefully at each stage of our study.
2. *Notes* on particular words and points of possible difficulty, especially as relating to the historical context, and to other parts of the Bible.
3. An *Interpretation* of the passage as it applied to those for whom it was written, and as we should understand it and apply its teaching in our lives today.

SPECIAL NOTES

The four Special Notes, on Angels, the Letters to the Churches, the symbolic use of Numbers in the Revelation as in other apocalyptic literature, and on the Devil and his works, have been separated from the sections dealing directly with the text, partly because of their length, and partly because each refers to more than one section.

STUDY SUGGESTIONS AND QUESTIONS

Suggestions for further study and review are included at the end of each section. Besides enabling students working alone to check their own progress, they provide subjects for individual and group research, and topics for discussion. They are of four main sorts:

1. *Words:* to help readers check and deepen their understanding of important words and phrases.
2. *Content:* to help readers check the work they have done, and make sure they have fully grasped the ideas and points of teaching given.
3. *Bible:* to relate the ideas and teaching in the Revelation with ideas and teaching found in other parts of the Bible.
4. *Application:* To help readers think out the practical relevance of John's words to their own lives and to the work of the Church in the world. Many of these are suitable for use in a group as well as for students working alone.

The best way to use these Study Suggestions is: first, re-read the Bible passage; second, read the appropriate section of the Guide once or twice; and then do the work suggested, either in writing or in group discussion, without looking at the Guide again unless instructed to do so.

The *Key to Study Suggestions* at the end of the Guide will enable you to check your work on those questions which can be checked in this way. In most cases the Key does not give the answer to a question: it shows where an answer is to be found.

Please note that all these suggestions are only *suggestions*. Some readers may not wish to use them. Some teachers may wish to select only those most relevant to the needs of their particular students, or to substitute questions of their own.

APPENDIX

The Appendix lists the first Roman Emperors from Julius Caesar (48–44 BC) to Hadrian (AD 117–138), with very brief notes on the character of each and the chief events of each reign. It thus helps to round out the picture given in the Introduction, of what life in the Roman Empire was like immediately before, during, and after the time when John was writing.

INDEX

The Index includes only the more important names of people and places and the main themes which appear in the Revelation or are discussed in the Guide. Bold-type page references are however provided to show where particular subjects are treated in detail.

BIBLE VERSION

The English translation of the Bible used in the Guide is the *Revised Standard Version of the Bible (Ecumenical Edition)* (RSV). Reference is also made to the *New English Bible* (NEB), the *Jerusalem Bible* (JB), and the *Good News Bible* (GNB), where these help to show the meaning more clearly, and in one or two cases to the *Authorized* (King James) *Version* (AV) and the *New International Version* (NIV).

Further Reading

INTRODUCTORY BOOKS

William Barclay, *Revelation* (Daily Study Bible). St Andrew Press, Edinburgh

T. F. Glasson, *The Revelation of John*, Cambridge University Press, 1965

L. Morris, *Revelation*. Tyndale Press, London, & Eerdmans, Grand Rapids, 1969

R. H. Preston & A. T. Hanson, *The Revelation of St John the Divine* (Torch Bible Commentaries). SCM Press, London, & Macmillan, New York, 1949

MORE ADVANCED BOOKS

G. R. Beasley-Murray, *The Book of Revelation* (New Century Bible). Oliphants, London, 1974

G. B. Caird, *The Revelation of St John the Divine* (NT Commentaries). Black, London, 1966 (specially recommended)

R. H. Mounce, *The Book of Revelation* (New International Commentary on the NT). Paternoster, Exeter, 1977

John Sweet, *Revelation* (SCM Pelican Commentaries). SCM Press, London, 1979 (specially recommended)

Introduction

Towards the end of the first century AD there appeared in Asia Minor a book which has fascinated and baffled Christians ever since it was written. Of all the books of the Bible none seems to be more baffling than the Revelation of John, but at the same time it is so fascinating, that once we start to read it carefully, it will hold us. Indeed, the very strangeness of its language gives the impression that here are some profound mysteries to be delved into.

That impression is very right. The Revelation of John deserves close study. But unless people are familiar with the sort of language John used, they can easily misinterpret his message. Many serious students of the Revelation have been led astray by their misunderstanding of its language.

The reason for such misunderstanding is obvious. Many people think that there is no other book quite like the Revelation to John. There are some passages of a similar kind in the books of Ezekiel, Zechariah, and Daniel, and the Greek version of the Old Testament contains the book 4 Esdras (sometimes confusingly called 2 Esdras), which some English translations include among the Apocrypha. But there is a widespread feeling that the Revelation is unique.

As a matter of fact, the period between 200 BC and AD 100 produced many writings of a similar kind. The Revelation of John was one of the last of them, and when this sort of book went out of fashion, these writings were no longer copied, and the existing copies were forgotten and left to moulder in the cellars of monasteries or synagogues, or thrown out altogether. Only during the present century have many copies been found again in forgotten corners of ancient monasteries or during excavations, especially in Egypt and the Holy Land, where the climate preserves most of what is buried under the sand.

The rediscovery of this 'apocalyptic' literature, as it was called (from the Greek word *apokalypsis* meaning 'revelation'), has helped tremendously to make it easier for us to understand the Revelation of John. We now no longer have to guess what his strange expressions and symbols mean.

But if we want to read the Revelation with understanding, we must keep some important points in mind. Whatever this book means to us (and we believe it means a great deal to us), it must also have meant something to the people for whom it was first written. If not, they would not have kept it and copied it, and it would never have been included in

1

the Bible. Moreover, however difficult, or even obscure, it may seem to us, John can never have wanted his book to be obscure (everybody writes in order to be understood). So before we begin to read the Revelation, we must try to answer some questions. Why did John write this book? When did he write it? Who was this John? And what is this strange form in which he wrote the Revelation?

Why?

There can be little doubt as to why John wrote the Revelation. The visions which this book describes showed John and his readers 'what must soon take place' (1.1), in order to warn, guide and comfort them. We must stress the importance of the word 'soon'. If we believe that John's visions were a genuine revelation from God, it is easy to see that he must have written them down in order to help people in the situation in which they would soon find themselves; not in order to answer the questions of people who were merely inquisitive. So most of his book would be about the present or the near future, with sometimes a reference to the recent past. John expected that in the very near future the Church would suffer persecution, and the purpose of the book was to warn people of what lay ahead, to comfort them in their distress, and to show them the way through. But for this purpose it was important that he should not only promise that there would be an end to the coming persecution. He had also to assure them that those who suffered for their faith were safe in God's hand, and that not only the forthcoming events, but history itself, would end according to God's plan.

However, we can define John's purpose a little more precisely. The letters to Sardis and Laodicea (3.1–6, 14–22) show clearly that some Churches were very much at home in the world. On the surface all was well; at that time the Church did not suffer any severe persecution, and it was tempting for Christians to think that it would be possible to be good and faithful disciples of Christ without suffering any hardship. John wanted to wake such Christians up. All is not well, he was saying. The Roman regime, benevolent though it might seem, was still totalitarian. It demanded people's total allegiance. The faithful should not be deceived, and should not give the State the total obedience it demanded. Total obedience was due to God alone.

Indeed, some Christians were already under pressure. John did not have to warn them of the perils ahead, for they had already experienced them. Not many Christians had become martyrs for their faith; in most cases, it seems, the penalty was no more than a short spell of imprisonment. But worse days were coming. To such people, who already saw the beginnings of the troubles to come, John gave the encouragement they needed, by reminding them that Christ was in command.

Thus John's message had two sides: 'Be warned! And be encouraged!

In spite of all opposition, He who loves us, and gave Himself for us, has already won the victory, and He will get us through!'

When?

What we have said about John's purpose, leads to the next question: when was there a time when such a book would have been required?

For a long time it was taken for granted that John must have written during a time of persecution, and the time which most writers on the subject suggested was the reign of Domitian, who was Emperor from AD 81–96. But we have no evidence that there was any persecution under Domitian. Certainly, in his later years he demanded to be called 'Lord and god', and some prominent Roman citizens were put to death for refusing to do so. A few Jews and Christians may have been among the victims. But there is no evidence that he took any measures aimed specifically at either Jews or Christians.

In view of the fact that, as far as we know, there was no real persecution under Domitian, John Robinson, in *Redating the New Testament*, argues that John must have written earlier, shortly after the persecution under Nero in AD 64–65. Until that time Christians had generally been protected by Roman law. The Christian faith was regarded as one form of the Jewish faith, and as Judaism was a *religio licita*, that is, a legally permitted religion, the Christians shared in that privilege. Indeed, Jews were in some ways specially privileged, in that they were the only people exempt from the obligation to worship the official gods of the Empire; and again, the Christians shared in that privilege. Gentile Christians were regarded as converts to a particular brand of Judaism, so they too were protected by the law.

The persecution of 64–65 was not, strictly speaking, a religious persecution. In 64 a large part of Rome was destroyed by fire, with terrible loss of life. The Emperor Nero, who was known to have ambitious plans for redeveloping the city, was suspected of arson, and in order to avert the suspicion, he accused the Christians. Large numbers of Christians were seized and put to death, often under appalling tortures. Peter and Paul were probably among the victims.

This first large-scale persecution was confined to Rome. Christians elsewhere heard of it, and were shocked by it, but were not directly affected. But one important thing had changed. The authorities had learned to distinguish between Jews and Christians, and Christianity stopped being a legally permitted religion. Christians were no longer under the protection of the law.

Robinson's argument is that the Revelation must have been written under the impact of that persecution under Nero. But must John have written in a time of persecution? He mentions only one martyr, Antipas (2.13), and takes it for granted that ten days in gaol is the worst most

John's purpose was to 'warn people of what lay ahead, comfort them in their distress, and show them the way through' (p. 2).

Bishop Desmond Tutu likewise warned the South African people today, both white and black, of the conflict and distress that might lie ahead, saying to Christians there: 'We have been given the ministry of reconciliation, but it cannot be a cheap reconciliation (it cost God the death of His Son).' In what ways can victims of oppression work for reconciliation with their oppressors?

Christians could expect. That sounds like harassment, but not like savage persecution. John must have written later than the days of Nero.

Nero's reign lasted only four more years (he committed suicide in AD 68), and his reputation was so bad, that later Emperors did not care to follow his example. Christians were no longer under the protection of the law, but this did not necessarily lead to persecution. Many other illegal cults were practised in the Empire, and even in Rome itself, without suffering any hardship whatsoever. And for some years the Church enjoyed relative peace. A few Christians did indeed suffer hardship, but they were exceptions.

All the same, the Church was heading for trouble, and the trouble would arise particularly from the worship of the Emperor. Some of the eastern provinces of the Roman Empire had once belonged to kingdoms where the rulers had been regarded as gods on earth. Now that they were under the Roman Emperor they looked upon him as a god. In 29 BC the city of Pergamum requested the privilege of dedicating a temple to the divine Augustus. The Romans received this request with amused smiles. To a Roman, Augustus was merely the head of state. Rome was, in name at least, a republic, and the Emperor was merely a servant of the Popular Assembly. But if peoples who were subject to Rome wanted to call him a god, they were welcome. So the request was granted, and the people of Pergamum built their temple for Augustus.

But this imperial cult soon spread to Rome itself. When Augustus died, the Senate declared that he had become a god, and this custom was continued at the death of later Emperors. Caligula (AD 37–41) pretended to be a god while he was still alive, but no one believed him (though no one dared to contradict him). But when in 88 Domitian demanded to be called 'Lord and god', he was taken seriously. Some people objected (and were punished severely), but most people accepted his claim. And in later years the worship of the Emperor became more and more an important part of the official religion of the Roman Empire.

Those among the authorities who took their religion seriously regarded the worship of the state gods and the Emperor as necessary for the security of the state: they did not want the gods to turn against Rome. Non-conformity, that is to say, a refusal to join in the state religion, was in their view dangerous to the state. But even those magistrates who did not take their religion seriously, still felt that people who did not join in the state ceremonies were enemies of the state.

The authorities were not inspired by excessive cruelty. They were in fact more humane than some tyrants of recent times. Their aim was not to kill but to convert. In many cases only one leading Christian was martyred to set an example, and the others were left unmolested. Considering the increasingly large numbers of Christians, there were surprisingly few martyrs. The authorities wanted their obedience, not their death.

The method was simple. As the Emperor Trajan wrote to Pliny, the governor of Bithynia (in what is now Turkey), 'These people must not be hunted out; if they are brought before you and the charge against them is proved, they must be punished, but in the case of anyone who denies that he is a Christian, and makes it clear that he is not by offering prayers to our gods, he is to be pardoned. . . .' Pliny had already written how he dealt with the matter: 'I have asked them in person if they are Christians, and if they admit it, I repeat the question a second and third time, with a warning of the punishment awaiting them. If they persist, I order them to be led away for execution.' Pliny thought it was a sad business that he had to punish them, for they were all people of exemplary conduct. But he was convinced that they must be made to conform, and was confident that 'a great many people could be reformed, if they were given the opportunity to repent.'

It is clear from his book that John wrote at a time when being a Christian was not yet punishable by death. But the clouds were gathering. Many Christians did not see it, or did not want to see it, but the state religion would soon claim many victims.

John must therefore have written after the time of relative peace which ended when Domitian claimed divine honours for himself in AD 88, and before the beginning of the reign of Trajan (AD 98–117). That is to say, the traditional date, towards the end of the reign of Domitian (AD 96) is probably correct.

Who?

For many centuries it was taken for granted that the Revelation of John was written by the same man who also wrote the Gospel according to John and the three Letters of John, and that this man was the apostle John.

But there are strong objections to that idea. The style and language of the Revelation are so different from those of the Gospel and the Letters, that it is difficult to think of the same man having written them all. The Gospel and the Letters were written in exquisite Greek, not exactly what pedants would call 'good Greek', but certainly by someone who used the language quite beautifully. The Revelation on the other hand, though it has a certain beauty of its own, was written in what most scholars would call a barbaric Greek. It was therefore tempting to think that, if these books were written by the same man, the Revelation must have been written when his Greek was still poor, and the other books later, when his mastery of the language had improved.

However, closer examination of John's language shows that the Revelation was not written by a man who was just beginning to learn

Greek. He had no problem about expressing himself clearly, and his Greek is usually perfectly easy to understand, easier sometimes than that of the great classical authors. It is the sort of Greek that a man like the apostle John might well have spoken since he was a child, a Greek not always grammatical, a Greek influenced by his native Aramaic and by the language of the Septuagint (the Greek version of the Old Testament), but definitely not the Greek of someone who is just learning the language.

Thus the language does not tell us who the author was, for there must have been thousands of Jews who had spoken Greek all their lives, but never learned to speak it like a native Greek. It does not even prove for certain that the John who wrote the Revelation did not write the Gospel and the Letters of John, for those books could have been written in Aramaic, and translated into Greek by someone who wrote a different style.

All that we can know must be found out from his book. He was a Jewish Christian called John. John (Jehohanan or Johanan in the Old Testament) was a common name; the Bible mentions at least twenty-five men of that name. It must have been his real name, for if it had been a pen-name he would have made it clear who was that famous John whose name he was using. But there is no reason to think that he must have been the same John who wrote the Gospel and the Letters: he could have been, but we do not know. And he could have been the apostle John, but again we do not know. We do know, however, that he was on the Island of Patmos 'on account of the word of God and the testimony of Jesus'. So he was a preacher of the gospel. We do not know if he was conducting a mission on that island, or whether he had been banished there, though the latter seems much more likely, especially as he wrote about sharing the tribulation of his readers (1.9). It also seems pretty certain that he was well known to the Churches in Asia Minor, for he took it for granted, when he wrote 'I, John, your brother', that his readers knew who he was.

How?

John called his book an 'Apocalypse', a Revelation, which tells us straight away what method he was using to convey his message. Revelation is an important notion. Through God alone can God be known; in other words, we can only know God if it pleases Him to reveal Himself to us. Thus Paul wrote that the gospel is the revelation of God's righteousness (Romans 1.16,17).

However, the word could also be used in a particular sense for writings of a particular kind, which we call 'apocalyptic'. Apocalyptic was born among the Jews after the nation had lost its political independence. Israel had been crushed under the power of gentile nations, and it seemed natural to ask whether that meant that the God of Israel had been defeated by the gods of those nations. People might believe in theory that the LORD God of Israel was the living God, beside whom the gods of the nations were of no account. But they saw the very real power of those gods all around them, and they seemed very mighty indeed.

Apocalyptic writers gave the answer to that question in a form required by those who were impressed by the power of the gods; a visionary manner using the imaginative language of ancient myths, both Canaanite myths with which the Israelites had long been familiar, and also Babylonian and Iranian myths, with which they had recently become acquainted. In their writings these writers told of visions in which it had been revealed to them that the powers which seem to rule the world are at best mere tools in the hand of the living God, or at worst enemies of His, who will be overcome and destroyed. Whatever strange turns the history of the world may take, and whatever may happen to individuals while the present age lasts, God has the whole world in His hand, and the end will be according to His plan.

An apocalypse presents, in language borrowed from myth, a summary of world history, and particularly of the end of history. Its chief purpose, however, was not to predict the future, but to warn, guide, and comfort the readers. In this respect the apocalyptic writers stood in the tradition of the Hebrew prophets, whose prophecies were not accurate predictions of the future, but warnings about the inevitable outcome of people's behaviour. Their task was not to satisfy inquisitive people's curiosity, but to comfort those who were distressed, and distress the comfortable.

The prophets and the apocalyptic writers wrote for their own times, but also looked forward to the future. However, the prophets saw the future as being to a great extent the outcome of people's actions. They believed that God's work was carried out largely through human beings. They knew that God has other hands besides ours to carry out his plans, but they emphasized the importance of human action.

The apocalyptic writers on the other hand laid far less stress on the human aspect. In their view the real field of God's action lay away from the human scene. They believed that the decisive battle which was to ensure God's victory was not fought by human combatants but by supernatural powers.

Thus these writers saw the future, when God will not only *be* King but will be *seen* to be King, not as the result of earthly events, but as a complete reversal of the whole creation, that is to say, as the coming of a new heaven and a new earth. And this in turn meant that the future of the individual, as they saw it, was no longer bound up in the future of the nation, but was to be brought about by the resurrection of the dead. On those two points the apocalyptic writers were given insights into important aspects of God's truth.

John used the same sort of language and word-pictures as earlier apocalyptic writers. As he was one of the last people to do so, later readers have found his book very difficult, and have sometimes thought that he was being obscure on purpose. Nothing could be further from the truth. He wanted to be understood, and he knew that his readers were simple people. And the first readers would have understood his language very well.

In every language people use symbols and metaphors. The trouble is that various languages use them differently. In Chinese tradition a dragon is a benevolent creature, to John a dragon represented evil powers. An Englishman regards a dog as a faithful companion, to John a dog was a dirty scavenger. In countries with a cold climate the sun is regarded as the giver of life, in hot and dry countries the sun is the 'copper fiend' which brings drought and famine. In some parts of the world white symbolizes mourning, but in other lands mourning is expressed by black.

Therefore we must not use our own understanding of certain symbols to interpret John's Revelation. We have to ask in every case what a particular symbol meant to John and his first readers. Fortunately much more is known about the origin, the usage, and the meaning of the symbols which John used than people sometimes think. De-coding the language of the Revelation is not an easy task; but it can be done, and in this Guide we shall attempt to do so. But we must beware of using our own imagination too freely, and we should not listen to the 'interpretations' given by people who want to use the Revelation for their own purposes. It is easy for people who care little for the truth to deceive those who accept all they are told. But we do not have to be so easily led, and there are sound scholars who can give us reliable guidance. They are not infallible, and they may disagree about the interpretation of some details, but it is not really too difficult to find out what John was trying to say.

The Revelation for Today

When John wrote the Revelation, it was highly relevant to his readers. But we may well ask, what does it mean to us? Most of the events for which John wanted to prepare people took place long ago. We may find it interesting to learn how he approached the problems of his time, and we may read his book as a source of historic information. But this is not our chief object in reading the Bible. We want to know how this book affects us, and what it has to teach us about how, as Christians, we should *live*.

As a matter of fact, the Revelation of John, a book written many centuries ago, and tailored precisely for the needs of particular people, has much to say to us too. The problems underlying the situation in which Christians found themselves in John's days are not so very different from those which have confronted Christians in later times. Consequently there have always been people who saw in some part of the Revelation an accurate picture of their own time, and they were right in thinking that John had something to say to them.

But we must be careful. One of the difficulties which many people have when they read the Bible, is that they forget that every part of the Bible was originally written for particular people in particular circumstances. We do not have that problem with other books, but many people feel that the Bible is not like other books. They tend to reason that, if the Bible is the Word of God, then every part of it must apply to all people. It therefore does not seem to matter, who wrote any particular part of it; when, where, or why he wrote; or who were the first people to read it. But if we believe that God is a living God, who cares for real people, we ought to see that His word cannot be like that.

Another mistake would be to expect guidance from texts taken at random, without asking what they meant when they were first written. There is a well-known story about a man who wanted to find guidance in the Bible by sticking a pin in it, opening the page where he had stuck the pin, and then, with his eyes closed, using the pin to point to the right verse. When he opened his eyes, he read, 'and he went and hanged himself' (Matt. 27.5b). Baffled at this 'answer', he tried again, and this time he read, 'Go and do likewise' (Luke 10.37b). Even more baffled, he tried a third time, and read, 'What you are going to do, do quickly' (John 13.27b). He had not yet learned that God's word is specific, spoken to real people in their actual circumstances.

Thus, for example, Abraham was called to leave Ur (Gen. 12), but I am not called to leave Ur, for I have never been there. Yet the story of Abraham's calling has much to say to us. If we read the story properly, it can tell us much about the way in which God guides His people, and about the obedience He requires of us.

Some commandments in the Bible apply to all people at all times. Other commandments may no longer apply at all, if they were given in view of particular circumstances which no longer exist or have any relevance for today. But the Bible contains more than commandments. The Bible is the story of God's continuing relationship with His people, the real living God and real people. If we do not see the people in the Bible as real people, and their lives as real human lives, then we cannot see ourselves in it, and we cannot hear the voice of the living God. God did not, and He does not, speak only in generalities. He speaks to people as they really are, in their particular circumstances at particular times.

The Revelation was originally written for Christians who had enjoyed

a time of relative peace, but were now beginning to face increasing pressure and danger. Their world was vastly different from ours. Yet the
pressures which they had to sustain, and the challenges which they had
to meet, were very similar to those which many people have to meet
today. Much has changed, but much more has remained the same.

For example, we shall only be able to see the relevance of Revelation
13, if we remember that the details of this chapter reflect what had
happened in the Roman Empire under Nero. That was the case even for
the first readers, for they too lived after Nero's days. There would never
be another ruler quite like Nero, and Christians had reason to be pro-
foundly thankful for that. But other tyrants would come, who were
different from Nero and yet attacking God's people just as Nero had
done.

And this line must be drawn further. John's vision was confined to the
Roman Empire. He and his first readers had no need to look further.
There will never be another Empire quite like Rome. Yet all totalitarian
regimes have much in common; they all display many of the same characteristics; we might say, there is a 'family likeness'. They are all different, yet in a deeper sense they are all the same. They have different
ideologies, but there is the same abuse of power. The slogans and the
tyrants come and go, but their oppressive tyranny keeps returning with
depressing monotony. Having a picture of the tyrant which John actually had in mind was helpful to the first readers, and can also help us to
see the family likeness in other, greater or smaller 'beasts'.

Throughout his book John shows things which become very important again and again in history. But they are not all important at all times,
or in all places, or to all people. Some parts may be extremely important
to us, but not to many other people; and other parts may be important to
some people, but not to us. The scenery changes, and we all play different parts, but the drama of human history is one story.

The Revelation of John is not the text of that drama. It is a commentary, or rather a series of commentaries, on the drama of human life and
history. Each of John's visions is a comment on the whole of human life,
history, and destiny. Each focuses on a different aspect, viewing it every
time from a different angle, but always seeing it in the light of Heaven.

The power of evil had, and has, its servants, who are able to inflict
terrible suffering on the faithful. Christians can expect this. But there is a
way through the minefield of adversities, and there is a glorious ending
to the story of human life. God is in command. Not only the individual
Christian, but the whole world is in God's hand. The power of evil is
strong, but in the end all its efforts are in vain. Whatever strange turns
the history of the world may take, in the end God's plan is carried out.
However strong the opposition, God's will prevails. If anyone thinks
these are just words, let him remember that Christ has already gained the

'Other tyrants would come, attacking God's people just as Nero had done . . . all totalitarian regimes have much in common' (p. 11).

Many of God's people, and many others as well, suffered and died in Uganda under the tyrannical regime of President Idi Amin – seen here reviewing his troops. How, if at all, can Christians help to prevent tyranny in the world?

victory on the cross. His cross is a solid fact: the victory has been won.

All this makes it very important that we should read John's book attentively. At first sight the Revelation makes a chaotic impression. But as we work through it we shall be able to see a definite plan.

We shall also discover that in several ways John differed from other apocalyptic writers. The Revelation of John is a revelation with a difference. Our first impression that this book is unique, is right after all. However, it seems best not to define those differences in advance, but to let John speak for himself.

STUDY SUGGESTIONS

WORDS

1. In what sense did the apocalyptic writers use the word 'revelation'?

CONTENT

2. What was the situation for the Church, when John wrote the Revelation? Was it a persecuted Church? Or was it a Church at rest? Give details.
3. What great change was brought about by the persecution of AD 64–65?
4. What was the 'Imperial cult', and how did it affect the Christians?
5. What do we know about the John who wrote the Revelation?
6. Why should it be important for us to know who wrote any book of the Bible, and why he wrote it?
7. Did the prophets of Israel chiefly aim to predict the future or to change the present?
8. Explain the chief differences between the prophets and the apocalyptic writers.
9. What important truths were first seen clearly by the apocalyptic writers?

BIBLE

10. What did Paul mean when he wrote that the righteousness of God is revealed in the gospel (Rom. 1.16, 17)?

APPLICATION

11. In what ways does the answer to Question 7 above affect us today?
12. Give examples of symbols traditionally used in your country, and of common symbols which have come to be used in modern times. Which, if any, of these symbols mean something else in other countries?

13. Why should it be important for us to know what any particular symbol meant for the writer of a book?

14. 'All this makes it very important that we should read John's book attentively' (p. 13). What are some of the points we should bear in mind in reading the Revelation? What are some mistaken ways of approaching the study of it that we should avoid?

1.1–8
Title and Preface

SUMMARY

1.1a: Title: 'Revelation of Jesus Christ'.
1.1b, 2: Subtitle, indicating in general terms what the book is about, and giving the name of the author.
1.3: How fortunate for the readers to have this book!
1.4–8: The preface, consisting of a greeting to the readers, and a doxology, a short praise-song, to Christ.

NOTES

1.1. Revelation of Jesus Christ. A 'revelation' was a particular sort of writing, setting forth things previously hidden, particularly God's plan for the world (see page 8).
Which God gave him. The phrase suggests that God had shown Jesus what must happen, and Jesus had shown John.
By sending his angel. This angel is not mentioned again until 19.9. We must probably picture this angel as a heavenly courier or guide, who accompanied John in his visions, and showed him the things at which he ought to look. But the angel himself was not important, so there was no need for John to keep mentioning him. When we tell our friends about a journey, we talk about the sights we have seen, rather than about the guide, and similarly John wrote about the visions he had seen, not about the angel.
1.3. Blessed is he who reads aloud. The word 'aloud' is not in the Greek, but is implied. In New Testament times reading was usually a group activity, with one person reading aloud to others. Most people could read, but books were very expensive, and few people could afford them. In Rome it was the fashion for authors to have reading parties, at which they would read parts of their books to invited guests. In later times it was the custom for monks at meals to listen to one of their number reading aloud. Here John was thinking of the Churches where the Revelation would be read to the congregation, just as lessons from Scripture are read aloud in Church services today.

This is of some importance for the interpretation of the Revelation (and of all the books of the Bible): the writers expected their books to be listened to carefully, rather than to be read silently.
1.4. The seven spirits who are before his throne. This expression was

probably inspired by the Jewish belief in seven archangels. But John was almost certainly not thinking of those. Seven is the number of divine perfection and completeness; and John was probably referring to the Holy Spirit, using the figure of seven to hint at His divine perfection.

1.5. Jesus Christ the faithful witness, the firstborn of the dead, and the ruler of kings on earth. The three attributes of Jesus are mentioned, because they were relevant to the first readers. The Christ in whom John and his readers believed, was the faithful witness who had revealed to them the truth about God; indeed, He *was* the truth about God (see John 14.6). He was the firstborn of the dead: His resurrection was the beginning of eternal life for all believers (see 1 Cor. 15). And He was the Ruler of kings on earth: powerful though earthly rulers might be, and frightening though their earthly power might be, Christ was in control.

To him who loves us. . . . This Ruler of kings on earth is not a stranger: He is that Jesus who loves His people; He has freed them from their sins by His own blood, He has made them into a new people under His rule, and they have been made priests to represent the human race before God.

Priests. A priest is a person who represents other people before God. In the Old Testament priests officiated at the offering of sacrifices and led people in prayer, and also prayed for them. But as go-betweens between God and the people they also represented God in certain functions, such as absolving people from their sins, and giving God's blessing to the congregation. (And it was laid down that only a priest could do these things; for it is God alone who can forgive sins and bless the people, and only priests, appointed by Him, can pronounce His forgiveness and His blessing.) When John says that Christ has made 'us', that is to say, all Christians, 'priests before God', he means that Christ has appointed the Christians to serve God on behalf of the whole human race. He was not writing about the order of the Church, and does not mention the fact that some people are ordained to carry out some specific God-given tasks in the Church. He simply observes that Christians serve God on behalf of all other people.

1.7. With the clouds. In the Old Testament clouds are a symbol of the presence of God. People are inclined to think that 'coming with the clouds' means that Jesus will be sitting on a cloud, and no doubt that is how some of the first readers would have pictured it. But that is not really what the expression means. 'Coming with the clouds' means that the coming of Jesus is a manifestation of God.

Every one who pierced him. This expression is derived from Zechariah 12.10–12, where God promises that He 'will pour out a spirit of compassion' on the house of David and the people of Jerusalem, so that, 'when they look on him whom they have pierced, they will mourn for him as one mourns for an only child'. The quotation suggests repentance, not punishment. Zechariah prophesied that Israel would repent.

But John speaks of 'all the tribes of the earth'. He may be hinting at the piercing of Jesus's side by a Roman soldier (John 19.34), but he is really thinking of all people who have rejected Jesus, and he foresees that at the end of time there will be world-wide repentance. But it will be a long time before that happens.

1.8. The Alpha and the Omega. These are the first and last letters of the Greek alphabet; the expression simply means, 'the first and the last', or 'the beginning and the end' (see v. 4).

The Almighty. The Greek word *pantokrator*, which is usually translated 'Almighty', really means 'the Ruler of all.' John was not trying to teach his readers a theory about God, but to assure them that God is completely in control of His creation. Later in the Revelation John used the same word for the Old Testament expression, 'the LORD of hosts'. This expression too speaks of God's power in practical terms: He is in command of His forces, so that His will be done.

INTERPRETATION

These verses contain the introductory matter to the book. The Greek title itself is simply, 'Revelation of Jesus Christ', not '*The* Revelation'. John was aware that there are other revelations (in fact, the Gospels also contain sayings of Jesus, which are 'revelations' in the sense in which the apocalyptic writers used the word, e.g. in Mark 13; Matt. 25). The writer of this revelation was a man called John, 'who bore witness to the word of God and to the testimony of Jesus', that is to say, he was a preacher of the gospel. John was clearly his real name (see p. 7). This is very un- usual. Most apocalyptic writers wrote their books in the name of some- one who had been dead a long time. Other writers often did this too, but did not actually pretend that the long-deceased person had written their books. Thus, for example, the book of Ecclesiastes was written under the name of Solomon, but the writer made it clear that Solomon had not actually written it (Solomon could not have written, 'I *was* king in Jerusalem', for he was king until he died – the RSV obscures this by translating 'I have been king. . . .', Eccles. 1.12). But the apocalyptic writers really did want people to think that their books had been written a long time ago. This made it possible for them to write about events which had already happened, but to write about them as if they had been predicted beforehand. As these 'predictions' had actually 'come true', the writers hoped that people would also believe the rest of their books. But this John did not use such tricks.

This Revelation is about 'what must soon take place'. The word 'soon' must be taken literally, and we must not read John's book as if it was a world history of the future. 'Soon' means 'within a short time'. It may be true that 'with the Lord one day is as a thousand years, and a thousand

17

years as one day' (2 Peter 3.8), but this is not what John meant. It is true that John was also pointing forward to the end of history, to the 'new heavens and a new earth', but most of his book concerned the near future.

It is tempting to try to find in the Revelation precise predictions about our own time. Many people have found in the Revelation somewhere a vision that seemed to fit their own situation so precisely, that they thought that John must have known in advance exactly what was going to happen. Thus, for example, people may recognize their own situation in chapter 13, and be tempted to think that Revelation 1—12 is now past, and chapters 14—22 will follow soon. But some parts of the Revelation seem to fit our own time so well, not because John predicted the distant future, but because the battle between God and the powers of evil is still carried on in the same way. What was true in John's days is still true today.

Of course, the whole point of John's book is the promise of the New Jerusalem at the end of history. But the majority of John's visions were concerned with the immediate future.

Therefore, how fortunate are these people to receive the Revelation! The Greek word *makarios*, translated 'blessed', does not always mean as much as the English seems to imply. The 'blessing' is the book itself: 'How fortunate you are,' John was saying 'to receive the revelation contained in this book'.

The preface consists of a greeting to seven Churches in Asia. This was not an unusual way of starting a book, and even now in some countries some writers still begin the prefaces to their books with the words, *lectori salutem*, 'Greetings to the reader', or *L.S.* for short. 'Asia' was the Roman province of that name, the western part of what is now Turkey (later the name was used for the whole continent).

Clearly then, this book was a circular letter to these seven Churches, where John was no doubt well known. But John was not only writing to them: the seven Churches represent the whole Christian Church, seven being a symbolic figure of fullness (see p. 69). John was writing, through these Churches, to the whole Church.

But the greeting comes, not from John, but from the eternal God: Father, Son, and Holy Spirit. Actually John did not put it quite like that. In later years the Church would begin to think about the relationship between God the Father, Jesus Christ the Son, and the Holy Spirit, and try to find suitable words to express the amazing teaching that the Father, the Son, and the Holy Spirit are three times the One God. That was long after John's days. Yet the message is clear: the greeting comes from the Father, the Son, and the Holy Spirit.

This is followed by a doxology, a 'praise-song'. Glory is ascribed to Christ as to God: 'To him who loves us and has freed us from our sins by his blood and made us a kingdom, priests to his God and Father, to him be glory and dominion for ever and ever. Amen.'

The preface ends with the promise that Christ will come soon, or, rather, that He *is coming* soon: He is on His way, and all will see Him. At present He is known to only a few, but then all will see Him and repent. John's wording expresses a certainty: Christ is already on His way.

To the preface is added the assurance that God is the beginning and the end, the Creator who made all things, the Protector who upholds all things, and the Perfecter with whom all things will end. He is the One who is and who was and who is to come, the Ruler of all.

STUDY SUGGESTIONS

WORDS

1. What is a priest?
2. What is the precise meaning of the word translated 'Almighty'?

CONTENT

3. What is unusual about John's having used his real name?
4. What is the precise meaning of the word translated 'soon' in v. 1, and what does this mean for the interpretation of this verse?
5. What did John mean when he called the readers of the Revelation 'blessed'?
6. What was the significance of John's writing to *seven* Churches?
7. What is significant about John's writing, not that Jesus will come soon, but *is coming* soon?

BIBLE

8. 'This is followed by a doxology . . . glory is ascribed to Christ as to God' (p. 18). All the following passages are about glory and blessing. Which of them are also doxologies? Exod. 18.10; Deut. 28.2–3; Pss 29.1, 2; 45.2, 3; 72.18, 19; 106.48; 135.21; Matt. 6.13; Luke 2.13, 14; John 12.27, 28; Rom. 11.33–36; 16.27; 2 Cor. 9.13–15.

APPLICATION

9. What is the reason why some parts of the Revelation reflect our own situation so precisely?
10. In what ways does the priesthood of all believers relate to the ordained priesthood or ministry?

Special Note A: Angels

John frequently refers to angels. Both the Hebrew and the Greek words simply mean a 'messenger'. Thus the Hebrew word is used in Genesis 32.3, for the messengers which Jacob sent to his brother Esau, and the Greek word is used in Luke 7.24, for the messengers sent by John the Baptist.

But the Hebrew word is used more often in the Old Testament for supernatural messengers of God. We are not told much about those angels. The writers were far more interested in the messages than in the messengers. Whenever God made His will known to people, but did so indirectly, we read that He sent an 'angel', a messenger. But the important thing was always the message from God, and the angel did not receive much attention.

In later years the Jews became more interested in the angels themselves, and developed a great deal of teaching about them. In particular it was believed that there were seven prominent angels, the archangels, who played a large part in God's government of His creation. This belief was probably inspired by the belief of the nations surrounding Israel that seven of their gods (identified with the sun, the moon, and the five planets known to them) were particularly powerful. The faith of Israel had no room for other gods beside the one living God, but the Jews felt there was reason to believe that there were seven powerful spirits, the archangels, waiting upon God to carry out His will.

In the New Testament angels chiefly have three functions:

1. In the first place they are messengers, who make God's will known to people. Thus the angel Gabriel (one of the archangels) was sent to Zechariah and to Mary to announce the births of John the Baptist and of Jesus, and 'the angel of the Lord' announced the birth of Jesus to some Judean shepherds (Luke 1, 2). In the Revelation an angel shows John all that God wants him to see, and other angels proclaim God's will. They are therefore very important, must be treated with respect, and must be listened to. But they must not be worshipped (19.10).

2. Angels carry out God's plans. Thus an angel set Peter free from prison (Acts 12.7), and in the Revelation angels carry out various God-given tasks.

3. Angels are used by God to show His special concern for certain groups of people or for certain individuals, such as the angels of the Churches in Revelation 1.20, and the angels of the little children in Matthew 18.10.

Occasionally the word 'angel' is used for servants of the power of evil, such as 'the angel of the bottomless pit' (Rev. 9.11), and Satan's 'angels' (2 Cor. 12.7; Rev. 12.7–9).

In several books of the Bible other names are also used for various supernatural beings. Isaiah mentions the seraphim, who worship the LORD (Isa. 6). Cherubim, according to the belief of other nations in the lands surrounding Israel, were the guardians of holy places, and were pictured as terrifying monsters. In the Old Testament cherubim guarded the entrance to the garden of Eden (Gen. 3.24), but their chief function was to carry God's throne (Psalm 80.1; 99.1), and images of cherubim covered the Ark of the Covenant, which was regarded as the throne used by God when He visited His temple (Exod. 25.19). The Bible gives us little information about those heavenly beings. That is partly because people would know what was meant by a seraph or a cherub, but chiefly because the important point about them was not what they were, but what they did.

The 'living creatures' in Ezekiel 1 and Revelation also belong among these supernatural beings. We shall discuss their function when we come to study chapter 4.

In conclusion, the Bible pays little attention to what angels and other supernatural beings are. All the attention is focused on what they *do* and what they *say*, because they act and speak for God.

STUDY SUGGESTION

Read the following passages, where angels are mentioned, and say in what way each passage agrees, or does not agree, with the above Special Note: Gen. 21.15–21; 22.1–13; 24.7; Judges 6.11–18; Ps. 103.20; Matt. 26.53; Luke 1.11, 26; 2.8–14; Acts 11.11–18; 12.6–11.

1.9–20
Christ appears to John

SUMMARY

1.9–11: John, on the island of Patmos, on a Sunday, hears behind him a voice commanding him to write to seven Churches in Asia.

1.12–16: He turns round, and sees seven lampstands, and in the midst of the lampstands a human figure of awe-inspiring appearance, holding seven stars in his right hand.

1.17–20: John is afraid and falls down at His feet, but the person appearing to him puts His hand upon him, tells him who He is, and says what is the significance of this vision.

NOTES

1.9. I, John, was on the island called Patmos. Patmos was a tiny rocky island in the Aegean Sea. The Romans used it as a place of banishment. John was there 'on account of the word of God and the testimony of Jesus'. This could mean that he had gone there to preach the gospel, but it is more likely that his preaching had offended the authorities, and they had banished him there.

1.10. I was in the Spirit, that is to say, in a state of ecstasy, or, as we might say, in a trance. But the word 'spirit' has many different meanings, and the Greek word has even more different meanings than the English. The English translators were probably right in thinking that John meant much more than just that he was 'in a trance'. They printed 'Spirit' with a capital S, to show that John was under the influence of the Holy Spirit. John was certainly not thinking of Paul's contrast between the spirit and the flesh (Rom. 8), but simply affirmed that the revelation he was about to receive came from the Holy Spirit.

On the Lord's day, that is to say, on a Sunday, the day of Christ's resurrection. This has always been the day of the week when Christians met for worship, if at all possible.

1.11. The seven Churches. There were more than seven Churches in the province of Asia (the New Testament mentions Alexandria Troas, and Colossae, and there were others), but seven was traditionally used as a figure of completeness (see p. 69). These seven Churches were chosen because they knew John, but they were meant to represent the whole Church. Even so we must not forget that the seven named were real Churches, each with their own particular problems.

A quick glance at these seven cities will not help us much with the interpretation of the letters in chapters 2 and 3, but may help us to remember that John was writing to real people.

Ephesus, on the coast near present-day Kusidasi, was the most important. In John's days it was one of the largest cities in the world, and for many years it remained an important port, but it declined after the Turks conquered it in 1420; the harbour is now silted up, and its ruins are some distance from the sea. The apostle Paul had founded the Church here.

Smyrna, present-day Izmir, was also a great port, and has remained so; it is now the largest city in the area. The Church suffered much when Turkey, a Muslim state, expelled the mainly Christian Greek population in 1922.

Pergamum now called Bergama, was a great religious and cultural

'John was on the island of Patmos', either as a missionary or because the authorities had banished him there (p. 22).

The steep hillsides and terraced fields of Patmos probably look much the same today as when John was alive. What other great Christians has God led to use times of exile or prison to write messages of warning or comfort for others to read?

centre, with famous shrines of the Greek gods Zeus and Asklepios, and also a temple dedicated to the Roman Emperor Augustus. The temple of Asklepios had a famous medical school attached to it; the city also had a flourishing book trade, and gave its name to parchment, which was first used there.

Thyatira (Akhisar) was renowned for the manufacture and dyeing of cloth; and *Sardis* had once been the capital of a powerful Lydian kingdom; in Roman times it had lost some of its ancient glory, but was still a great city; the present village of Sart is insignificant.

Philadelphia (Alesehir) was a prosperous town, but was particularly noted as a centre of learning; it was sometimes called 'little Athens', comparing it with Athens, the ancient seat of Greek learning. And finally *Laodicea*, now a splendid ruin, was a wealthy centre of the wool trade; it was destroyed by an earthquake in 65, but rebuilt within a short time, an achievement of which the citizens were justly proud.

1.13. One like a son of man. A 'son of man' simply means a human being. Much has been written about the term 'the son of man' as used in the Gospels, but that is not relevant to this vision. John may have known Gospel stories in which Jesus spoke of 'the Son of man', probably meaning Himself, but John was not referring to those. John's vision, however, was influenced by Daniel's vision of 'one like a son of man', that is to say, a human figure, to whom 'was given dominion and glory and kingdom, that all peoples, nations and languages should serve him; his dominion is an everlasting dominion, which shall not pass away, and his kingdom one that shall not be destroyed' (Dan. 7.13–14).

As angels were usually pictured in human form, some interpreters take the view that John saw Jesus in angelic form. But we may well ask, if that is what John had in mind, why did he not say so? It seems more likely that John meant that he saw, not an angel, but a human figure.

Clothed . . . The details of the description are derived from traditional sources. The robe and girdle were part of the High Priest's dress (Exod. 28.4), the white hair belongs to the Ancient of Days (Dan. 7.9), the bronze feet are those of Ezekiel's living creatures (Ezek. 1.7), but in John's vision these features merely serve to depict an impressive and awe-inspiring figure.

1.16. From his mouth issued a sharp two-edged sword. The Ruler of all the earth is the Judge. It may be significant that the sword is not in His right hand but issues from His mouth. This could simply be part of the picture, for the right hand holds seven stars. But it probably shows that the kingdom of Christ is established not by a sword in His hand but by the sword of His mouth: not by force of arms but by the preaching of the gospel. But the sword must be taken seriously: it establishes justice, and separates the righteous from the wicked.

1.17. Fear not. These words occur frequently in the Bible (see, for example, Gen. 15.1; Judges. 6.23; 1 Sam. 12.20; Matt. 1.20; 28.5; Luke 1.13, 30; 5.10; John 12.15; Acts 27.24). The fear which people have of their gods shows how wrong things are between God and us. Even John, who ought to have known better, did not remember that God is not against us but for us.

I am the first and the last. These words show that 'I' here is God. But notice also that there is no break between this verse and the next.

1.18. I died . . . so this 'I' is Jesus. In later years the Church has tried hard to find the right words for the relationship between the Father and the Son (see p. 18). John makes no such attempt. But what he says about God equally applies to Christ, and what he says about Christ equally applies to God.

Death and Hades. In Greek myth Hades is the god of the dead, and this name is also used for the underworld, that is to say, the realm of the dead, the place where the dead are. In the Old Testament the realm of the dead was called *Sheol*, and according to the belief of most Old Testament writers, the dead in *Sheol* were really dead: they were not immortal spirits. In New Testament times this belief was changed to some extent, but we shall never understand the New Testament hope of the resurrection, if we do not recognize that the dead are really dead. God alone is able, by His creative power, to raise the dead, to make the dead live. Here again Jesus does what God does. Jesus holds the keys of death and Hades. He is able, through the resurrection, to make the dead live, and to give them eternal life.

INTERPRETATION

John introduces his first vision by telling his readers that he was on the island of Patmos on account of his preaching of the gospel, and that, though he was far away, he was in fellowship with them, and that one Sunday, while they were meeting for worship, he received a message for them.

This first vision was not really a 'heavenly vision'. John was shown the real state of affairs, not in heaven, but on earth. Things on earth are not quite what they seem, and before he was shown anything else, he was shown how things really stand.

When John heard a voice and looked round, the first things that he saw were seven lampstands. At this stage he did not know what they signified. But in the midst of the lampstands he saw a human figure holding seven stars in His right hand. Here was a symbol which John recognized at once. It had long been the belief that the stars govern life on earth. Particular power was attributed to the sun, the moon, and the five planets known to ancient peoples. The importance of the sun for all life on earth is clear. Without the heat of the sun there would be no life.

But this same heat could also be a serious threat in times of drought. Thus the sun was regarded as a mighty god. The moon may seem less important to modern city dwellers, but to ancient peoples the moon was an impressive sight. In desert lands it is also a great helper to people who want to travel without the scorching heat of the day, and in Bible times people engaged in inter-city travel were often fervent worshippers of the moon. Just as in many areas today, the work of fishermen and farmers was planned in relation to the phases of the moon; and at that time they too were often moon worshippers. The planets seemed to move freely among the 'fixed' stars, and they were regarded as powerful gods. In fact, we still call them by the names of ancient gods, and when modern astronomers discover a new planet, they give it the name of a Roman god. With modern astronomers this is simply the continuation of an old custom, but ancient peoples were completely serious in regarding the planets as mighty gods.

Many Christians tend to regard the gods and powers in which other religions believe, as mere nothings. As we realize that the gods are not the living God, we are inclined to think that they do not exist at all. Particularly when we hear the myths which people tell about their gods, we are tempted to think that we are listening to mere fairy tales, charming stories with no truth in them. But myths are not just fanciful stories: a myth is a particular way of telling a truth.

No religion worships, or ever worshipped, mere inventions of the imagination. What people worship, and what they worshipped in John's days, are, and were, the realities of life.

And just as today there are many different religions, so in ancient Rome there was a great variety of religious belief and practice. But, in whatever form, or under whatever name they were worshipped, they were realities.

Thus, for example, Venus was not just a beautiful girl, who featured in charming stories, but the sexual urge by which every human being is affected. Mars was not a warrior-hero from tales about wars, but the actual bloody conflict between peoples, and once he was in action, no one could stop him. Mercury was not merely a good-looking boy with wings on his feet, who carried messages for the other gods, but the world of commerce and finance. And so we could go on. Actually the gods we mentioned were much more complex than we have shown: they were much more than mere personifications of earthly realities. But the point ought to be clear: the gods were not God, but they were realities with which people had to reckon.

The same is still true today. Whether we think in terms of the gods which our fathers used to worship, or in terms of mysterious powers which we sense around us, or in terms of a so-called 'modern' view of the world in which we reckon only with the power of naked realities, it is unwise to underestimate the powers which are active in the world.

The first readers of the Revelation saw the power of those gods all around them. Not only did they see the temples which dominated the cities, and the crowds worshipping there. They saw how the gods actually dominated the daily lives of people: in the market place, where most of the meat that was sold had first been dedicated to a god; in the law courts, where oaths were sworn by a god, and justice was done in the name of the gods; on the battle field, where the soldiers fought for their nation and their gods; in the homes, where no meal was proper without an act of worship. The riches amassed by successful merchants, and the bribes accepted by many officials, showed that Mercury was more than a name, and the brothels in every town showed the power of Venus. The gods were very powerful indeed.

So this is what John saw: he saw Him who has the whole world in His hand. His vision illustrated the words of Jesus in Matthew 28.18: 'All authority in heaven and on earth has been given to me'. Mighty though they seem to be, the powers which are active in the world, and which seem to govern all that happens, are subordinate to Him who holds the seven stars.

John's first reaction was fear. So he had to be reassured. Some people have pointed out that v. 17 seems to contradict v. 16: how could He who appeared to John hold the seven stars in His right hand, and put His right hand on John? But we must not take this too literally. John had to use such language as he knew to tell his readers what his vision had shown him, and we need not worry if his language is not always consistent – as long as we know what he means. The movement of the hand was a comforting and protective gesture: John need not be afraid, for he was under the protection of Him to whom all authority belongs.

John was then told who it was who was appearing to him. He who has the whole world in His hand is the same Christ who died, and is alive for evermore. He to whom all authority has been given is the same Jesus, who walked the roads of Galilee. But He also holds the keys of the realm of death. His almighty power is power to save.

Next, John was told that 'the seven lampstands are the seven Churches'. They were not a heavenly counterpart of the Churches. They were the Churches as they were on earth, harassed by enemies, exposed to the threats of persecution, and also suffering from their own shortcomings and sins. These Churches looked as if they might be snuffed out any minute—very much like some Churches today—but Christ was in their midst.

'And the seven stars are the angels of the seven Churches': the forces which have power over the world are in the hand of the risen Christ, and must therefore serve the good of His people, indeed, they must serve as the guardian angels of the Church. We find here, expressed in the language of apocalyptic, the same truth which Paul had expressed in different terms: 'We know that He (that is, God) makes all things work together for good for those who love God, who are called according to His purpose' (Rom. 8.28, new translation).

STUDY SUGGESTIONS

WORDS

1. What is a 'son of man'? (Before answering this question, look at such passages as Dan. 7.1–14; Ezek. 2.1; Mark 13.24–27; Rev. 1.12–16.)
2. What do the New Testament writers mean by 'Hades'?
3. In v. 20 John uses the word 'mystery', that is to say, something that is hidden, but revealed to a few people. Why should he have used the word 'mystery' here?

CONTENT

4. Why are the names of the seven Churches important to us?
5. What was the first thing that John saw when he turned round?
6. What were the seven stars, and what did they mean to John?
7. What is the significance of vv. 17, 18?
8. What did it mean when John was told that the seven stars were 'the angels of the seven Churches', and why was this important to John?

BIBLE

9. Compare John's vision with Isaiah's vision in Isa. 6, and Ezekiel's vision in Ezek. 1. What are the most striking differences?

APPLICATION

10. Do the gods chiefly worshipped by people in your country today have the same sort of power as the ancient gods in the Roman Empire? Give examples.
11. In what sense can money and sex be regarded as gods of the modern age? What other such gods can you think of?
12. Many people today say that they have no religion. Does that mean that they have no gods? If not, what does it mean? Give examples to support your answer.

2.1–7
The Letter to Ephesus

SUMMARY

2.1: Addressee and sender.
2.2, 3: The Church at Ephesus is praised for its zeal and perseverance.
2.4, 5: But the Christians there no longer show that quality of love which they showed at first. They must remember how they started, and return to that first love, or their lampstand will be removed.
2.6: Yet it is right that they should resist false teaching.
2.7: 'He who conquers' will gain eternal life.

NOTES

2.2. Who call themselves apostles but are not. The word 'apostle' means someone who has been sent, a special messenger. The writers of the Gospels and the Acts used it of those twelve of the Lord's disciples who had received from Him a direct commission to preach the good news.

Sometimes the words 'disciple' and 'apostle' are used carelessly as if they meant the same thing, but a disciple is anyone who follows Jesus, and that means every Christian, whereas an apostle is someone with a special task. In Paul's days it was a burning question whether or not he really was an apostle. He had not been a follower of Jesus when He was on earth and appointed His apostles, but Jesus had appeared to Paul after His resurrection, and only then appointed him to preach the gospel.

But although the writers of the books of the New Testament were very careful of the way in which they used the word 'apostle', many other Christians were not, and there were some preachers who called themselves 'apostles', but taught things which did not follow the teaching of Jesus Himself. These were the men who called themselves apostles but were not.

2.6. Nicolaitans. It is not certain what the Nicolaitans taught. There is a tradition which says that Nicolaus, a convert mentioned in Acts 6.5, at first became an extreme ascetic, and later changed his ideas completely and became an 'antinomian', that is to say, he regarded obedience to the law, not only the Old Testament Law but any law, as contrary to the Christian faith. There were, in fact, some antinomians in the early Church, but there is no reason to think that the Nicolaus of Acts 6 had anything to do with them.

Most antinomians believe that people who are filled with the Holy Spirit need not be worried about the sins of the body. They say that what we do in the body does not affect the spirit, and therefore does not matter. Other interpreters think that the teaching of the Nicolaitans was Gnostic in nature, and that they believed that what we believe is more important than how we behave. But the body is our body, and we belong to God; what we do in the body is important to God. Heretics of the sort we have described often quote Paul in support of their teaching, but Paul had made it very clear, when he wrote to the Christians in Rome, that the Christian faith entails a Christian life: 'Are we to continue in sin, that grace may abound? By no means!' (Rom. 6.1).

2.7. The tree of life. The tree of life is mentioned in the Paradise story (Gen. 2.9; 3.2), and again in Revelation 22.2, where it provides food for the life eternal (see note and interpretation for Rev. 22.2).

The paradise of God. John uses the word 'paradise' in a sense which differs from the common Jewish usage of his days. It was widely believed that the dead, while they were waiting for the resurrection and the Last Judgement, were either in Hades, or in Paradise, depending on how they had lived their earthly lives. But here John is clearly thinking of the City of God, which he was to see in a later vision, but which he was already expecting (see notes and interpretation for chapters 21, 22).

INTERPRETATION

After the opening vision of chapter 1, John has a message for each of the seven Churches. The first Church he addresses is Ephesus. This was probably the first city reached by the messenger who was to carry the Revelation to the various Churches, and who after Ephesus would visit Smyrna, Pergamum, Thyatira, Sardis, Philadelphia, and Laodicea in that order.

This letter is addressed to 'the angel of the Church in Ephesus'. By 'angel' John meant the man who was to receive the letter and read it to the congregation; perhaps the secretary of the local Church, or the person in whose house the services were held. But it seems strange that John chose this word 'angel', which could only be confusing after his mentioning 'the angels of the Churches' at the end of chapter 1. He probably meant to show that the state of the Church, and, indeed, the state of every single congregation, is closely linked to Christ's government of the world. He certainly did not mean that the letter was to be shown to the powers which seem to govern the world, and we need not try to think of ways in which he could possibly do this. But the people in Ephesus, and we ourselves, need to know that whatever happens in any Christian Church, however small, affects Christ's government.

The Church at Ephesus had much to recommend it. It had not only resisted pressure from outside, but also taken great care to preserve the purity of the gospel. Its members had tested certain men who called themselves apostles, and found them to be false, and had made sure that no false teaching was preached in their Church.

The false preachers, who were not allowed to preach in Ephesus, were followers of a man called Nicolaus. We do not know what they preached, but that does not affect the interpretation of these verses. It is right for Churches to ensure that the gospel is preached and taught properly.

The Ephesians' concern for the purity of the gospel was praiseworthy. But something had happened which often follows when we are especially zealous for the truth. At first the attempt to rule out heresies is inspired by an honest zeal for the truth and a sincere love for those who follow wrong teaching. But soon people get angry, violent emotions flare up, and it all ends in bitter quarrelling, in which the Christian love is in danger of dying altogether. This is a serious danger at all times, especially in Churches which want to keep closely to the teaching of the Bible.

That is what had happened in Ephesus. People there had 'tested the spirits to see whether they were of God' (see 1 John 4.1), and had not believed the spirit of false prophets. But in testing the spirits they had lost the love which they once had. And so, although they might claim to have prophetic powers to understand all mysteries and all knowledge, and to have faith, yet they had no love, therefore they were nothing (see 1 Cor. 13.2). They had taken the first step on that disastrous road which leads to Christian people's quarrelling with each other and even persecuting each other.

If we have no love, we are nothing. We certainly cannot be 'the light of the world' (see Matt. 5.14–16). So the Ephesians were warned that, if they did not repent, their lampstand would be removed, that is to say, they would be removed from the Lord's presence. That judgement was meant as a warning, not only to the Ephesians, but to all Christians whose zeal for the truth threatens to harden their hearts towards other Christians, whom they believe to be in error.

This message ends with the promise, that 'he who conquers' will receive eternal life sustained by God Himself. Every one of these seven messages ends with a similar promise of life and fellowship with God.

'He who conquers' could generally mean anyone who overcomes all temptations and remains faithful, but here it refers specifically to martyrs: in the persecution that was to come, being faithful to Christ could mean facing danger and even death.

John was not suggesting that every faithful Christian would suffer martyrdom, nor that only martyrs would gain eternal life, nor that other Christians would be second class citizens in the City of God. Other Christians were given promises similar to those given to 'him who con-

31

quers' (2.10; 3.4, 20). But the martyrs were singled out in order to strengthen the Christians in the trials which were lying ahead. It may be exciting to read about people suffering and dying for the gospel, but it is much less exciting actually to suffer and to die. Courage in the face of torture and death is difficult to achieve and rare to find. If we have not suffered ourselves, it is easy to expect that other people will remain faithful, but if we ourselves have been tortured, we know how difficult it really is.

When persecution did come, many Christians died for their faith, but many others denied their faith. Most Christians, however, did not suffer at all, and those people who had suffered no hardship were often loudest in condemning the lapsed Christians. On the other hand, Christians who had suffered but had survived were much less likely to condemn, for they knew how difficult it was, and understood their lapsed brothers and sisters.

The sort of courage needed for martyrdom is very different from that required in battle. In battle we can actively do something, and, moreover, we are not alone. It is also different from the courage needed in rescue efforts. It may take great courage to try to rescue someone from drowning or from a fire, and we may be alone whilst making the attempt, but at least we are doing something. But the martyr is all alone, and he is quite powerless and unable to do anything. It has been said that under torture everyone will break sooner or later. That is not quite true. Many courageous men and women have remained true to what they believed to be right even under the most terrible tortures. But it does need extraordinary strength and courage.

John's first readers who might have real suffering and perhaps martyrdom ahead of them, needed the encouragement of knowing that they were not truly alone, and that the Lord was with them. The ordeal which they had to face was their opportunity to share in His passion and death, but also in His resurrection.

STUDY SUGGESTIONS

WORDS

1. Explain the difference between a disciple and an apostle.
2. What does the expression 'he who conquers' mean?
3. What did the Jews of John's days mean by the word 'paradise'? And how did John use it?

CONTENT

4. What was praise-worthy about the Church at Ephesus?
5. What was the particular sin of the Christians at Ephesus?

6. What signs, if any, are there in this letter that the troubles for which John wanted to prepare his readers were already beginning?

BIBLE

7. Compare the teaching of this letter with Paul's teaching on Christian love in 1 Cor. 13.

APPLICATION

8. What occasions can you think of in the history of the Christian Church, when the sin of the Ephesians had dreadful consequences?
9. What signs, if any, are there of the sin of the Ephesians in your own Church?

2.8–11
The Letter to Smyrna

SUMMARY

2.9: The Lord knows about the Church's troubles.
2.10: The Christians at Smyrna must not be afraid: they will suffer, but their suffering will lead to better things.
2.11: 'He who conquers' will receive eternal life.

NOTES

2.8. Who died and came to life. The Church in Smyrna seemed to be in a poor condition, almost as if it was a dying Church. It was good for the Christians there to know that they followed Him who died and rose from the dead.
2.9. Poverty. It was a common thought in some Jewish circles that godliness and poverty go together. John and the Smyrniote Christians may have known Jesus's saying about how difficult it is 'for a rich man to enter the kingdom of God' (Mark 10.25).
But you are rich. The poor Christians at Smyrna have riches which the world cannot give, not in material goods but in the love of God.
2.10. The devil. The Greek word for 'devil' is *diabolos*, meaning 'slanderer'. This word is used in the New Testament for the chief opponent to God's plans and the greatest enemy of the Church. We shall discuss his being a slanderer more fully in Special Note D.
Ten days. Some interpreters have taken this to mean the time between the arrest of the Christians and their trial, which would lead to their conviction and execution. But it seems more natural to take John's

33

words literally, and to interpret the ten days as evidence that the authorities at Smyrna did not want to make martyrs, but tried to wear the Christians down by comparatively mild treatment. Even so, ten days in gaol would not have been a holiday!

The crown of life. The Greek word *stephanos*, translated by 'crown', actually means a 'garland'. John was referring to the garlands presented to the winners at the Olympic and other games, just as medals are presented to winners today. The *stephanos* of life could mean the gold medal, not for boxing or running, but for *living*; or it could mean a 'first prize' consisting of eternal life. As the expression is ambiguous, it is quite likely that both are meant: those who remain faithful to the end will receive the gold medal for living, and the prize itself will be eternal life.

2.11. The second death, that is to say, the death penalty at the Last Judgement. See also note on the reference to 'the second death' in 20.14.

INTERPRETATION

The Church at Smyrna receives no criticism, only encouragement. The congregation there was poor, and under considerable pressure, being harassed not only by the authorities but also by the local synagogue.

The synagogue at Smyrna was called a 'synagogue of Satan' not because it was a Jewish meeting place, but because the Jews of Smyrna were hostile to the Christians. We must stress this, because many interpreters have been inclined to misconstrue this and similar phrases in the New Testament, especially in the writings of Paul, John the Evangelist, and John the writer of the Revelation. Thus John the Evangelist often refers to the enemies of Jesus simply as 'the Jews' (John 1.19; 2.18; 5.16, 18; 6.41, etc), but we must remember that Jesus and John were themselves Jews, and when John wrote 'the Jews', he meant 'we', or 'our own people'. Similarly, when Paul expressed his disagreement with certain aspects of Jewish teaching, he was not attacking the Jews as a nation; in fact he could not do so, for he was himself a Jew. Here too the Jesus who appeared to John was a Jew, and so was John himself.

Many Christians in John's days were Jews. But even those who were not, the gentile Christians, regarded themselves as converts to the Jewish faith, and they thought of the Jews as being their own people. So, when the Christians in Smyrna suffered at the hands of Smyrniote Jews, they felt that they were suffering at the hands of their own people, which made it so much harder.

One hesitates to mention it, after all that Jews have suffered at the hands of people who called themselves Christians, but in those early days Christians did sometimes suffer at the hand of Jews. That was the case in Smyrna, and that is why the Jews there are called a 'synagogue of Satan'.

'Crown' here and in the other letters to Churches can mean 'the gold medal for living . . . or the prize of eternal life' (p. 34).

The student in Singapore receiving his degree – the prize for working faithfully through his training – is now equipped for life in his chosen profession. What sort of 'training' helps to equip a Christian for eternal life?

But we must also remember that God has not abandoned His people. God remains true to His promises. Christians are to call the Jewish people to faith in Christ by word and example, and never by coercion (see Rom. 9—11). People who call themselves Christians, but indulge in any sort of anti-semitism or any hostility to the Jewish people, are a 'Church of Satan'.

The Church at Smyrna already suffered persecution, but only a mild form of persecution. At that time, as we have seen, the worst that Christians there were likely to suffer was ten days in gaol. But mild persecution is often more devastating to the well-being of the Church than severe and bloody persecution. Many people are more likely to deny their faith for fear of being laughed at than for fear of a cross or a firing squad. Peter was not boasting, when he said, 'Lord, I am ready to go with you to prison and to death', and he did much later go to prison and to death for his Lord's sake (Acts 12.3; John 21.18–19); yet he denied his Lord for the sake of a mocking remark (Mark 14.66–72). At the time of the Second World War there was a young Dutchman who never liked to speak openly about his Christian faith, but during the Nazi occupation of his country, when his obedience to the will of Christ led to his arrest (he had stolen food coupons for Jews who were in hiding), he faced a firing squad without flinching.

Bloody persecution often breeds resistance and courage, and sometimes arouses sympathy for the victims. The authorities in Smyrna had a better idea. Apart from token sentences for those convicted of the 'crime' of being Christians, they would stop Christians from holding any positions of influence. Christians were also made to seem ridiculous by tales told against them (the theatre gave many opportunities for that purpose). John did not describe all this in so many words, for his readers knew it by experience. Modern readers will not find it difficult to get the picture, for the same methods are still used. There are books, plays, and films, which pretend to give no more than harmless entertainment, and which never openly attack the Christian faith, but which contain some unpleasant or ridiculous characters, of whom we are told in passing that they are Christians.

But the 'soft' persecution would not last. The time would come when to remain faithful might mean to face death. This is what often happens when persuasion and harassment, aided by some mockery, have no effect: the unbelieving world goes on to take stronger measures.

Clearly the Church at Smyrna would not allow itself to be intimidated. What the Smyrniote Christians needed was not criticism but encouragement, and that is what they receive. The Lord promises that they will receive the crown of life, the highest prize for living. This prize is life eternal.

STUDY SUGGESTIONS

WORDS

1. Compare the use of the word 'tested' here with the way in which it is used in 1 John 4.1, and with the word 'test' in James 1.12.

CONTENT

2. Comment on the contrast between poverty and riches in v. 9.
3. How would the devil 'throw' some of the Christians at Smyrna 'in prison'?

BIBLE

4. What is the importance of Romans chapters 9—11 in connection with the 'synagogue of Satan' in v. 9?

APPLICATION

5. Explain why 'soft' persecution is so dangerous.
6. Have you yourself, or has anyone you know, suffered any sort of persecution, or unpleasantness, on account of being a Christian? If so, what form did it take, and how did you (or they) react to it?

2.12–17

The Letter to Pergamum

SUMMARY

2.12–13: The Lord knows the dangers to which the Church at Pergamum is exposed, and the trials which the Christians there have already suffered.
2.14–16: But the Pergamenian Christians are too lax towards false teaching, and if they do not repent, the heretics will find in Christ a determined opponent.
2.17: 'He who conquers' will receive the food of eternal life, and intimate fellowship with Christ.

NOTES

2.12. Sharp two-edged sword. These words point forward to v. 16, where the Lord threatens to use His sword to defend His truth.
2.13. Where Satan's throne is. We do not know for certain what is meant by 'Satan's throne'. There are at least three possibilities.
1. People who are familiar with Greek art think of Pergamum as the

site of a particularly spectacular altar to the god Zeus. The altar itself stood on a huge platform surrounded by colonnades, and the whole structure looked like an enormous throne.

2. The city also had a famous shrine of Asklepios, a god of healing. This temple was a great centre of pilgrimage, and had a medical school of worldwide reputation attached to it. This god's symbol was a snake, which may have suggested to John associations with 'that ancient serpent, who is called the Devil and Satan, the deceiver of the whole world' (12.9).

3. But most probably 'Satan's throne' refers to the fact that Pergamum was the first city to build a temple for the worship of a Roman Emperor (see p. 5), and had remained very devoted to the imperial cult. This imperial cult was the testing ground of the Christian faith, as it was the Christians' non-participation in the worship of the Emperor that usually led to their persecution. It was at this point that Satan made his most determined attack.

2.13. My witness. The Greek word *martys*, meaning 'witness', was later used particularly for a person who was put to death for his faith. The English word 'martyr' is properly used only for someone who died for his faith (though sometimes people do use it in a less serious sense today).

2.14. Balaam was a prophet, hired by Balak, king of Moab, to curse the Israelites. When he was prevented from doing so, he advised Balak to tempt the Israelites to idolatry by inviting them to a sacrificial meal (Numbers 22; 25; 31.16).

Food sacrificed to idols. According to Acts 15 the Jerusalem Church advised gentile converts to abstain from food sacrificed to idols. However, Christians interpreted this advice in different ways. Paul clearly regarded it as meaning that Christians should not take part in sacrificial meals, but were otherwise free to eat whatever was put in front of them, and to buy whatever was sold in the market. He argued that as an idol had no real existence, the fact that something had been offered to an idol meant nothing: a piece of meat was not affected by having been laid on an altar, and Christians could eat it with a clear conscience. This was of considerable importance, as most of the meat sold in the market came from temples, where it had been sacrificed to a god (but only a token part was burnt on the altar, and the rest was sold). However, as Paul pointed out, love is more important than food, and Christian freedom is defined by Christian love. Therefore, if you know that a fellow Christian is not sure that an idol is nothing, and may be offended or led astray by your eating, then do not do it. Also, if you are in the home of a non-Christian friend, and he makes an issue of it, then do not eat what he gives you (see especially 1 Cor. 8.8–13; 10.23).

Practise immorality. This expression was often used to denote religious infidelity: being unfaithful to God was similar to being unfaithful to one's wife or husband, only worse. But both in Numbers 25 and here it should probably be taken literally.

The hidden manna. God had fed His people in the wilderness with manna. Here John was referring to the food of eternal life, the fruit of the tree of life; but he may also have been hinting at the foretaste of that food of life, which Christians enjoy even now, when they partake of the Eucharist, or Lord's Supper.

2.17. A new name. People who are close to each other often use private names which no one else knows. A new name hints at a new relationship. But a new name also suggests a new beginning, a new life. In some Churches new converts, when they are baptized, take new names. So those 'who conquer' are promised a new life in a close relationship with Christ. At the same time the 'new name which no one knows' hints at the mystery of Christ which will not be revealed until the end (see 19.12).

INTERPRETATION

After the Church at Ephesus, which was criticized so severely, and the Church at Smyrna, which received so much encouragement, we meet a Church which had both good and bad sides.

Pergamum was not an easy city for Christians to live in, and it must have been a great comfort for the Christians there to know that the Lord knew what they were experiencing.

Hostility to the Church was more determined and more vicious here than in many other towns. There had been real persecution, and a Christian called Antipas had been put to death to encourage the others to forsake their faith, and to discourage people from becoming Christians. But the congregation had remained faithful.

However, the Pergamenian Church had been less successful in resisting on another front. The devil knows that it is easier to catch flies with honey than with vinegar, and the danger to this particular Church lay in too much tolerance. In those days Christians had particular problems with such everyday things as buying meat in the market and having meals with non-Christian friends. As we saw, most meat sold in the market had been supplied by some temple, where it had been dedicated to some god. Most meals included a short religious ceremony, such as a prayer to one of the gods, or the pouring out of some wine in honour of a god, rather like saying grace in a Jewish or Christian home. What were Christians to do about such things? Paul had already found it necessary to give some advice on the subject (see Rom. 14; 1 Cor. 8–10). His advice to the Romans differed slightly from his advice given to the Corinthians: every Church has to find its own way of living a Christian life in its own situation. We do not know what sort of rules the Churches in Asia followed. But it seems clear from this message to Pergamum that the Christians there had adopted a life-style very similar to that of their environment, so that to all intents and purposes people could not tell the difference between a Pergamenian Christian and an unbeliever.

This adaptation to the non-Christian environment had not been confined to comparatively harmless practices; in such situations it rarely is. The Pergamenian Christians had adopted an equally permissive attitude to the lax morality of the times. That was an understandable error: moralism is the enemy of the gospel; Christ came not to condemn but to save. But Christian freedom means the freedom to do God's will, and that is where this Church had failed. The Christians at Pergamum had taken a firm stand against the authorities, and some had suffered for that; but they were inclined not to take private sins very seriously.

Yet they were not deliberately denying the gospel. If they were asked if they were Christians they would say so. They would rather not be asked, and they made no demonstration of their beliefs; but if they were put to the test, they had the courage of their convictions, and were prepared to die for their Lord.

The permissiveness of this Church was criticized, but not as severely as the Ephesians' lack of love. And John made it quite clear that the Lord's quarrel was not with the Church as a whole, but only with those of its members whose teaching and practice went against the gospel. Nevertheless the whole Church was called to repent.

Here too 'he who conquers' is promised eternal life. The 'hidden manna' means the food of the blessed in heaven. The 'new name' on the stone probably means the name of Christ (see 19.12): the stone is His seal, and certifies that the recipient belongs to the Lord. The 'conqueror' is therefore promised the most intimate fellowship with Christ. The name which no one else knows hints at that intimacy.

STUDY SUGGESTIONS

WORD

1. What are 'martyrs', and what does the word mean?

CONTENT

2. In what way is the two-edged sword relevant to the message to the Church at Pergamum?
3. Compare Christ's criticism of the easy-going Pergamenian Church with His criticism of the strict Church at Ephesus. Which of the two is criticized more severely, and why?

BIBLE

4. (a) Compare Paul's advice to the Romans with his advice to the Corinthians on matters of food, as set out in Rom. 14 on the one hand and 1 Cor. 8.8–13 and 10.23 on the other.
    (b) In what ways, if any, is Jesus's advice in Luke 10.7–8 relevant to this question?

APPLICATION

5. We saw that there are at least three possible interpretations of what John meant by the words 'where Satan dwells'. What clear indications, if any, do you know of, as to where Satan dwells in the world today?
6. Christians in the ancient Church had problems about 'food sacrificed to idols' and about having meals with non-Christians. What problems of that sort do Christians experience in the world today?
7. (a) Some Churches demand a very strict code of conduct from their members. Give examples from your own and other Churches, and comment on this practice in the light of the letters to the Churches at Ephesus and Pergamum.
    (b) Other Churches do not lay down any rules for the conduct of their members. Again, give examples and comment on this practice.

2.18–29
The Letter to Thyatira

SUMMARY

2.19: Christ is aware of the love and faith, service, and patient endurance of this Church, and its growth in the Christian life.
2.20–23: But some people in this Church are following false teaching, and they must be dealt with.
2.24, 25: The other Christians, who have not been affected by false teaching, are urged to hold on to what they have.
2.26–29: To 'him who conquers' the Lord will give great power.

NOTES

2.20. The woman Jezebel. 'Jezebel' was almost certainly not the woman's real name. John was calling her by the name of Ahab's wife, who had led the people of Israel to practise idolatry (1 Kings 18). Her name was (and still is) used for a woman who leads people astray, or generally for a bad woman. Here the name draws attention to the evil which the 'prophetess' of Thyatira was doing.

Prophetess. Prophets and prophetesses in the early Church were inspired preachers, who preached and taught, but also exercised leadership. As they believed themselves to be inspired by the Holy Spirit, it was not always easy to distinguish between true and false prophecy. That was not a new problem. Some of the Old Testament prophets had already had to battle against false prophets, the obvious example being Jeremiah's conflict with Hananiah (see Jer. 28). Paul too met this problem, and laid down that only a preacher who proclaimed that Jesus is Lord could be regarded as truly inspired by the Holy Spirit (see 1 Cor. 12.3; 14.29). At about the same time that John wrote the Revelation, the Church began to deal with this problem by insisting on the authority of an ordained ministry, and Clement of Rome wrote about the three orders of bishops, presbyters, and deacons (1 Clement 42–47).

2.21. I gave her time. 'Jezebel' had evidently been tackled before about her preaching, perhaps by John himself. She was probably quite sincere, and had a small but loyal following in the congregation, and so far the Church had not been willing to silence her.

2.23. Searches mind and heart. Here Christ is said to do what some Old Testament writers described God as doing (see e.g. Jer. 17.10).

2.26. Power over the nations. 'Authority over the nations' (NEB) is a better translation. Those who faithfully follow Christ have not always the power to overcome the nations, but they do have the authority to do so, not by the sword but by their faithful witness.

INTERPRETATION

The Church at Thyatira had much in common with that in Pergamum, and at first sight there does not seem to be much difference between the teaching of Balaam and that of Jezebel. But we get the impression that Jezebel's teaching was more aggressive, and also that it was carefully thought out. The 'deep things of Satan' do not mean that her followers practised some sort of devil worship, but that they regarded themselves as having been initiated into some secret knowledge. There are three possibilities:

1. The first is that they practised some sort of magic. The belief in hidden powers was widespread, and magicians, sorcerers, medicine men, and all kinds of people claiming supernatural powers played a great role, as they still do. Christians were not immune from the attraction of such practices, and it may even be that Jezebel was a kind of Christian sorceress.

2. The second possibility is that the expression 'the deep things of Satan' was meant to be sarcastic, and that Jezebel and her followers

'Her followers regarded themselves as having some secret knowledge. People claiming supernatural powers played a great role, and still do' (p. 42).

Many people, both in the West and in the Third World, claim to have access to secret knowledge and wisdom, like this 'fakir' or holy man with shaven head, and his followers, in Karachi. What sorts of special knowledge or powers do some Christian congregations claim, and what effect can it have on their relationships with other people?

spoke of 'the deep things of God'. She may have claimed that she had visions or dreams, in which she had learned mysteries about God which nobody else knew. If this was the case, her followers would probably look down upon the other, ordinary, Christians, who did not have such special knowledge.

3. The third possibility, which is perhaps the most likely, is that the 'deep things of Satan' means that she taught that the Satan does not really exist, and that there is no such thing as evil: the secret of Satan is that he is not real. If that was so, then there could be no sin, and morality would be irrelevant. In practice the belief that evil is not real does not always make people bad, but it does make them look upon sin as not really serious, and also makes the 'enlightened' people despise the simple folk who try to live godly lives.

This sort of teaching, that evil is not real, is attractive only to a particular sort of intellectual. Ordinary folk feel instinctively that some deeds are good and others are bad, even if they do not always agree upon which are the good and which are the bad deeds. Jezebel does not seem to have had many followers, though they were very loyal to her. But the Church at Thyatira is criticized for allowing her to preach and to practise her teaching within the congregation.

However, the majority had not fallen for her, and they were given no new instructions: they were only encouraged to hold fast to what they had received.

The promise to the 'conqueror' makes it clear that evil is real: it is something that must be destroyed, as when earthen pots are broken in pieces; and it will be the privilege of the faithful to receive the authority to do that. This first part of the promise is not concerned with the life to come: in the New Jerusalem there will be no need for iron rods to break up misshapen vessels, that is to say, for faithful Christians to demolish false teaching or ungodly conduct. It is here and now that the faithful need and receive that authority. The night of evil is dark, but the faithful are promised the morning star which heralds the day—which is Christ (22.16), who leads them to perpetual light.

STUDY SUGGESTIONS

WORD

1. Jezebel is called a 'prophetess'. What does the word mean?

CONTENT

2. What is the special significance of v. 19?
3. What could 'the deep things of Satan' mean?

4. In what way(s) did the false teaching in Thyatira differ from that in Pergamum?
5. What authority did John promise that the faithful would receive?

BIBLE

6. At first sight there seems to be a great difference between the historic Jezebel and the Thyatiran heresy. Read carefully 1 Kings 16.29–33 and 21.1–14, and say what similarities, if any, there are between Ahab's Jezebel and John's 'Jezebel'.

APPLICATION

7. Both Jeremiah and Paul spoke about distinguishing between true and false prophets, and so did the writer of the Letters of John (see 1 John 4.1–6). But how can *we* know the difference?
8. Sorcery, witchcraft, and similar practices are still carried on. Give any examples you can, of such practices in your own country, whether outside or inside the Church.
9. There are still people in some Churches, who claim to have had some special revelation, or to have some special knowledge about God. What is your opinion of such claims?
10. The criticism levelled at Jezebel and her followers suggests that we should hold on to the 'simple gospel', and some Christians think this means that ignorance is godly, and that serious and critical study of the Bible and of the Church's teaching is not necessary. What is your opinion?

3.1–6
The Letter to Sardis

SUMMARY

3.1: The Lord knows that this apparently lively Church is really dead.
3.2, 3: That judgement is here slightly modified: the Sardian Christians are at the point of death. There is still time for them to wake up, if they do not want the Lord to give them a rude awakening.
3.4: However, some of the Christians are alive.
3.5, 6: 'He who conquers' will appear unsullied before God's judgement, and his name will remain in the book of life.

NOTES

3.1. The seven stars. The Christians at Sardis, who regard worldly

45

success and riches as very important, are reminded that Christ has the whole world in His hand (see note on 1.16).

3.2. Perfect in the sight of my God. The Greek word here translated 'perfect', means 'filled up', or 'full'. It is not the same word as used in Matthew 5.48: 'You, therefore, must be perfect, as your heavenly Father is perfect'. But, no matter which word is used, the 'perfection' expected of a Christian is not that he should be without any faults, but that he should be wholly on one side, on God's side. Good deeds are very important indeed, but it is even more important to be entirely on God's side.

3.3. Remember . . . The Sardians are told nothing new. All they have to do is to remember the gospel and live by it.

Like a thief, that is to say, suddenly, unexpectedly (see Luke 12.39–40; 1 Thess. 5.2, 4).

3.4. Not soiled their garments. The Christians had 'put on Christ', an expression which Paul used to mean baptism (Gal. 3.27). But in Sardis many of them had 'soiled their garments' by denying Christ, not by what they said but by what they did.

3.5. White garments suggest the clean white woollen or linen robes worn by Near Eastern peoples as festive dress: the life eternal is a feast that never ends. In the Revelation white, the colour of light, is also the colour connected with Christ, so the faithful are promised that in some respects they will be like Christ, and close to Him. And white garments also mean the 'good deeds of the saints' (19.8, though the word 'white' is not used there).

The book of life: the roll or list of citizens of the City of God. That roll had been made up 'before the foundation of the world' (13.8; 17.8). It is the book of God's grace, containing the names of those whom He has chosen. But God is a living God, always in contact with His creation, and He is able to revise the book of life, as He chooses. So He is able, if the Sardians do not repent, to delete names from it. We shall have to look more closely at the book of life, when we come to the interpretation of the Last Judgement (20.11–14).

I will confess his name. At the Last Judgement Christ will plead on behalf of His people. The two-edged sword of the opening vision (1.16) seemed to suggest that Jesus will be the Judge. But we do not have to think that the Last Judgement will be conducted according to the rules of earthly law courts.

INTERPRETATION

The Church at Sardis seemed to be a flourishing Church, which had learned to live to its own satisfaction in a world hostile to the gospel. We do not hear of any persecution, and we can assume that this Church had found a place for itself in the life of the city. Here Christians were respected, and Christianity was respectable.

We do not know in detail, how this was achieved, but there have been so many Churches like the Church at Sardis, that we can make a fairly accurate guess.

Christians must not seek martyrdom for its own sake. If necessary they must be prepared to pay the price of persecution, and even to die for their beliefs, but there is nothing dishonourable in seeking peace for the Church. The Gospels record sayings of Jesus which prepared His disciples for hardship and martyrdom, but also His saying to the Pharisees: 'Render to Caesar the things that are Caesar's and to God the things that are God's' (Mark 12.17). And both Paul's letters and the Acts of the Apostles show that the early Christians tried to avoid conflict if that was at all possible. The Church can rightly and properly try to keep the peace even with a hostile state, and that is what Christians have usually attempted to do.

In the Roman Empire religious bodies which were not recognized by the state, and therefore illegal, could usually find ways of escaping the attention of the authorities. It was not even necessary to meet in secret. All that was needed was to pay some token worship to the gods of the state, and particularly to the Emperor. As long as some token observance of the state religion was complied with, Rome was extremely tolerant of 'illegal' cults. Thus, although these cults were officially prohibited in Rome, Caligula was able to introduce the worship of Isis and Osiris there, and Claudius did the same with the cult of Cybele and Attis.

As we saw, if Christians were taken to court they were asked to make an offering to some of the gods and to the Emperor, and 'to revile the name of Christ'. But if they sacrificed to the gods and the Emperor voluntarily, no one would take them to court, and they would not be asked 'to revile the name of Christ'. Many people regarded the state religion as a mere formality, and joined in its rites even if they did not believe in the Roman gods, or did not believe that the Emperor was a god. Maybe some Christians too thought that sacrificing to the gods and the Emperor was a meaningless ceremony, which need not be taken seriously. And perhaps that was how the Christians in Sardis escaped persecution, but we do not know for certain.

We do know from this letter, however, that somehow or other the Church at Sardis had managed to become respectable in its pagan environment, that some of the richer and more influential people there were Christians, and that the members of the congregation were very pleased with the favourable position they had gained.

But all this had not been achieved without serious damage to their spiritual life. Here, as in Pergamum, it was not easy to distinguish a Christian from an unbeliever – and that in a city which had a bad name for its riotous living. This apparently lively and flourishing Church had little inner life. Its faith had become shallow, and few of its members continued to preach a distinctively Christian message or to live in a distinctively Christian way.

There are Churches to be found in many parts of the world which are very 'respectable', and are on friendly terms with governments and with unbelievers, but which, like the Church at Sardis, have no inner life.

The promise to 'him who conquers', and to faithful Christians generally, is directly related to 'living the gospel'. The white garments, as John was to tell his readers later, represent the 'good deeds of the saints', the evidence of their Christian living. And Christ will confess their names before His Father, as they have confessed His name before the world.

STUDY SUGGESTIONS

WORDS

1. What does the expression 'the book of life' mean?

CONTENT

2. What was the condition of the Church at Sardis?
3. What sort of perfection does God require of His people?
4. What is the significance of 'remember' (v. 3)?
5. What does 'white' mean in the Revelation?

BIBLE

6. Compare the promise to 'him who conquers' with the teaching of Jesus in Matthew 7.21–23.

APPLICATION

7. 'There are Churches in many parts of the world which are very 'respectable', but which, like the Church at Sardis, have no inner life' (p. 48). If you know of any such Churches, give examples. In what circumstances do you think congregations are chiefly tempted to become shallow and 'respectable' in this way?
8. Some Churches try to build up the fellowship among the members of the congregation by 'worldly' functions, such as garden parties, teas, meals, concerts and similar things, and also to gain new members through inviting people to such functions, and by such activities as youth clubs, bands, and sports. What are the advantages of doing this, and what are the dangers?

3.7–13
The Letter to Philadelphia

SUMMARY

3.8a. The Lord knows the works of the Christians at Philadelphia.
3.8b–11. The Lord promises His help and support in the time of trial which is ahead, and assures the Philadelphians that He is coming soon.
3.12, 13: 'He who conquers' will be a lasting monument in the Temple of God.

NOTES

3.7. The key of David. This expression is derived from Isaiah 22.22, where the 'key of David' is simply the key of the Royal Palace in Jerusalem. When Eliakim received that key, he received the authority to decide who should, and who should not, be admitted to the royal presence. Here 'the key of David' means the authority to decide who is, and who is not, to be admitted to God's presence.

3.8. An open door, that is to say, in this case, access to God.

3.9. Synagogue of Satan. The local synagogue at Philadelphia had evidently excluded Christians from membership of the synagogue. As we saw, Christians in those days felt strongly that they belonged to Israel, so this was a severe blow to them. Moreover, when Christians were no longer regarded as Jews, they became liable to suffer persecution. As we have emphasized before, John was himself a Jew, and we must not take the expression in an anti-Jewish or anti-Semitic sense. The synagogue at Philadelphia was criticized, not for being Jewish, but for being hostile to the Christians (see p. 34).

3.12. A pillar, not a pillar to support the roof, but a free-standing pillar as a lasting monument. Then as now it was customary to erect such pillars or columns to celebrate the lives or victories of great leaders.

The temple of my God. According to Revelation 21.22 there is no temple in the new Jerusalem, but we must not stress the apparent contradiction. The word 'temple' here simply means the place where God is, the same as it does in 11.19. In 21.22 John means that in the new Jerusalem there is no need for any special place set aside for worship, because God fills the entire Holy City (see also 21.2, 11).

The new Jerusalem which comes down from my God. It would be a more literal, and probably more correct, translation, to say, 'The new Jerusalem which *is coming down* from my God'. When we compare this verse with Revelation 21, where the same expression occurs twice (vv. 2, 10), we see that John is not writing of a future event but of a quality of the City of God. The essential nature of the new Jerusalem is that it is created by God, and is forever coming down out of heaven from God. People do not have to wait for the 'new heavens' and the 'new earth' (21.1); they can even now enter the City of God, they can even now be citizens of the heavenly city.

INTERPRETATION

The Church at Philadelphia was very different from that in Sardis. It was poor, small, and harassed both by the pagan citizens and the local synagogue; but its members had not strayed from the way. The Lord does not criticize this Church; like its sister Church in Smyrna, it receives only encouragement.

The Christians here had found many doors closed to them. They had been evicted from the synagogue, and probably had also been barred from various offices. But Christ, who has 'the key of David', had set before them an open door. That open door was the gate of the heavenly city, God's dwelling place. Christ had given them access to God. This was much more important than access to the synagogue, to the homes of their neighbours, or to high office. And it also meant that they would find a way through their trials. Verse 10 seems to suggest that this Church would not suffer persecution, but that cannot be the meaning, as the promise to the 'conqueror' shows that there will be martyrs. Rather, the Philadelphian Church is promised that it will win through and win the crown of life, the ultimate prize.

This message shows that the Church at Philadelphia had made a good beginning. The fact that this Church has survived through many troubles, and is still alive today in its Muslim environment, shows that its foundations were well laid. Smyrna, the other Church praised in these letters to the seven Churches, is another Church in the area which survives today.

The promises to the Christians of Philadelphia are abundant. They will receive the crown of life, they will be lasting monuments in the presence of God, they will be marked as belonging to God, and as citizens of His Holy City, carrying its passport, and they will be bound intimately to the Lord Jesus. The promises to 'him who conquers' are great indeed, but the crown has already been given to the whole Church.

STUDY SUGGESTIONS

CONTENT

1. The message to the Church at Philadelphia says much about keys, about opening and shutting, and about an open door. What was the significance of all this?
2. What had the synagogue at Philadelphia done to be called a 'synagogue of Satan'? In what sense, if any, does this expression have an anti-Jewish meaning?
3. What does the expression 'kept my word' (v. 8) mean?
4. Was Philadelphia the only Church that had to face trouble?
5. What was the 'crown' mentioned in v. 11?
6. What is the significance of the New Jerusalem 'coming down'?

BIBLE

7. What is the difference between the 'pillar' of v. 12, and the 'pillars' mentioned in Galatians 1.9?
8. Look at such passages as Mark 15.45—16.8; Luke 13.22–30; John 10.7; 20.19–29, which all mention doors. What connection, if any, do these have with the letter to Philadelphia?

APPLICATION

9. What comfort does the letter to Philadelphia give to many Christians today, perhaps to members of your own Church?
10. Do you think it is easier or more difficult for a small and poor Church to 'endure' and 'conquer' in the world today, than it is for a large and rich one? Give reasons for your answer.

3.14–22
The Letter to Laodicea

SUMMARY

3.15–17. The Laodiceans are rather pleased with themselves, but they are lukewarm.

3.18–20. Their Lord, who loves them, calls them to repent.

3.21. 'He who conquers' will reign with Christ.

NOTES

3.14. Amen. This word comes from a Hebrew root meaning, 'that which is firm', and especially, 'that which is reliable'. We use the word at the end of our prayers to indicate that God is absolutely reliable, and that we are certain that He will hear our prayers. Here 'Amen' means the same as the words which follow: 'the faithful and true witness'.

3.17. Poor, blind, naked. There is some irony in these words: Laodicea was a banking centre, it had a medical school specializing in eye diseases, and it had a prosperous wool trade. In contrast with those earthly riches – which are good in themselves, and should not be despised – the Christians there were spiritually poor, blind, and naked; they needed the riches, the white garments, and the true sight, which Christ was offering.

3.20. I stand at the door and knock. Christ asks to be admitted to this Church (not merely to the lives of individual Christians). We may recall the story of an African who felt very despondent at having discovered that he was not welcome in a 'white' Church, and was comforted by a vision of Christ, who said to him: 'Never mind, brother, I have tried to get into that Church for years, and never yet managed'. In Laodicea Christ felt shut out of His own Church!

Eat with him. A meal uniquely binds people together. The story is told of a man who gave hospitality to someone who had escaped from justice, and gave him a meal. When he found out that he had given hospitality to the murderer of his own son, he yet did not hand him over to the police but helped him on his way, for the bonds of hospitality were sacred.

INTERPRETATION

The condition of the Laodicean Church seems to have been similar to that of the Church at Sardis, but there were differences. Here too the congregation seem to have been fairly wealthy, the members were respectable citizens, and the Church had escaped the attention of the authorities. The Christians here seem to have regarded religion as a private matter, something which satisfied their spiritual needs but did not really affect their lives in the world. Out of the rich variety of cults practised around them they had chosen Christianity—after all, people must have some sort of religion, but there was no fire in them. They were neither cold nor hot, like the sort of tepid food you want to spit out: the picture is marvellously descriptive.

Yet these Christians were not aware that they lacked anything. They did not realize that what they took for the gold of true faith was mere tinsel; they had their eyes closed to the reality of their lives and saw only what they wanted to see. Their Lord advises them to accept the gold of the gospel which He offers, to take the righteousness with which He is able and willing to clothe them, and to let Him open their eyes so that they may see the truth.

This Church is reprimanded severely. The severity, however, is a sign of love. Sentimentality or indifference may condone sins, but love must sometimes be severe. Christ does not want to lose His people – for in spite of everything they are *His* people. He wants to come into their lives and have fellowship with them, now in the Eucharist, the Lord's Supper, and later at the messianic banquet.

STUDY SUGGESTIONS

WORDS

1. What does the word 'Amen' mean? How is it used, and why?

CONTENT

2. What did the Laodicean Christians think of themselves, and what did Christ think of them?
3. What does this letter teach us about criticizing others – and ourselves.

BIBLE

4. 'As I myself have conquered' (v. 21). In what ways do these words correspond with John 19.30?

APPLICATION

5. If you know of any Churches like the Church in Laodicea, say why you think they are like that, and what you think ought to be done about it.
6. One reader of 3.15 said that 'Would that you were cold or hot!' means that it does not matter what you believe, as long as you believe fervently, and act on what you believe. What is your opinion?

Special Note B
The Letters to the Seven Churches

We may be tempted to regard the letters to the seven Churches as some kind of foreword, unconnected with the real subject of the Revelation. But that would be a mistake. The Revelation was meant to warn, comfort, and guide people, and the letters are an important part of the book as a whole.

We must also beware of thinking that each message was meant only for the Church to which it was addressed specifically. Every one of the messages ends with the words, 'He who has an ear, let him hear what the Spirit says to the *Churches*', and every one was meant to be read, and taken to heart, by all the Churches in Asia, and, indeed, by all Churches everywhere. The seven Churches stand for the whole Church, and those which are criticized are examples of the sort of things that can go wrong in any Church.

The fault of the Ephesian Church can be found wherever people are over-zealous about creating a perfect congregation of saints. They may try to do this by over-emphasizing pure doctrine, as was the case at Ephesus. Or they may be too critical about the way in which other Christians conduct their lives. A Church which takes either its teaching or its morals too seriously, can very easily become self-righteous, and indulge in finding fault with other people's conduct or with other people's teaching, so that the love which should sustain the Christian fellowship dies.

Unfortunately the example of the Ephesians has often been followed in the history of the Church, and Christians have often regarded each other as enemies instead of brothers and sisters. Today the older Orthodox, Roman Catholic, and Protestant Churches, which used to fight each other and even persecuted each other, have repented of their past sins in this respect, and are trying to understand each other and, as far as they can, to help and support each other. But there are still Christians who look upon other Christians, not as erring brothers and sisters who must be persuaded, but as enemies who must be defeated. The Letter to Ephesus ought to be a warning to such over-zealous Christians.

Pergamum is the example of a permissive sort of Christianity. Many preachers today who want to be popular at all costs, and who never criticize any kind of conduct, however bad, would have been very much at home there. John does not suggest that the Pergamenian Christians themselves were living disreputable lives, any more than their modern counterparts are. But they forgot, as many Christians still forget, that the Church has a very clear message to proclaim, and a quite distinct life to live. True, Christians are sinners, the same as other people. But they have heard and believed the gospel, they know that they are God's children, and they ought, as far as they possibly can, to live as God's children.

The heretics of Thyatira were typical of those people who are not content with the simple gospel, but claim to have some special spiritual knowledge. We have to be clear about this. John did not suggest that ignorance is bliss, and that Christians should know as little as possible. He did not write the Revelation to keep people ignorant, but to inform them about God's truth. Most of the biblical writers were highly intelligent and very knowledgeable. Thus, for example, the writer of Genesis 1 was far ahead of most people of his time in knowledge of the world.

Amos, Isaiah, and Jeremiah were much better informed about the political scene of their days than even the politicians were. Paul was probably the greatest thinker of his time. But we must not allow ourselves to be deceived by people who use clever arguments to prove what they know is not true. And we must be very suspicious of people who claim that God has given them special knowledge, which is not available to other people.

There have always been Christians like those in Sardis, who have adapted themselves to their environment, so that, except for their going to Church on a Sunday, no one would know that they were Christians. If necessary such Christians would probably have the courage of their convictions, but they usually manage to keep out of danger. Even if they live under decidedly anti-Christian governments, they usually manage to keep excellent relationships with the authorities. A good example were the 'German Christians', as they called themselves, those among the Christians in Germany who were prepared to collaborate with the Nazis. They did not actually take part in the Nazi atrocities, but as long as they were allowed to have their Sunday services they shut their eyes to such things as the concentration camps and the attempt by the government to exterminate the Jews, the gypsies, and other racial minorities. Many Churches in countries where Christians are a minority, and where the people or the government do not favour Christianity, are inclined to 'lie low', and not to draw attention to themselves. If we are lucky enough to live in a country where there is no risk attached to being a Christian, we should not condemn less fortunate Christians who keep silent for safety reasons, and in some situations this may be the only way in which the Church can survive. But on the other hand, there are situations in which a disciple of Christ cannot remain silent, and must speak up, even at the risk of his life.

The Laodicean sin is also widespread. We all know the sort of people who regard themselves as good Christians, perhaps even as pillars of the Church, and if they have the money probably contribute generously, but who never really do anything about their faith. If they are asked to render any kind of Christian service, whether for the Church, or for their neighbours, or for the community, they always say they have something more urgent to do. Most of them attend the services sometimes, but not very often. They believe in God, but He is not very important to them. Thus we find that in some parts of America, and even of Africa, it may be fashionable for businessmen to belong to a Church, without their having much interest in the gospel.

In contrast with those Churches there were, and are, also Churches and individual Christians, who carry on faithfully with their Christian witness and their Christian lives without being discouraged, Christians like those in Smyrna and Philadelphia. Some of these Churches may be small, poor, and harassed by their environment, but they carry on. They may have one disappointment after another, and their work and witness may not always meet with success, but they will not be discouraged or intimidated.

These seven letters put the whole Church under the Master's scrutiny. But the Lord came not to condemn but to save. Every one of the messages ends with a word of encouragement, comfort, and hope. Faithfulness to the end receives its reward. It is true that we should not serve God in the hope of any reward other than that of knowing that we are doing His will; but He knows our weakness, and wants to encourage us with the promise that our pains will bear fruit.

Finally, we must bear in mind that the letters to the seven Churches are part of John's vision of Christ in the midst of the seven lampstands, holding the seven stars. In spite of the Lord's criticism of much that is wrong in the Churches, He is in the midst of His Church. He knows its problems, and, indeed, the problems of every congregation everywhere. He knows of the Church's achievements and its sins, and He is concerned about the life of His people; in fact He is involved in every aspect of our lives, and He is determined to save us. And He has the seven stars in His hand: all authority belongs to Him. He has the power to do whatever He desires to do, and if He intends to stand by us, no one will be able to overcome us. Much will happen in the world, much that is terrible and frightening, but through it all we who are God's people can rely on Him who is in the midst of the seven lampstands and holds the seven stars.

STUDY SUGGESTIONS

APPLICATION

1. Does your Church show any signs of the fault of the Ephesians? If so, what is being done, or could be done about it?
2. In what way, if any, does your Church show an inclination to be too easy on false teaching or lax morals?
3. If we avoid the fault of the Ephesians, we easily fall into the fault of the Pergamenians; and if we avoid the fault of the Pergamenians, we easily fall into the fault of the Ephesians. How can both faults be avoided?
4. Describe any modern cults you know of, which practice the faults mentioned in the letter to Thyatira.
5. Do you know of any Churches that 'keep silent'? If so, what are their chief reasons? Is such silence always to be condemned? In what circumstances is it especially important for Christians to speak up?
6. Do you know of any 'fashionable' congregations within your own

'God knows our weakness and encourages us with the promise that our pains will bear fruit' (p. 56).

Some of the runners in this American students' marathon race will take much longer than others to reach the finish. But even the weakest can receive the 'reward' of knowing that God is with them, and this helps them to do their best. In what ways is this sort of marathon *not* like the 'race' that Christians run in the world?

denomination, which seem to be flourishing, but whose members are lukewarm? If so, what are the chief reasons for it, and what, if anything, do you think that they should do about it?

7. A minister, who was conducting the evening service in a Church where the morning service had been conducted by someone else, began his sermon with the words, 'This morning you got the poison, tonight I am giving you the antidote.' Why do you think he said this, and what would have been your reaction if you had been a member of that congregation?

4.1–11
The Heavenly Worship

SUMMARY

4.1: John sees an open door in heaven, and is invited to go in.
4.2–5: He sees God's throne, surrounded by twenty-four elders.
4.6a: In front of the throne is something like a sea of glass.
4.6b–8: Four living creatures worship God day and night.
4.9–11: The worship of the twenty-four elders.

NOTES

An open door. The motif of the 'open door' was derived from the early belief that the sky was a vast dome supporting the heavens (the English word 'firmament', which literally means a 'firm structure', still reflects that belief). The 'open door' meant an opening in the structure through which one could see what was beyond. But even in John's days that belief was out of date. The 'open door' is here merely picture-language meaning that John was allowed to see that which is normally hidden from human eyes.

In heaven. John does not refer to the intermediate spheres, which people believed to exist between heaven and earth. The general belief was that there were intelligent beings, not on other planets, but in a number of stages between the earth and the highest heaven. John must have known about such beliefs, and probably shared them himself, but he does not mention them. His visions were practical, and only dealt with what concerns us: God's heaven and the world in which we live.

4.3. Jasper and carnelian. We cannot always be certain of the meaning of ancient names of precious stones. The word translated 'jasper' perhaps means a diamond, though it is actually a brightly-coloured form of chalcedony. So also is 'carnelian', which is usually red, the colour of blood – or fire. More important is that the brightness and colour of the stones suggest the presence of God.

4.4. Twenty-four elders. Some interpreters think that John meant angels, but angels are never called 'elders', and John used the word 'angel' quite often. So, if he had meant angels, he would have said so. Others think that the elders represent the twenty-four heads of priestly families who had to be present in the Temple at the great festivals; but that would only explain the number, it would not explain what the elders in John's vision represented. Others again think of the 'men of old' of Hebrews 11.2, who were also called *presbyteroi*, 'elders'. But the most natural explanation is that the twenty-four elders represent God's chosen people from Israel and the Church, represented on earth by the twelve tribes and the twelve apostles.

4.6. Round the throne, on each side of the throne. The Greek text is awkward, and not quite clear; but it is not really important to have an accurate picture; to the first readers this would have been just as vague as it is to us. We find the same vagueness in 5.6. Perhaps John himself found it difficult afterwards to remember exactly how the scene had looked.

Four living creatures. These four living creatures are also mentioned in Ezekiel 1. Ezekiel's vision was given to him in a form which he could understand, using picture-language with which he was familiar. We find the ox, the lion, and the eagle in the sky, in the constellations Taurus, Leo, and Aquila, whilst Scorpio was called by some ancient astrologers 'the Man'. Three of the four are signs of the Zodiac, but that cannot mean anything here, for Aquila is not among those signs, and never was. The four constellations mentioned cover the four corners of the sky, and we could say, as Ezekiel did, that they hold up the throne of heaven.

However, interesting though that may be, it does not tell us what the living creatures meant to John. In Ezekiel 1 the message was clear: the powers which hold up the heavens serve to carry God's throne. But here the four creatures do not carry anything: they worship.

However, in Jewish tradition the creatures of Ezekiel 1 were regarded as representing the whole creation praising the Creator. Popular opinion divided all living creatures into four groups: human beings, domestic animals, wild beasts, and creatures of sea and air. The man, the ox, the lion, and the eagle represented those four groups. And this is what the vision of the four living creatures must have conveyed to John: they worshipped God as representatives of the whole creation.

4.8. Full of eyes all round and within. Stars were often called 'eyes'. 'Full of eyes' would originally have meant that the four constellations in the sky were full of stars. Even in a vision John could not actually have *seen* the eyes within, but the idea simply belonged to the picture. However, John was not thinking of stars, and to him the eyes probably signified that the four creatures were wide awake as they sang to the Lord.

Holy, holy, holy. This was the hymn of the seraphs in Isaiah 6.3. This hymn of heavenly worship, known in Greek as the *Trisagion*, or in Latin as the *Sanctus*, was regarded as a pattern for worship, not only in heaven, but also on earth. It was part of the liturgy of the synagogue, and Clement of Rome, a bishop of that city who wrote a Letter to the Corinthians at about the same time that John wrote the Revelation, seems to infer that it was also part of Christian worship (1 Clement 34.6–7).

4.11. Our Lord and God. The Roman Emperor was often addressed by those words, and Domitian insisted on being called 'lord and god'. Absolute rulers claim for themselves the authority and honour which belong to God alone.

INTERPRETATION

The first vision had shown John how things really stand on earth: in spite of appearances, Christ is in the midst of His Church, and has the whole world in His hand. In this second vision John was shown a vision of heaven. The 'open door' is John's way of saying that he was granted access to the presence of God, and also links this vision with the letter to Philadelphia: the faithful there were also promised access to God. John was shown what is in store for them, and what is in store for all the faithful. Most important of all that is to take place is the coming of Christ. The Church does not look forward to a number of unrelated events, but to a *person*, Jesus Christ, and the coming of Christ means that God is close by, and can be approached.

So John was shown a reality which is usually hidden from human eyes. We can never really put into exact words what heaven actually is. If we want to speak about heaven at all, we have to do as John did, and use pictures. We might say that heaven is the reality beyond time, the universe when all history is past. As human beings we live in time, but 'eternity', God's 'time', if that is the right word, must be totally different from our time, an eternal present, in which the outcome of all that happens is already completed. In heaven the past, the present, and the future are one. But if we say such things, we are still using picture language, and we do not really make things any clearer. It would be foolish to think that we could define heaven adequately. All that we say about that reality which underlies our own reality, can only be said in pictures or symbols, and we should be deluding ourselves if we thought otherwise.

We should also be mistaken if we took vv. 2 and 3 for an attempt to describe God. In fact, John does not even use the word 'God', but speaks of 'One seated on a throne'. The vision of God is indescribable, and these verses must not be taken literally; they merely hint at that which is beyond understanding or imagination. It stands to reason that God, who is infinite, must be beyond our finite understanding. That is why there is no biblical 'concept' or definition of God. Of course, various biblical writers did have some sort of concept in their minds when they wrote about God – after all, no one can speak or write without thinking. But what they worshipped was not their concepts, their thoughts or ideas about God, but the living God Himself, who is beyond our thinking.

Even so these verses do tell us *something* about God. He who cannot be described, and whose name is not given, was seated on a throne. To most people today a throne is merely a piece of furniture, used on certain solemn occasions, and it is difficult for us to understand what a throne meant to John and his readers. We find it difficult to imagine the awe which filled people when they saw their rulers from a distance seated on a throne, or the trembling with which they would approach the throne when invited to do so. We should also remember the power which rulers actually wielded in ancient times, and the fear which they instilled in their subjects. He who sat on a throne really had authority and power, and He who sits on the throne of heaven has all authority and power in the universe. Flashes of lightning and peals of thunder leave no doubt that all the natural forces of the universe are at His command.

It is difficult to think what John may have meant by saying that the rainbow round the throne looked like an emerald. But there can be little doubt as to what the rainbow signified. In Genesis 9.12–17, at the end of the story of the flood, the rainbow is the pledge of God's faithfulness. He who sits on the throne, who is the Ruler of all, and whose will is sure to be carried out, is also the One who is faithful to His promises and to His people.

We must think of the sea of glass, or rather, something like a sea of glass, against the background of the manner in which people looked upon the sea. Their attitude was ambiguous, rather like that of fishermen today. On the one hand the sea was important as a link of communication. Without a regular supply of wheat from overseas, Rome and some other cities would starve; and to many men the sea was their livelihood. On the other hand people were frightened of it; with their small ships they were helpless in storms; the sea could be terrifying, and it could never be trusted.

Consequently the sea could easily be identified with the powers of death, or be regarded as a manifestation of threatening chaos, and the Jews and other Semitic nations certainly thought of it in this way. In the story of the Flood (Genesis 6—8) the power of God is shown not only in His ability to send the flood, but even more in His ability to contain it. In this connection we should also remember the wonder which people felt at Jesus's ability to still the storm and calm the sea: 'Who then is this, that even wind and sea obey Him?' (Mark 4.41).

The sea then is a treacherous and dangerous element, and we should not be surprised that people thought of it as representing the powers of chaos which threatened to overwhelm God's good creation. But what John saw was like a sea of glass, like crystal. Chaos may still threaten, but the threat is idle. Whatever may happen in the world, in the presence of God there is peace.

He who is seated on the throne is worshipped by twenty-four elders and four living creatures. Some interpreters will not say more than that the elders and cherubs are heavenly beings, like the angels, whose task it is to praise God. But John's words suggest something more precise. For one thing, he does not speak of 'cherubs' but of 'living creatures', as Ezekiel had done (Ezek. 1.5). This suggests that the four living creatures represent the whole of the living creation (see note on v. 6 above). Not just mankind, but the whole universe was created to praise the Lord.

The twenty-four elders must then represent God's people, twelve representing Israel, and twelve representing the Church (see note on v. 4).

The heavenly worship takes a form similar to the praise of God in Isaiah 6, with only slight variation. There is, however, a subtle difference between the worship of the living creatures and that of the elders. The twenty-four elders have more to say; they interpret the Sanctus, so to speak, rather than merely repeating it. Also, whilst the living creatures worship God in the third person, and do not address Him directly, the elders do speak to Him directly. The whole creation proclaims the glory of God, but the faithful have a direct and intimate relationship with Him.

John, however, was not wanting to focus attention on either the living creatures or the elders. We must therefore not inquire too closely into what they really are, and not take the symbolic description given by John too seriously. The important point is that they worship Him who is seated on the throne. All their attention, and all John's attention, was focused on Him, and so should our attention be.

STUDY SUGGESTIONS

WORDS

1. Explain the significance of the word 'throne' in this passage.

CONTENT

2. Give John's reasons for not trying to describe God.
3. What is the significance of the open door?
4. What is the significance of the rainbow?

5. What would the white garments (v. 4) suggest?
6. Why was it important that what John saw before the throne was like a sea of *glass*, like *crystal*?
7. What do the flashes of lightning and peals of thunder mean?
8. What do the four living creatures represent? In what way is it significant that John did not call them 'cherubs'?
9. Comment on the difference between the worship of the twenty-four elders and that of the four living creatures.

BIBLE

10. There are certain differences between the four living creatures as described in Ezekiel 1 and those described in Revelation 4. What are those differences? And why should there be such differences?

APPLICATION

11. What, if anything, does the worship of the four living creatures suggest about the relationship between human beings and the rest of creation? (You may find it helpful to read again Genesis chapters 1—3 before answering this question.)
12. What does the worship of the elders suggest about our own relationship with God?
13. What can we learn from this scene of the heavenly worship about the ways in which we should worship God on earth?

5.1–14
The Lamb of God

SUMMARY

5.1–4: John sees in the hand of Him who sits on the throne a scroll, sealed with seven seals, which no one is able to open.
5.5: One of the elders tells him that the Lion of the tribe of Judah can open the scroll and its seals.
5.6: John sees a Lamb, standing slaughtered.
5.7: The Lamb takes the scroll.
5.8–14: The living creatures, the elders, a host of angels, and every creature in creation, worship the Lamb.

NOTES

5.1. A scroll. The Greek word, *'biblion'*, could also mean a folded and sealed document such as a will. A will would become effective at the opening of the seals, and some interpreters think that John saw such a document containing God's will. The seven seals seem to support that. But it is more likely that John saw a scroll; God is not dead, and the idea of a last will does not seem right. The idea of a Book of Destiny is also found in other apocalypses, and suits the context of John's vision very well.

5.3. No one in heaven or on earth or under the earth was able to open the scroll. No doubt God was able to open it, but no creature was able to do so.

5.5. The Lion of the tribe of Judah, the Root of David. See Genesis 9.9–10: 'Judah is a lion's whelp; from the prey, my son, you have gone up. He stooped down, he couched as a lion, and as a lioness; who dares rouse him up? The sceptre shall not depart from Judah, nor the ruler's staff from between his feet, until he comes to whom it belongs; and to him shall be the obedience of the peoples.' This was a favourite messianic text, as was Isaiah 11.10: 'On that day the root of Jesse shall stand as an ensign to the peoples; him shall the nations seek, and his dwellings shall be glorious.'

5.6. Between the throne and the four living creatures and among the elders. John's Greek is not quite clear. He probably meant, 'In the very middle of the throne, inside the circle of living creatures and the circle of elders' (NEB). But it is not really necessary to have an accurate picture (see note on 4.6).

A Lamb. The Greek word which John has used for 'lamb' (*arnion*) is not the word used by other New Testament writers (*amnos*). Some scholars have therefore thought that John meant a 'ram', such as the ram mentioned in Daniel 8.3, and also in other apocalyptic writings. But it seems more reasonable to take the word *arnion* to mean what it normally means, a lamb, and to connect the Lamb of this vision with Isaiah 53; Acts 8.32; and 1 Peter 1.19; and especially with John 1.29 and 36, where John the Baptist calls Jesus 'the Lamb of God'. The writer of the Revelation seems to have used the term 'the Lamb' quite naturally as one of the names of Jesus, and to have taken it for granted that his readers knew that 'the Lamb' meant Jesus.

As though it had been slain. This translation is misleading; 'a Lamb that seemed to have been sacrificed' (JB) is better, but still does not make it clear that the Lamb *had* been sacrificed. What John meant to say was that it had been killed, and that he could still see that it had been killed. **Which are the seven spirits of God.** A comparison with 1.4 and 4.5 shows that we must not take John's symbols too literally.

5.8 The prayers of the saints. In the New Testament 'the saints' simply means 'the Christians' (see, for example, Acts 9.32, 41; Romans 1.7; 15.25; 2 Cor. 1.1; 13.13). Their prayers are brought before God and the

Lamb to sing Their praise, but also with the purpose that God may use their prayers in the government of His universe. More is said about this in chapter 8.

5.9. Ransom, literally 'purchase'. The Greek word is uncommon in the New Testament: Paul uses it twice ('you were bought with a price', in 1 Cor. 6.20 and 7.23), and it is used once in 2 Peter, and twice in the Revelation. But it is linked closely to the idea of redemption, which means, in ancient Greek usage, either the purchase of a slave to set him free, or the ransoming of a prisoner of war. By His Cross Jesus has set us free from the slavery of sin. His death was a 'ransom for many', the price paid for our redemption (Mark 10.15; the Greek word used by Mark is not related to that used by John). But we must not think of that as a sales agreement, and it would be absurd to ask to whom the price was paid. The point of these expressions is that the Cross of Jesus was the one thing that was necessary to achieve our redemption.

Men. Most English Bibles translate the Greek word *anthropoi* by 'men'. But an *anthropos* is a 'human being', who could be a man or a woman, and *anthropoi* are 'human beings', that is to say, men *and* women. The Greek word for 'man' (*aner*) does not occur in the Revelation at all, and when we read 'men', we should take it to mean 'men and women'.

Blood suggests a connection on the one hand with the blood shed in animal sacrifices, on the other hand with the Passover lamb.

Animal sacrifices can have very different purposes, but in most cases, if the sacrifice is to be meaningful, the animal must belong to the person who makes the sacrifice. That is to say, the giver must give something of his own, in a sense he must be giving part of himself. Thus the sacrificial animal can be regarded as representing the giver. Similarly the sacrifice of Jesus on the Cross can be seen as a sacrifice made on our behalf.

But the Gospel according to John pays particular attention to the connection between the Cross of Jesus and the Passover lamb. This evangelist points out that the crucifixion took place at the time when the Passover lambs were killed, and that not a bone of Jesus was broken, as was prescribed for the Passover lamb (John 19.14 36; see Exod. 12.46 and Num. 9.12). At the Passover the Passover lamb was killed in remembrance of the time when the Israelites were liberated from bondage in Egypt, when the blood of the Passover lamb had been used as a sign to set apart God's people who were to be set free. The parallel with the Cross is less than perfect. In this hymn Christ is praised for having redeemed His people by shedding His blood, by giving His life.

5.10. A kingdom. The Greek word means 'royal government' rather than a territory.

They shall reign. The ancient manuscripts are fairly evenly divided between 'they reign' and 'they shall reign'. We can now no longer find out what John actually wrote, but either would make sense. Whatever their position was on earth, in heaven the believers already share in Jesus's royal government. But on earth too the royal government of Christ will be made visible in God's good time, and His people will share in it.

5.11. The voice of many angels. The whole heavenly host joins in worshipping the Lamb.

5.12. Worthy is the Lamb who was slain. Worship is offered to the Lamb as to God. Once more it is stressed that He was slain (the form of the Greek word indicates that the effect is lasting): the Cross reveals God's very self.

5.13. Every creature. In the world that John and his first readers knew, the worshippers of Christ were a minority, the same as they are in the world that we know. But in heaven, where the future is already present, the whole creation joins in praising God.

INTERPRETATION

The vision described in chapter 4 was grand, and it was a great privilege for John to have seen it, but it was also rather remote. He knew, and his readers knew, that in heaven, with God, there is peace. But we live on earth, and here we have pain and sickness and sorrow, famine and violence and war, and death. The peace and joy of heaven do not touch us. Or do they?

John sees a scroll in the right hand of God, a book so full, that the letters had to be cramped all over both sides of the pages – which should not surprise us, for it is the book of human destiny. This book is sealed with seven seals, which seems to suggest a testament, but as John saw later, it contains God's 'will' in another sense. Ultimately our history and destiny are in God's hand, and God's 'will' will be done, but much of what happens before the end is not of God's doing.

The seals emphasize that the contents of the book are hidden. For who is able to open the seals? Who can fathom the mysteries of human history and destiny?

Simple people suspect that there must be some meaning to it all, wise people have tried to fathom its mysteries, and cynics have tried to tell us that there is no such thing as meaning, and that life and history are governed by mere chance. What is the truth? To John in his vision it seemed tragic that no one was found worthy to open the scroll, so that no one was able to discover the secret, and he wept.

But then things begin to happen. So far the scene has been one of eternal rest. But now John discovers that in the peace of heaven things do happen, things which are closely connected with events on earth.

The language (both the language which John hears and his own language in which he describes what he sees) is symbolic. When one of the elders says, 'Weep not, the Lion of the tribe of Judah, the Root of David

66

has conquered', John does not expect to see a lion, and certainly not the root of a tree. What he does expect to see is a conquering hero. Both he and his readers would have been familiar with the Old Testament writers' use of the lion as a symbol of courage and nobility of character (see e.g. Prov. 28.1), and of the 'root' or 'stump' of Jesse or David to mean the Messiah (see note on 5.5, and compare also Rom. 15.23).

But when John looks, he sees 'a Lamb standing, as though it had been slain, with seven horns and seven eyes.' Again, we must not think that John saw a monstrous animal looking like a lamb with seven horns and seven eyes. The Lamb was Jesus, and the seven horns symbolize His power, the seven eyes His ability to search, and see, and know all things. And He is standing 'as slaughtered' because He still bears the wounds of His passion and death; in other words, like Thomas, John saw the risen Christ, victorious over death, but still bearing His wounds (see John 20.26–29).

But the contrast between the Lion and the Lamb was deliberate and meaningful. The Lion turns out to be the Lamb, that same Jesus who died on the Cross: God's victory was won, not on a battlefield but in the passion and death of Christ.

Jesus alone is able to break the seals of the book of human destiny, He alone can uncover and handle its mysteries. Not only is He worthy to reveal its secrets, but He actually holds it in His hand, and He knows what to do with it.

Before the contents of the scroll are disclosed, it is good to know who holds it in His hand. Our destiny is not dependent on a cold and heartless fate, nor subject to mere chance, nor in the hand of a capricious god whom we cannot trust: it is in the hand of the Lamb who was slain.

That is why it was necessary for John to see the wounds of Jesus, for these wounds are the signs of His love. Jesus does not just speak nice words to His people: He actually shared their burdens and suffered their pains, even the pain of death. Indeed, the vision of the Lamb standing as slaughtered suggests more: He still shares the burdens and pains of His people. Our pains hurt Him more than they hurt us. But as He is victorious over sin, and pain, and death, so He will bring us through our own.

The contrast between chapters 4 and 5 contains a paradox which we shall never be able to resolve rationally, but which reveals God's very heart. God is secure in His eternal peace, but in Jesus Christ He has chosen to make Himself vulnerable, and to share the pains of His creatures. He who holds our destiny in His hand shared that destiny with us, lived a human life with all its joys and sorrows, took our burdens upon Himself, even the burden of our sins, and died for us on the Cross. And He is still the same, now and always, sharing our burdens and sorrows. Because He holds it all in His hand, life cannot ultimately be tragic.

John now hears a new tone in the heavenly worship. It is not merely that worship is now offered both to God and the Lamb, but also that our salvation is made one of the main themes of the praise offered to God. He who is seated on the throne and the Lamb are praised, not only because God has created all things, but because the Lamb loves us and has given Himself for us. The real mystery of God is the mystery of His love.

STUDY SUGGESTIONS

WORDS

1. What did the word 'the Lamb' mean to John and his readers?

CONTENTS

2. What was the significance of the seals?
3. What could the scroll be, and what do *you* think it was?
4. Why was it so sad that no one could break the seals?
5. What is the meaning of the contrast between the Lion and the Lamb?
6. Does the description of the Lamb, as given by John, mean that this is what the heavenly Christ looks like? If not, what does it mean?
7. What is the meaning of 'standing as though slaughtered'?
8. In what way does the heavenly worship described in this chapter differ from that in chapter 4, and what is the significance of that difference?
9. Who joins in the heavenly worship?

BIBLE

10. Why should David have been mentioned in v. 5?
11. What did the Second Isaiah say about the Suffering Servant (see Isa. 53, especially v. 7)?

APPLICATION

12. What do the words 'as slaughtered' mean to us today? What do they *not* mean?

Special Note C
Numbers in the Revelation

Numbers play a large part in the Revelation, as, indeed, they did in the ancient world generally, and still do in many parts of the world. Thus three and seven were sacred numbers to most ancient peoples, and it is not by accident that among the gods of India the Triad of Brahma, Shiva, and Vishnu is most highly venerated, or that Buddhist teaching is contained in three sacred Scriptures. Four is a sacred number to many peoples in Africa. Thirteen was an unlucky number to Babylonians, Indians, Greeks and Aztecs, and is still unlucky to many Europeans (though there are some people today who regard it as lucky).

In the Bible, One is the number of Him who is unique. 'Hear, O Israel, the LORD is our God; the LORD is one' (Deut. 6.4) – not only in the sense that there is no other God, but in the sense that there could be no other one like Him. And 'there is one body and one Spirit, just as you were called to the one hope that belongs to your call, one Lord, one faith, one baptism, one God and Father of us all' (Eph. 4.4–6a).

Two was the minimum number of witnesses required by the Old Testament Law to establish the truth (Deut. 19.15); the Revelation also has two faithful witnesses (11.3).

Three was regarded as a divine number. It is rarely used in the Bible explicitly as the number relating to God, though there is the remarkable story in Genesis 18, where the LORD appears to Abraham in the guise of three men, and there are a number of instances where things closely connected with God come in threes.

Four is the number of the created world: there are four corners of the earth and four seasons.

Seven is three plus four, and is the number of completeness and perfection. There were thought to be seven chief heavenly bodies (the sun, the moon and the five planets then known), seven days in the week, seven archangels, seven spirits of God. Seven Churches in Asia represent the universal Church; God's work in the Revelation is completed in sevens; and John uses a division into seven in several parts of his book.

Six is seven minus one, and is the number of *in*completeness. In the Revelation it is used particularly either as the number of the devil, who aims to be equal with God but cannot quite manage it, or as the number of human effort, which can never reach the perfect seven of God's work.

Eight was later used for God's new creation, and Sunday was regarded as the eighth day, rather than the first of seven, but this number plays no part in the Revelation.

Ten is simply a round number, the number of fingers on both hands. Ten, a thousand, and ten thousand are used rather vaguely by Bible writers, simply to mean very large numbers. And multiplication by ten or by a thousand is used to intensify other numbers, such as the twelve thousand from each tribe in 7.5–8.

Twelve, four times three, is, like seven, a number of completeness or perfection. There are twelve months, twelve tribes of Israel, twelve apostles, a thousand times twelve times twelve firstfruits of the elect (see notes and interpretation of chapter 7).

However, the importance of the numbers in the Revelation is not exhausted by their symbolic significance. Though John occasionally uses such expressions as 'myriads of myriads', and 'a great multitude which no man could number', he usually gives finite numbers. These numbers must not be taken literally, for they were chosen for their symbolic meaning, but they are *finite* numbers. The works of evil are six (the idea of seven deadly sins was of much later origin). In times of great distress we sometimes have the feeling that there is no end to all the troubles in the world. Scarcely have we escaped from one peril but another danger confronts us. Scarcely have we managed to cope with one calamity but another overtakes us. Scarcely have we lived through one war but another threatens. In folk tales, when the perils have been overcome, the hero and heroine 'live happily ever after'; but in real life new troubles will arise, and new problems will have to be faced. There seems to be no end to it all. But John saw that there *is* an end to it all. God makes an end. The number of dangers, troubles, and disasters is six, not literally of course, but it is a *limited* number, and it does not add up to the whole of our destiny, the full seven of God's plan.

For God's plans are also given in finite numbers. His work of creation and redemption is completed in sevens and twelves. They are numbers of fulness and perfection, which must not be taken literally, but which are nevertheless specific. God's works are not a mass without definition, they are distinct and individual; and the redeemed are not just a mass of people: they too are distinct and individual, and every one is known to God and loved by God.

STUDY SUGGESTIONS

1. Which numbers are of special significance in your own environment, and why?
2. What is the significance in the Bible of each of the following numbers:
   one? two? three? six? seven? twelve?

3. Apart from their symbolic meaning, what else is important about the numbers in the Revelation?

6.1–8
The First Four Seals

SUMMARY

6.1, 2: At the opening of the first seal John sees a rider on a white horse, who goes out conquering and to conquer.

6.3, 4: At the opening of the second seal John sees a rider on a red horse, who brings war.

6.5, 6: At the opening of the third seal John sees a rider on a black horse, who brings famine

6.7, 8: At the opening of the fourth seal John sees a rider on a pale horse, who brings death.

NOTES

6.1. One of the living creatures. The connection of the four living creatures with the four corners of the earth (see note on 4.6) links this vision in a formal way with Zechariah 6, where the prophet records a vision of four horse-drawn chariots, which represent the four winds. But John may have seen a more intimate link between the creatures and the horses. As the four living creatures represent the whole creation, the call, 'Come!' suggests that the whole creation longs for the completion of God's plans.

6.2. A white horse. The colours of the horses are the same as those described in Zechariah 6.2–3 (though the dappled grey is here called 'pale'); but John puts the white horse first, leaving the others in the order red, black, pale. This seems to suggest that John attached a particular significance to the white horse. White is the colour of daylight.

A bow. The image of the four horses seems to have been used first in Iran (called Persia in the Bible, and Parthia in John's days). Parthian cavalry were the only horsemen using a bow (other mounted soldiers used spears or swords), and many interpreters have explained the four horsemen as a symbol for the threat of a Parthian invasion. Some commentators have been even more precise, and have interpreted the first horseman as a Parthian invasion, the second as troubles within the Roman Empire, such as the revolt of Boudicca in Britain, the third as the sort of troubles that follow after strife, and the fourth as the collapse of the Roman

Empire through famine and pestilence. But we must distinguish between the source of the images and the way in which John used them. It may be interesting to know where John got his pictures from, but it is much more important to see how he used them, and what he meant by them (see the Interpretation below).

6.4. Bright red, the colour of blood.

6.5. Black, the colour of the night.

Balance. Coins were often weighed rather than counted (coins were minted of gold, silver, or copper, and they were literally worth their weight in gold, silver, or copper; a coin with the edge scraped off was worth less than its face value, and the only way to avoid being cheated was by weighing the coins). In times of scarcity the price of food rises, and more money is needed.

6.6. A quart of wheat for a denarius, and three quarts of barley for a denarius; but do not harm oil and wine. A denarius was a Roman coin; its value was supposed to be equal to a man's daily wages, though in fact many men had to work several days for one denarius. The four things mentioned were among the daily necessities of life (wine was the everyday drink, and was not regarded as a luxury); John was simply referring to a year when the harvest has been bad, but not so bad that all the necessities were scarce. Still, people cannot live on wine and olive oil, and the scarcity of wheat and barley did mean famine.

6.7. A pale horse. John has altered the colour from the traditional dappled grey to pale. Pale is the colour of death.

6.8. The wild beasts of the earth. The picture is that of a city, devastated by war, famine, and pestilence, which has been abandoned by the survivors, and left to wild animals to scavenge among the ruins.

INTERPRETATION

This chapter has some special difficulties. Some interpreters have remarked that it seems strange that the Lamb who was slain is there represented as an Avenger, who brings death and destruction. But that is not what John actually says. True, the scroll is in the hand of the Lamb, and He will decide what is to be done with it; but that does not mean that He brings about the events which the book describes. The Lamb has not written the scroll, but is opening its seals. The opening of the seals means that He shows John, and through John the Church, what the book contains.

It also means that the sequence of the seals does not necessarily reflect a sequence of events. It reflects the order in which John was shown certain aspects of human history, but the events may well take place in a different order, or at the same time, or frequently repeat themselves.

Much in this chapter is traditional. War, strife, famine, pestilence,

72

persecution, and portents in the sky had been mentioned in other apocalyptic writings, and we should note that Jesus Himself had spoken about them (Mark 13, Matthew 24, Luke 13).

The chief difficulty lies in the white horse. We are told that the riders on the other three horses bring about terrible disasters. Most interpreters take it for granted that all four horses must have similar functions, and that therefore the white horseman too must be a bringer of disaster. Thus it is widely thought that 'the four horsemen of the Apocalypse represent conquest, slaughter, famine, and death'.

But John does not actually say so. On the contrary, the picture of the first horseman is wholly positive, though mysterious: 'He had a bow, and a crown was given him, and he went out conquering and to conquer'. He is a conquering hero, of that there is no doubt, but John says nothing about the horrors of war or about anybody being slain. This rider seems to be out on a campaign of conquest in which no blood is shed. This is scarcely a fair description of the terrors of war.

If the white horse does not refer to the disasters of war, is there any way of knowing what it does mean? White is usually connected with Christ and His saints. The white horse therefore seems to hint at Christ. True, the colours of the horses were traditional, but John was never careless, and often altered the meaning of traditional pictures to suit his message. Moreover, the Lamb is He who conquered (5.5), and a *stephanos*, a crown or garland, is granted by Christ to His faithful people (2.10; 3.11).

Thus at the opening of the first seal John sees a rider on a white horse setting out quietly on his triumphant course, a horseman who seems to be connected with Christ. Whatever may happen in the world, he is already on the scene. He had already been given a crown (the necessary authority) and a bow (the necessary equipment); and it is not surprising that many people find him terrifying. But those who know God can be secure in knowing that he has gone out to conquer, and that nothing will be able to stop him from carrying out his purpose.

The rider on the white horse offers peace, but his coming inaugurates the arrival of the other horsemen, who are the bringers of man-made disasters. We may argue that famine, pestilence, and the attacks of animals of prey are not always man-made calamities, but in this vision John sees war and its results. It all starts with war; war brings about scarcity of food, high prices and inflation; and finally the war-ravaged land is visited by famine, epidemics, and jackals and vultures. The picture is all the more terrifying because the riders do not seem to be in control: in a headlong gallop the horses trample everything under their hooves. This is not a prediction of any particular war, but a comment on human violence generally. Nations and individuals very often begin using violence in only a limited way, but once the violence has been

'In this vision John sees war and its results . . . violence has a way of escalating' (p. 75).

Even the armies sent, like this Tanzanian soldier, to 'liberate' victims of aggression usually end by causing more destruction, and refugees fleeing from danger, as in Laos, may find themselves facing captivity or starvation instead. Do you think there will ever be an end to war in the world, and if so what will make it end?

unleashed there is no stopping it. Violence has a way of escalating.

The riders are men. Violence is caused by people. At this point we might almost have forgotten the man on the white horse. When we see the violence in the world we may easily forget that God too, in His own mysterious way, works through human beings. However, the man on the white horse is still on the scene. We may be tempted to look for a more precise interpretation than we have attempted before, and interpret the first horseman either as the victorious course of the gospel, or as Christ Himself. But the figure is too mysterious for such precision to be justified. The rider on the white horse is closely connected with Christ, he is on the scene, and he conquers; that is all we are told.

STUDY SUGGESTIONS

CONTENT

1. What is the significance of the colours of the four horses?
2. What is the connection between the horses and the four living creatures.
3. For what reason or reasons do you think that John may have changed the traditional order of the four colours of the horses?
4. The four horsemen are often interpreted as meaning war, slaughter, famine, and death? What other interpretation or interpretations can you suggest?
5. In what respect were the disasters of the third and fourth horsemen man-made?

BIBLE

6. There are several differences between Zechariah's vision of horsemen (Zech. 6) and John's. Leaving out the less important differences, what is the *chief* difference between the visions?

APPLICATION

7. In what respect can some of the troubles in the world today be said to be man-made? (Remember that war is not the only way in which people can cause disasters.)

6.9–11
The Fifth Seal

SUMMARY

John sees the dead who have been killed for their loyalty to the word of God, and hears their cry for vindication.

NOTES

6.9. Under the altar. The altar was not mentioned in the vision of the heavenly worship in chapter 4, but the picture is that of a heavenly altar like its earthly counterpart in the Temple in Jerusalem. The death of a martyr is pictured as a sacrifice on that heavenly altar. This idea gave rise to the custom of building churches with the altar over the grave of a martyr (see also the interpretation of chapter 7).

Souls. In the Old Testament 'soul' is used to translate the Hebrew word *nefesh. Nefesh*, however, does not mean something apart from the body; it means a body which is alive. In English the opposite of a soul is a body, but in Hebrew the opposite of a 'soul' is a corpse or a dead object. In Greek the word *psyche* did mean the same as our word 'soul', but the New Testament writers used it in the same sense as the Hebrew *nefesh*. In most cases the correct translation would be 'person' or 'human being' or just 'living creature' (for it could also be used for animals). John's use of the word here, referring to 'dead souls' therefore seems to be a contradiction in terms, but he may already be pointing forward to the vision he describes in chapter 7.

6.10. Judge and avenge. The Greek words were not used in quite the same way as their English translations. *Krinein* chiefly means to declare someone guilty or innocent; it is usually translated 'to judge', and in the New Testament it often means 'to condemn', but here it clearly means 'to condemn the guilty and to declare the martyrs innocent'. *Ekdikein* is not merely 'to avenge', but also 'to justify', 'to vindicate' a person. The RSV translation is not wrong, but does not do justice to the vindication of the Christian martyrs.

6.11. Until the number . . . should be complete, that is to say, the number of all those whom Christ has chosen to share in His trials.

INTERPRETATION

At the opening of the fifth seal John is shown that while all those disasters had befallen the world, the Church also had suffered, and he sees 'the souls of those who had been slain for the word of God and for the witness they had borne' (v. 9). The world had suffered self-inflicted calamities, the Church had suffered persecution.

Once again we must beware of taking John's words literally. The image of the altar under which he saw the souls was probably inspired by the great altar in the Temple at Jerusalem, where the blood of the victims was drained away in a hollow under the rock. 'Souls' as we understand the word today cannot be seen, but here as elsewhere in the Bible the word simply means 'people'. So John sees the men and women who have been martyred for their faith, and who are, of course, dead. Their 'crying out' is meant figuratively, like the 'crying out' of Abel's blood in Genesis 4.10: their death is a call for God's judgement and vindication. Vindication of the innocent includes the condemnation and punishment of the guilty, but that is not where the emphasis lies.

Their vindication will be made public at the Last Judgement, but even now the martyrs are already pronounced innocent: 'they were given each a white robe', as a token of their innocence and their relationship with Christ, 'and told to rest a little longer'.

STUDY SUGGESTIONS

WORDS

1. Read the following passages: Gen. 2.7; 12.5; Exod. 1.5; Pss 6.3–4; 23.3; 33.20; Matt. 11.29; 16.26; Mark 14.34; Luke 12.20. In all those the original Hebrew or Greek text contains the Hebrew or Greek word for 'soul', and the AV translates 'soul', but in some cases the RSV uses 'living being' or 'person'. In what way or ways, and with what meaning did the Bible writers use the word 'soul'?

CONTENT

2. What do the words 'under the altar' suggest?
3. What was the important thing about the vindication of the martyrs?

BIBLE

4. What very important teaching about vindication do we find in the story of Solomon's first judgement (1 Kings 3.16–28)?

APPLICATION

5. In what way(s) was the vision of the dead martyrs relevant to John's first readers, and in what way(s) is it relevant to harassed or persecuted Christians today?
6. Some Christians are greatly inspired and strengthened in their faith

by reading about the lives and deaths of martyrs and heroes of the Church. Others, however, say that such stories make them depressed and discouraged, because they feel weak, cowardly, and uncertain of their faith, by comparison. What is your own reaction to such stories, and how do you think people can be helped to find inspiration in them, rather than discouragement?

6.12–17
The Sixth Seal

SUMMARY

At the opening of the sixth seal John witnesses terrible events in the natural world, and sees how all people, high and low, are terrified at these dreadful 'acts of God'.

NOTES

6.12. Earthquake. This vision is reminiscent of a real volcanic eruption, with the earthquake, the sun being darkened by the cloud of debris thrown up by the volcano, red-hot stones falling like stars from heaven, and trees falling and buildings collapsing as the ground itself is set in motion. In fact, these verses recall at several points Pliny's description of the eruption of Vesuvius in AD 79, of which he had been an eye-witness. John could not have read Pliny's report, which was not published until later, but he may have heard stories from other witnesses. Moreover, Asia Minor was itself an earthquake area, and Laodicea had been destroyed by an earthquake in AD 65. But great portents in the natural world were also part of the language regularly used by apocalyptic writers. Thus, whilst a real event, still remembered throughout the ancient world, lent the colours to John's vision, we must not forget that this vision had the whole world and all human history in view. The disasters show the natural world as hostile to the human race; indeed it may seem to be reverting to chaos and so becoming hostile to God. But the Lamb still holds the book with the seals, He still has the whole world in His hand.

6.15. Kings of the earth ... and every one, slave and free. God's judgement on the proud is a theme which recurs often in the Bible. The belief that God 'has scattered the proud in the imagination of their hearts' is expressed not only in the Magnificat (Luke 1.46–55) but in many parts of the Scripture. Here, however, the poor too are terrified of God's wrath.

6.16. The wrath of the Lamb. The belief that God is against us is typical of the wrong relationship between God and ourselves. This leads to the fear which many people have of their gods, and to the appalling rituals which some nations have devised to pacify their gods, such as the Canaanites sacrificing their children, and many other nations offering human sacrifices. In this vision even the Lamb, the crucified One who still bears the signs of His love, causes terror in the hearts of those who do not believe in Him.

6.17. That day. The day of God's judgement, as announced by the prophets (see Amos 8.8; Joel 2.11; Nahum 1.6; Malachi 3.2).

INTERPRETATION

At the opening of the sixth seal John sees another aspect of the human condition: the natural disasters which devastate the world. John's language seems to suggest supernatural events, but, if we allow for the peculiarities of apocalyptic writings, vv. 12–14 contain a good description of how people might experience a terrible volcanic eruption.

In contrast with the man-made disasters inaugurated by the horsemen, this part of the vision presents us with a natural catastrophe, an example of the sort of things which people call 'acts of God'. The vision gives only one example, but it represents all the hostility with which the natural world confronts us. Our own time has given many dreadful examples of such events, floods in India and Holland, earthquakes in China and Japan, in Italy and the United States, drought and famine in Africa. The paradise story had already made it clear that sin not only estranges people from God, and makes them hostile to each other, but that the power of evil also makes the natural world hostile to us (Gen. 3.16–19).

Natural disasters seem to arise spontaneously, and people are quick to see in them the hand of God. At such times people who have not taken much notice of God, and have certainly not been grateful for His mercies, or tried honestly to do His will, suddenly speak of 'acts of God'. Some, indeed, turn to God, and call on Him for help. Others, as John was shown in this vision, want to hide 'from the face of Him who is seated on the throne, and from the wrath of the Lamb'.

STUDY SUGGESTIONS

CONTENT

1. In what respect do the events following the sixth seal differ from those following the earlier seals?

2. Why should a volcanic eruption be particularly suitable to give a picture of absolute terror?
3. What is significant about certain people being mentioned specifically in v. 15?

BIBLE

4. The paradise story does not mention natural disasters. In what way(s) does it indicate that nature has become hostile to us?

APPLICATION

5. Is it wise to call natural disasters 'acts of God'? Give reasons for your answer.

7.1–17
The First Fruits of the Redeemed

SUMMARY

7.1–3: Four angels hold back the four winds to give an opportunity for the servants of God to be sealed.

7.4–8: John hears the number of those who are sealed, a hundred and forty-four thousand, twelve thousand from each of the twelve tribes of Israel.

7.9–17: John looks, and sees a multitude which no one can number, standing round the throne worshipping God; and is told that these are those who have come out of the great tribulation.

NOTES

7.1. After this I saw. John is now shown, not something that will happen after the events of chapter 6, but another side of the truth. While all those terrible things are going on in the world, there is another side to reality, God's side.

The four winds of the earth are here regarded as destructive forces (anyone who has seen the results of a hurricane will know why). The 'angels' hold back their destructive force.

7.2. The seal of the living God. Seals were used for various purposes, just as they are today: to protect a document from being tampered with by unauthorized persons (as with the scroll with the seven seals), to guarantee that a document came from the person whose seal it bore, or to establish to whom certain things belonged. Here the seal is used to show which people belong to God. The image is derived from Ezekiel 9, where a mark is put on the foreheads of those among the people of Jerusalem who are penitent, to show that they belong to God and are under His protection. The idea is closely related to the practice of tattooing and other forms of marking still used in many parts of the world today. It seems that the ancient Kenites were tattooed with a sign that they belonged to the LORD. Both in the Kenite practice and in Ezekiel the mark used seems to have been the letter *taw*, which in very early Hebrew script was written either + or ×. We do not know when exactly it became the practice in Christian baptism to mark the person baptized with the sign of the cross, a sign that not only reminded the believers of the cross of Christ, but was also the initial letter of the name of Christ in Greek (spelled *XPISTOS* in Greek capital letters). John may already have known this custom, but even if he did not, baptism was the sign that a person belonged to Christ.

7.4. Israel. The much discussed question whether John meant the natural Israel or the 'new Israel', the Church, takes no account of the fact that the early Christians did not see the relationship between Israel and the Church as one of contrast or even of difference. Paul looked upon the Church simply as an extension of the 'Israel of God' (see Romans 11.17–24; the parable of the olive tree shows that Paul did not know much about how trees are actually propagated, but there can be no doubt as to what he meant). We have no reason to think that other Christians saw the relationship between Israel and the Church otherwise.

But 'Israel' had rarely been a purely racial concept. True, Ezra had put great emphasis on racial purity, and in Jesus's days descent from Abraham was regarded as a great privilege (see John 8.33). But, on the other hand, early in the history of the nation whole tribes had been incorporated into Israel (such as, for example, the Kenites), and individuals had also frequently been admitted and had become faithful members of Israel (Ruth is a famous example). In New Testament times the Scribes and Pharisees would 'traverse sea and land to make a single proselyte' (Matt. 23.15), and long after those days the whole Khazar nation was converted to the Jewish faith. Thus Israel was both a nation and another name for God's people, and the name is used here in that double sense. But it remains the 'natural' Israel: the list of the twelve tribes is enough to show this, even if the tribes are enumerated in an unusual form.

7.7. Levi. This tribe was usually left out when counting the twelve; in this list Dan is left out.

7.8. Joseph. This tribe was divided into Manasseh and Ephraim; as Manasseh is mentioned in v. 6, 'Joseph' here means Ephraim.

7.9. I looked. John looks at the 144,000 he has just heard enumerated, and sees, not only the remnant of Israel but a great multitude 'from every nation, from all tribes and peoples and tongues'.

Palm branches were carried in procession to celebrate a victory, here the victory of Christ over sin and death, in which the martyrs share.

7.10. Salvation. The NEB translation is 'victory', which could be the meaning of the Aramaic word at the back of John's mind. But that is mere guesswork. The Greek word used by John suggests total well-being: the salvation worked by Christ is not merely salvation *from* sin and death, but above all salvation *for* a new life with God.

Belongs to our God . . . and to the Lamb. Salvation is not something that the faithful have gained for themselves: it was God's gift to them. He alone has it in His hand, and He alone can give it.

7.14. 'Sir, you know'. How could John have known that those who are dead to the world are alive with God? The early Christians did expect the resurrection of the dead to a new eternal life, but had no clear ideas about what happened immediately after death. Paul speaks of 'those who are asleep' (1 Thess. 5.13).

'These are they who have come out of the great tribulation'. The dead martyrs are alive with God. Whatever may happen to other Christians when they die, the martyrs are certainly already in heaven even now. In later centuries the word 'Saint' was used particularly for those Christians, not only martyrs but others too, of whom it was believed to be certain that they are already in heaven.

Washed their robes. Salvation belongs to God alone, and is His alone to give. But receiving the gift of salvation also calls for serious effort on the part of the people who receive it.

He . . . will shelter them with his presence. The Greek means literally 'He will spread his tent over them'. In 21.3 the same verb means, 'He will dwell with them', and in John 1.14 it is used to say that the Word 'dwelled among us'. He who is seated on the throne is Himself covering them with His protection.

7.16. They shall hunger no more . . . In the world to come the blessed will not go short of anything they need. John clearly hints at the spiritual 'food' which sustains the life eternal. But we must not over-spiritualize the words. The blessings of heaven will be very substantial. In a world where many people go hungry it is good to know that there are no shortages in heaven. The many times food is mentioned also ought to remind us that food is important, and that, while the present world lasts, Christians have the task to feed the hungry (see James 2.14–17).

The sun shall not strike them. People living in temperate climates will find it difficult to feel the weight of this phrase. But those who live in a hot climate will appreciate the need for shelter from the heat of the sun.

7.17. The Lamb . . . will be their shepherd. This seems to be a reversal of roles. But the Lamb is the Lord of His people. The word 'shepherd' had long been a term used for any ruler (see e.g. Jer. 2.8), and also for God (e.g. Pss. 23 and 80.2). In the Gospel according to John we find both terms used for Jesus: 'Behold the Lamb of God' (John 1.29); and 'I am the good Shepherd' (John 10.11).

God will wipe away every tear from their eyes, in fulfilment of Isaiah 25.8. The phrase also reminds us of Isaiah 66.13: 'As one whom his mother comforts, so I will comfort you'.

INTERPRETATION

Some scholars feel that this chapter does not fit in the context, and regard it as an insertion, added after John's time by an editor. True, this chapter is an interlude, but it is closely connected with chapter 6, and the contrast between the two chapters is meaningful. Without this vision the Revelation would be incomplete.

In the midst of all the destruction which John had just seen, we might well wonder, would any room be left for God's people? John is now shown that in the midst of the disastrous course of the world there is a holding back. By God's grace there is an opportunity for the redeemed to be marked out. Those whom God has chosen will not be lost in the confusion of the world.

John is then told the number of the redeemed from Israel. The numbers, twelve thousand from every tribe, a hundred and forty-four thousand in all, are symbolic: they mean a full count. Not one of God's people is lost. 'Israel' here means the real, natural Israel, it is not a code-name for the Church.

But when John looks at this Israel of God, he sees a multitude which no one can number, not only from Israel, but from every nation, from all tribes and peoples and tongues. God has not forsaken His people Israel, nor has He become unfaithful to His promises. But His mercy extends far beyond the chosen nation, and gentiles have joined from east and west, from north and south, from wherever people live. This wideness of God's mercy was a source of constant wonder to the early Christians.

Many readers have wondered what the relationship is between the hundred and forty-four thousand and the multitude which no one can number. Were they meant to be two different groups, the 144,000 perhaps meaning the nation of Israel and the 'multitude' meaning the Church, or were they both the same? The text certainly seems to suggest that the multitude which John saw were the same people whom he had heard being counted before. The spoken words and the vision explain each other. The Israel of God is not confined to the chosen nation but includes faithful from all races and nations. The *words* had reminded John that God had remained faithful to Israel; the multitude which he *saw* showed him that God's mercy is worldwide. God's salvation of the world cannot be separated from His faithfulness to Israel (see Romans 9—11).

The emphasis is on the martyrs, 'they that have come out of the great tribulation'. They are the first fruits of the redeemed. Those same people whose earthly life is ended, those same people whom John had just seen as the dead victims of persecution (6.9–11), are actually alive with God.

It is not said that they are the only ones in heaven. They are the first fruits, and the light falls on them. They are the people who have remained faithful to the end. Yet it is not their faithfulness that has saved them. Salvation belongs to God and to the Lamb, and is God's gift alone. But they have 'washed their robes and made them white in the blood of the Lamb'. By Christ's sacrifice of Himself they have been made fit to enter into the presence of God and to share in the heavenly worship. The Revelation continually stresses the need for patience, steadfastness, and faithfulness, and describes in detail the fruits they bear; but it also shows clearly that salvation is God's work. God does not save people because they have served Him; they serve Him because He has saved them. Even so, the service is real, and receives its reward.

The reward for serving God on earth is serving Him in heaven. John mentions no details about this service in heaven, other than showing the redeemed praising God, or, more precisely, singing His praise. Heaven is full of song. For the service of God is not a burden but a joy.

In God's presence people are protected and secure, they are supplied with all that they need, and – the picture becomes more and more tender – 'God will wipe away every tear from their eyes'.

STUDY SUGGESTIONS

WORDS

1. In what two senses is the word 'Israel' used in the Bible? What is the connection between the two meanings?
2. Apart from a man who looks after sheep, what does the word 'shepherd' mean?

CONTENT

3. What was the task of the four angels mentioned in v. 1?
4. What was the meaning of 'being sealed'?
5. What is the connection between the 144,000 from Israel and the great multitude from every nation?
6. 'Salvation belongs to our God . . .' What is the full meaning of this saying?
7. Whom did John mean by 'they who have come out of the great tribulation'?

'The emphasis is on the martyrs . . . who have remained faithful to the end. Yet it is not their faithfulness that has saved them' (p. 84).

In 1977 Archbishop Janani Luwum of Uganda was arrested and killed because he had the courage to stand up and protest against the cruel and oppressive regime of President Amin and his government. If not his faithfulness, what was it that 'saved' Janani Luwum, who died for his faith?

8. Explain how Jesus is both a Lamb and a Shepherd.

BIBLE

9. In what way does Romans 9—11 help us to understand Revelation 7?

APPLICATION

10. The words 'they shall hunger no more' are clearly a great comfort to people who have not enough to eat. But do they also hint at a task which Christians must carry out on earth? If so, what task?
11. 'They have washed their robes and made them white in the blood of the Lamb'. How would you explain this statement to someone who said that this does not make sense?
12. How would you answer someone who asked, 'Is it *only* those who have "come out of the great tribulation" who will receive the gift of salvation and share in the worship of God in heaven?'?

8.1
The Seventh Seal

This verse completes the vision of the Lamb and the scroll with seven seals. When the Lamb opened the seventh seal, there was silence in heaven for about half an hour.

INTERPRETATION

We might expect the opening of the seventh seal to show the end. Now at last the ultimate mystery of our destiny will be revealed. The silence of heaven is indeed the end, the eternal sabbath rest towards which the whole of history is moving; but John was allowed to see it only for a short time, about half an hour. He gets a glimpse of the blissful end, but no more.

Not all those who have studied the Revelation agree with that interpretation. Some prefer to think of the Revelation as describing a succession of events, and regard the half hour's silence as merely an interlude between the events described before and the events described later. But if we regard the Revelation as a timetable of future events, in which chapter 8 must follow chapters 6 and 7, some parts become quite inexplicable, such as chapter 13, which describes events which had already taken place when John wrote. Moreover, seven is the number of completeness, and the sequence of seven must be complete.

So we take it that John wrote this verse to conclude the vision of the seven seals. After describing this vision John went on to tell of other visions, showing other summaries of human history, each with another emphasis, each from a different point of view, but every time in the light of heaven. In each of these visions John was led to the end, but the end was not actually shown. This was repeated several times until the very last vision, which he described at the end of the Revelation, in which the New Heavens and the New Earth were shown at last.

The effect of that repetition is, that we become aware of the long time history is going to last. The vision of the seals was complete in itself. It showed the sort of things that will happen in the world as long as people live on earth. It showed the hardships which the Church will suffer, not always, but very often. It also showed that God's people are in His hand, and that their salvation has already been achieved. And in this verse 8.1 it showed that there will be an end, and that His servants may look forward to the peace of heaven (see also 22.3–4).

But taken by itself the vision of the seals can have the effect that with every disaster that befalls the world or the Church people may say, 'This is a sure sign of the end'. As a matter of fact, people have often said precisely that: 'The end is near'. However, the end was not yet. Jesus had already warned against that mistake, when He said, 'When you hear of wars and rumours of wars, do not be alarmed; this must take place, but the end is not yet' (Mark 13.7).

The way in which the Revelation unfolds contains the same warning. In every vision, at the very point where we should expect the Last Judgement and then the end, we find the beginning of another picture of human history. Again and again the showing of the end is put off, and comes only at the end of the Revelation itself. Though near by the standards of heaven, the end is still in the far future, or at least may still be in the far future by our reckoning. John did not know any more than we do, how long it would still be, but he was aware that the end would not be the next day.

These various summaries of human history gave John an opportunity to see it all from several different points of view. There is more to human history than could be shown in the vision of the seals.

So, the vision of the Lamb and the scroll with the seven seals must be read as complete in itself. Much of it is saddening, but then a large part of human history is the story of human folly and sin. However, this is also the story of what is, and remains, God's world. While three of the horsemen take their violent course through the world, there is also the Rider on the white horse, who gains the victory. Although God's people suffer on earth, He does not forget them, and their place in heaven is assured. And whatever devious courses the world may take, its ultimate end will be the peace of heaven.

STUDY SUGGESTIONS

1. What does the *seventh* seal suggest?
2. What does 'silence' suggest in connection with Gen. 2.1–3?
3. What is the particular importance of this verse?
4. Some Christians say that since Jesus said that 'wars and rumours of war. . . . must take place' there is no point in trying to bring about peace between the nations of the world: peace can only be achieved in heaven. What is your opinion?

8.2–13
The First Four Trumpets

SUMMARY

8.2–5: In a new vision John sees 'the seven angels who stand before God', to whom seven trumpets are given. Another angel, with a censer, brings the prayers of the saints before God, and then throws fire from the altar on the earth. There follow thunder, loud noises, lightning, and an earthquake.

8.6, 7: The blowing of the first trumpet affects the plant life.

8.8, 9: The blowing of the second trumpet affects the sea.

8.10, 11: The blowing of the third trumpet affects the fresh water.

8.12: The blowing of the fourth trumpet affects the sun, the moon, and the stars.

8.13: An eagle announces the woes to follow at the blasts of the remaining three trumpets.

NOTES

8.2. The seven angels. John probably meant the seven archangels of Jewish tradition (see Special Note A, p. 20).

8.3. Incense to mingle with the prayers of the saints. Incense was used in many religions. In Israel it was regarded as a symbol of the prayers of the faithful. So the meaning of John's vision was that the prayers of the faithful actually do reach God.

8.5. Threw it on the earth. This picture is derived from Ezekiel's vision of burning coals from God's throne being scattered over Jerusalem (Ezek. 9—10). The burning coals may suggest cleansing, as they do in Isaiah 6. John, in his vision, saw a close connection between the prayers of all the saints and the events which take place in the world.

8.7. The first angel blew his trumpet. The blowing of the trumpets is meant as a warning, like the ringing of bells in medieval European cities, or the use of air-raid sirens in wartime today, or, indeed, as horns are still used in many countries. God's trumpets warn people of the coming judgement, and call them to repentance.

Hail and fire. Severe thunderstorms are sometimes accompanied by hail, and are regarded by many people as specially important instances of God's speaking. The Book of Wisdom in the Apocrypha mentions the combination of hail and fire (lightning) as a miracle in which God made the fire 'forget its native power' (Wisdom 16.22–23).

Mixed with blood. A reminder of the first plague of Egypt (Exod. 7.18).

8.8. A great mountain. John may be recalling Jeremiah 51.25, where the prophet calls Babylon a 'destroying mountain', and announces its fall. Perhaps John was already pointing forward to the fall of 'Babylon' as described later in the Revelation.

8.10. A great star fell from heaven. This may be another reference to an Old Testament prophecy of the fall of Babylon (Isa. 14.3–20). Jeremiah and Isaiah were referring to ancient Babylon on the river Euphrates, a state that had attempted to usurp the authority which belongs only to God. Later in the Revelation John used 'Babylon' as a code-name for Rome, and for any authoritarian state.

8.11. Wormwood, used nowadays to flavour such drinks as vermouth and absinthe, was believed in ancient times to be poisonous. If the great star is the state which claims for itself absolute authority, then the worm-wood suggests the poisoning of the atmosphere of righteousness. Old Testament writers thought of 'righteousness' not simply as a virtue, but as an atmosphere in which people could live in the right relationship with God and with each other. Unjust rulers could, and often did, 'pollute' or 'poison' this righteousness (see e.g. Amos 5.7).

It may seem strange to find these references to an ungodly state in visions which speak of natural disasters. But there is a close connection between bad government and wasted natural resources. Some centuries of Turkish misrule left Canaan (now Israel and Jordan), which was once a land of milk and honey, a desert. In India the state of Bihar, rich in natural resources, suffered similarly because the central government was not interested in it and neglected it.

8.12. Was darkened. Darkness was the last but one of the plagues of Egypt (Exod. 10.21–23).

INTERPRETATION

Many interpreters take verses 1–5 together, and regard the vision of the trumpets as forming part of the vision of the seventh seal. This second series is then regarded as a glance back, from another aspect, and from the peace of heaven, to the same human history to which the first series (the visions of the seals) referred. This makes no real difference to the interpretation of what follows. But it seems better to regard v. 2 as a new start.

The new aspect is suggested by the angel with the censer. The story of the human race is accompanied by the prayers of the saints. By 'saints' John meant the Christians, both those on earth and those in heaven. John was not referring to particularly good or saintly people. Prayer is something that every Christian does.

We may feel at times that no-one listens to our prayers. But they are carried before God's throne, and He hears them, listens to them, and responds to them. Verse 5 illustrates their effectiveness: the angel took the censer and filled it with fire from the altar and threw it on the earth. God is the sovereign Lord, who governs His creation as He chooses, but He chooses to use the prayers of His people in governing His world.

But what is the content of these prayers? John says nothing about that at this point, but he hints at it in 9.20–21: 'The rest of mankind . . . did not repent.'. Christians pray to God for many things. They praise Him, they thank Him for His mercies, and they ask Him for many favours for themselves and for other people; but whatever else they may bring before God in their prayers, they are sure also to ask that people may repent.

The opportunity to repent is provided in many and various ways. Several of these are mentioned in the Revelation. Thus chapters 10 and 11 stress the importance of the preaching of the gospel: John is told, 'You must again prophesy' (10.11), and two witnesses prophesy in the holy city (11.3). The Rider on the white horse in 19.11–16 also emphasizes the importance of the word of God. But here, in chapter 8, John describes some terrifying events which ought to lead people to repentance. John does not actually say that God causes these disasters, but he sees them happening at the blasts of the trumpets, which means that they are under God's control, and can happen only at His appointed time.

The picture-language which John uses to describe the terrible disasters of this vision is borrowed partly from the Old Testament (Exod. 7.18; 10.21–23; Isa. 14.3–20; Jer. 51.25; Amos 5.7), and partly from various apocalyptic writings. Though John regards these events as supernatural, he shows their effect in the natural world: in the plant life, the sea, the fresh water, and the sky. More important, however, is that they are spectacular and terrifying. John emphasizes the terrifying effect by increasing the amount of damage they do from the damage done in the first series (one third is damaged, as against one quarter in 6.8). These dreadful events are meant to make people sit up and take notice, so that perhaps they may repent. But in spite of the terrible things which are happening all around them, the faithful need not be afraid, for they know that God is in control.

STUDY SUGGESTIONS

WORDS

1. The meaning of the Greek word usually translated 'righteousness' differs in many ways from the meaning of the English word. What difference is suggested by the word 'wormwood' in v. 11?

CONTENT

2. What does the scene described by John in vv. 2–5 tell us about prayer?
3. Why did John include references to 'Babylon' in his description of *natural* disasters?
4. What ought to be the effect on people of terrible disasters?

BIBLE

5. Two of the four plagues mentioned reminded John of the plagues of Egypt (see Exod. chapters 7—13). In what way were the disasters seen by John similar to the plagues of Egypt?

APPLICATION

6. What if anything does the scene in vv. 2–5 tell us about our own prayers?
7. What would be your answer if someone said, 'There is no point in praying, for God already knows our needs, and He knows better than we do what is to be done about them'?
8. There are many man-made deserts in the world, and many other places where human beings have ruined their natural resources. If you know of any (apart from those mentioned), say or find out how they were caused, and what if anything is being done to repair the damage. What can Christians do to prevent such disasters in the future?
9. Give examples of other ways in which governments or individuals have been responsible for waste of natural and other resources.

9.1–21

The Fifth and Sixth Trumpets

SUMMARY

9.1–12: At the blast of the fifth trumpet, a star fallen from heaven opens the shaft of the bottomless pit. From the smoke from the pit come monstrous locusts. These locusts torture those of mankind who do not have the seal of God on their foreheads, but are not allowed to harm any plants.

9.13–19: The sixth trumpet releases four destructive angels, and a host of monstrous cavalry.

9.20, 21: But the survivors of these plagues do not repent.

NOTES

9.1. A star fallen from heaven. As we saw (p. 25), stars were identified with supernatural beings, especially with gods, but also with angels, and some interpreters suggest that the star mentioned here means an archangel. But John's words remind us of the story of the fall of Lucifer, an ancient folk-tale which Isaiah had used as a figure of the fall of the king of Babylon (Isa. 14.2). Moreover, John does not say that he saw a star *falling* from heaven, but *fallen* from heaven. He had not, in his vision, seen the star falling, but he had seen a fallen star, that is to say, a fallen supernatural being. In other words, he saw a supernatural being which was closely associated with the power of evil.

In later centuries Christians have expanded the story of the fall of Lucifer, and many believe that Satan and his army of evil spirits were created as angels, but rebelled against God, and became His enemies. But John did not write about such details; he simply stated that he saw 'a star fallen from heaven', a supernatural being, but not heavenly, as God's angels, but 'fallen', 'hellish'.

The bottomless pit. This image is derived from the ancient belief that the power of evil had its home deep under the earth. We can easily see how people came to believe this: the poisonous fumes coming out of the ground in volcanic areas, and the destruction caused by lava and debris thrown up by volcanic eruptions are enough to explain this ancient belief. We now know much more about what causes fumes to come out of the earth, and what causes the earth to tremble and volcanoes to erupt, and we know that there is no home of evil under the earth. In fact, it is doubtful if John believed seriously that the home of evil was under the earth. But the 'bottomless pit' was a useful picture for him to use, when he wanted to write about the source of all evil.

9.3. Locusts are a terrible plague. When a swarm of locusts comes down on a field of corn, it takes only a very short time before there is not a green blade or a grain of corn left: every last scrap is eaten. Many Old Testament writers used the image of locusts to describe invading enemies, and locust swarms were widely regarded as signs of God's anger. Locusts were the eighth plague of Egypt (Exod. 10.12–20). But John was probably also thinking of the locust plague which the prophet Joel described as 'destruction from the Almighty' (Joel 4.15).

9.4. Not to harm the grass . . . but only those of mankind who have not the seal of God. These words suggest that the locusts seen by John in his vision mean demonic powers. These have no effect in the natural world, nor on the faithful, but only on those who are not God's people. The evils described in this vision affect only those who are unwilling or unable to resist their power. The powers of evil are real, but they have only such power as people give them. Witchcraft was practised widely in the ancient world, as it still is today. It is dangerous to think that 'there is nothing in it', and even more dangerous to be inquisitive about it, and to try it, for it gains real power over the people who practise it. Spiritual evils have no power over us, if we resist them from the start, but if we try to use them, they gain real power over us.

9.5. Five months. As far as we know, a five-month period had no special meaning for John, and to give it a meaning of our own, as some people do, does not help us to understand this passage. John simply gave a specific figure for a limited period of time, to show that the power of evil even over its willing victims is strictly limited.

9.7. In appearance. The details of John's description in vv. 7–10 come from various sources, but all serve to show how terrible these evils are. **What looked like crowns of gold.** Crowns are given by Christ to His faithful people (see note on 2.10). The servants of evil can only have 'what *looks like* crowns of gold'. The riches of evil are mere tinsel, not real gold.

9.11. The angel of the bottomless pit is probably the same as the 'fallen star'.

9.13. The golden altar, that is to say, the altar of incense. Some interpreters suggest that God sent the plague described in this vision in answer to the prayers of the faithful.

9.15. The hour, the day, the month and the year. The devil may cause the evils that afflict the human race, but God holds the times in His hand.

9.16. The troops of cavalry. Whilst vv. 1–2 emphasized the demonic origin of spiritual evils, these verses stress the human element. The 'troops of cavalry' were clearly inspired by the threat of a Parthian invasion, which, if successful, would have destroyed the civilization of the eastern Mediterranean world as John knew it. The four angels seem to have the function of letting loose the Parthian cavalry to cross the river Euphrates. But the horses in the vision have demonic features, and, terrifying though the Parthian cavalry may have been, they certainly did not look like the monsters described by John. John was using metaphors derived from the Parthian peril to give a picture of spiritual terrors. In Jewish tradition witchcraft was often thought of as coming from beyond the Euphrates (see Num. 22.5, where we are told that Balaam came from 'near the River', which probably means the Euphrates; and Isa. 2.6, where 'from the east' probably means, 'from beyond the Euphrates').

9.20. Did not repent. Both the prayers of the faithful and God's own work aim at the sinners' repentance. But there are many people who will not repent, even when they suffer the consequences of their own folly.

The works of their hands. This was a common expression for idolatry (see, for example, 1 Chron. 32.19; Isa. 2.8; 37.19; Jer. 1.16; 32.30; Micah 5.6). This verse confirms that this chapter refers to the evils of the mind, particularly to such evils as witchcraft, but also to idolatry in general. It may be true that 'an idol is nothing' (1 Cor. 8.4), but it is also true that 'where your treasure is, there will your heart be also' (Matt. 6.21). Anything that we worship becomes our god, and gains power over us.

INTERPRETATION

The fifth and sixth trumpets introduce events of much greater horror than those of John's earlier visions. They show clearly that God is not the creator of evil. He is sufficiently in control of His world to determine the time when the evil strikes, but it comes from a realm of darkness.

We no longer believe that this realm of darkness is located under the earth, but we should still be able to see that John wants to convey something that is very real. Evil is not of God. It is anti-godly in nature. Its ruler is here called *Abaddon* or *Apollyon*, words which mean the 'Destroyer', for its aim is to lay waste God's good creation.

Many people today claim that the Jewish and Christian faiths, and the demands which they make on us, restrict our liberty, and prohibit a full natural life. Unbelief is thus presented as life-enhancing, and many unbelievers pride themselves on their free and satisfying lives. But in fact God alone gives true life, and gives it abundantly. A life without God may seem easier, but it is also much emptier and less satisfying than a life with God. Just as people who have bought a machine will ruin their machine if they disregard the maker's instructions, so people who do not obey their Creator's instructions ruin their lives. God's enemy is out to destroy; God is determined to save.

These woes do not touch the natural world, nor do they harm those who have 'the seal of God on their foreheads'. Christians suffer as much as other people, and sometimes more than other people, but they do not suffer the pains that come from being unrepentant, and demonic forces have no power over them.

For the woes shown in this vision are demonic ills, which means in practice that they work on people's minds. This explains why John describes them in terms which otherwise would be self-contradictory.

The first woe may remind us of the hallucinations sometimes suffered by victims of alcoholic poisoning. John was certainly not thinking of alcoholism, but he was thinking of an evil which poisons the mind.

The second woe stresses the human side of spiritual evils. These evils are spread by human beings, driven by demonic forces (the 'cavalry' of John's vision ride on monstrous horses). They bring witchcraft, pseudo-religion, and all the weird beliefs and practices which were common in the Roman Empire, and which are still with us today; and for our own time we might add such evils as drug abuse.

Spiritual dangers have a double nature. They are human, and in a sense we could say that they exist in the mind. But they are demonic in origin and character. Their effects are terrible, but, apart from the damage they do to human bodies, they do not affect the realm of nature ('they were told not to harm the grass of the earth or any green growth or any tree'), nor any of God's own people ('but only those of mankind who have not the seal of God on their foreheads').

When they see the results of their evil ways, it would be sensible for people to change their ideas, and to stop their evil practices. But many people do not change their ways. Indeed, many people cannot change them, for the power of evil is very real. People become the slaves of their own bad practices.

Ultimately God makes all things work together for good, and even the devil's works will be turned to a good purpose. But in the short term the devil seems to have it all his own way. Even when the devil shows his true colours, and people see the damage he does, they still do not take the warning, and do not repent.

Actually, of course, some people do come to their senses and repent. But John was shown that the majority do not. Repentance, in any case, is not usually brought about by people seeing the evil of their ways, but by the preaching of the gospel.

STUDY SUGGESTIONS

CONTENTS

1. What does the star fallen from heaven mean?
2. (a) What does v. 4 tell us about the nature of the evils described in this chapter?

'Spiritual evils are spread by human beings . . . people become the slaves of their own bad habits' (p. 95) – and not only their own. The callous greed of drug dealers is what finally ruins the lives of young people like these, who may start on soft drugs like cannabis through their own weakness but then move on to the horrors of heroin or LSD. What do *you* consider the most dangerous 'spiritual evils' of today?

(b) What does the word 'cavalry' suggest about these evils?
(c) And what does the description of their horses signify?
3. 'On their heads were what looked like crowns of gold' (v. 7). Can you explain why John did not simply say, 'On their heads were golden crowns'?
4. What do the names 'Abaddon' and 'Apollyon' mean, and what is important about these names?
5. What was significant about the river Euphrates?

APPLICATION
6. What special warning does this chapter contain for us today?
7. Many people have experienced how difficult, or even impossible, it is to give up bad practices. What does this show? What, if any, bad practices are common in your own country? What if anything can be done to help people give up bad practices?
8. What comfort can Christians draw from v. 4?

10.1–11
The Little Scroll

SUMMARY

10.1, 2: John sees a mighty angel with a little scroll.
10.3: When the angel calls out, the seven thunders sound.
10.4: John is about to write down what he has heard, but is not allowed to do so.
10.5–7: The angel cries out that there must be no more delay.
10.8–11: John is told to take the little scroll and eat it. He finds it sweet in his mouth, but bitter in his stomach. He is then told to prophesy.

NOTES

10.1. Another angel coming down. Unlike the 'star' in 9.1, this angel is not 'fallen', but is 'coming down'; he was sent by God to make His will known. Some interpreters think of the angel Gabriel. The description of his appearance shows that he was in close contact with God. Clouds were believed to be blankets or cloaks wrapped round heavenly beings, but in the Old Testament clouds are regarded as a symbol of God's presence. The rainbow hints at God's faithfulness, as in the story of the Flood (Gen. 9.13); and the pillars of fire bring to mind the Exodus (Exod. 13.21, 22).

10.2. His right foot on the sea, and his left foot on the land, that is to say, he covered both sea and land, in other words, the whole world.

10.3. The seven thunders. Seven being the number of perfection, was therefore the number of God (see Special Note C, p. 69).

10.4. Seal up what the seven thunders have said. Why was John not allowed to tell this? If we consider the context, it is clear that everything is moving towards 'the end', that is to say, the Last Judgement. The 'thunders' may have referred to that Judgement, which John must not yet announce.

10.6. That there should be no more delay. The angel calls for an immediate Judgement.

10.7. The mystery of God. In the New Testament the 'mystery of God' invariably means His hidden purpose as revealed in the gospel. But that means that His chief purpose is not the punishment of the wicked but the salvation of the repentant. And this in turn means that there must, after all, be delay, to give time for as many people as possible to repent.

10.8. Go, take the scroll. The preaching of the gospel is the task, not of an angel, but of John and his fellow preachers.

10.9. Take it and eat. The idea of a prophet swallowing a scroll is derived from Ezekiel 2.8—3.3. Neither in Ezekiel nor here should we understand the words literally. The prophet was to 'eat' the scroll in order to make its contents thoroughly his own. In modern English we should say, he had 'to swallow and digest it'.

INTERPRETATION

Now would seem to be the time for the seventh, the last trumpet, but again there is an interruption. A mighty angel arrives with an open book, and seven thunders announce . . . what? The End? John is not allowed to tell. The angel insists that there must be no more delay.

But a voice from heaven decides otherwise, and tells John to take the scroll and swallow it. We are not told whose voice this is, but probably it is the voice of Christ. It is He who holds back the Last Judgement. It would not make any difference if we interpreted John as meaning that God holds back the Judgement, for the Father, the Son, and the Holy Spirit are three times the One God. True, John did not formulate the relationship between the Father and the Son in those words, but he would have known, as John the Evangelist knew, that 'the Son can do nothing of his own accord' (John 5.19). There is still time to repent.

John emphasizes that the scroll is open. This book is not like the scroll with seven seals: it contains no secrets. This second scroll is the known word of God, it is what God has said for all to hear in the Scriptures of the Old Testament and in the coming of Christ. Some Christians have thought that this scroll represents the Bible, but that would be defining it too precisely, for the little scroll certainly includes the message about Jesus Christ, which in John's days was not yet part of the Scripture. It would be better to say that it is the gospel, or God's word, and to remember that to all the biblical writers, including John, God's 'word' meant the spoken word, the word spoken by Moses and the prophets, and by Jesus and the apostles.

The idea of a prophet eating a scroll, both here and in Ezekiel, is symbolic, but meaningful. The things which we eat are digested, and become part of us. So what John was told to do, was to 'read, mark, learn, and inwardly digest' the gospel (Book of Common Prayer, Collect for the second Sunday in Advent). This scroll was sweet to the taste but, in Ezekiel's words, 'full of lamentation and woe', or, in John's words, 'When I had eaten it my stomach was made bitter'. God's word is a joy to receive, but it contains a judgement and criticism of human life, which is very painful. Also, it brings about a parting of the ways, and condemns those who reject it. Both Ezekiel and John rejoiced at the privilege of receiving God's word and being allowed to preach it, but they had no pleasure in pronouncing judgement.

John, however, did not receive God's word on his own behalf alone. He received the Revelation for the Church, and the next vision shows that the gospel was given to the whole Church, to take and swallow and digest, to preach, and to live.

STUDY SUGGESTIONS

WORD

1. What does the word 'prophesy' in v. 11 suggest, and how does this compare with what we have said about prophets and prophecy on p. 42 and in the note on 2.20?

CONTENT

2. What do the cloud, the rainbow, and the pillars of fire signify?
3. For what reason was the call of the angel in vv. 6–7 not carried out?
4. (a) In what way does the little scroll differ from the scroll with seven seals in chapter 5?
   (b) What is meant by the statement that this scroll was sweet in the mouth but bitter in the stomach?

BIBLE

5. Compare the vision of Ezek. 2.8—3.11 with John's vision as described in chapter 10.
6. What bearing if any does Amos 3.7 have on this chapter?

APPLICATION

7. What was the practical significance of v. 11 for John, and what message, if any, does it have for Christians today?

11.1–14
The Two Witnesses

SUMMARY

11.1, 2: John is given a measuring rod to measure the temple of God, but not the outer court, because that is given over to the nations, who are trampling all over the city.

11.3–6: Great power is given to two faithful witnesses.

11.7–10: The death of the two witnesses.

11.11, 12: The resurrection and ascension of the two witnesses.

11.13: A great earthquake devastates a tenth of the city.

11.14: The announcement that two woes have passed, and a third woe is soon to come.

NOTES

11.1. A measuring rod. Measuring rods were used by builders, so the giving of this rod to John implies that there is something to build or to restore.

The temple. The Greek word translated 'temple' means the 'house' of God, that is to say, the actual shrine itself without the court and the outbuildings. The same word was used in the Greek translation of the Old Testament for the larger part of the actual Temple building in Jerusalem, where the altar of incense stood (1 Kings 6.5). But before John's time this word, 'temple', had already been used as an expression for God's people (see e.g. 1 Cor. 3.16, 17). We must therefore ask does 'temple' here mean a building or people (see Interpretation below)?

11.2. The court was part of the temple complex. The Temple at Jerusalem had more than one court, the altar of sacrifice being in the centre court.

The holy city. Here again we may have a double meaning. The Greek word *polis* for 'city' could mean the buildings, but its chief meaning was a community of people (see notes and interpretation for 21.1–8).

Forty-two months, that is, three and a half years, half of the sacred number seven. The numbers are derived, with some slight alteration, from Daniel 7.25 and 12.11, 12.

11.3. One thousand two hundred and sixty days is the equivalent of the forty-two months of v. 2. Clearly the two numbers must be symbolic. They represent the time when 'the nations' trample over 'the holy city'. The faithful witnesses must continue to preach as long as the present condition of the world lasts.

11.4. The two olive trees. In Zechariah 4.14 two olive trees refer to Zerubbabel (of the royal family) and the high priest Joshua. Some people see here a reminder that Christ has made His faithful people kings and priests (see 1.6 and 5.10).

The two lampstands. Some interpreters link the lampstands also with Zechariah's vision (Zech. 4.2). Zechariah's vision and John's are connected by the idea that people, like lamps, can carry light. Faithful Christians carry the light of Christ into the world (see Matt. 5.15, 16). But there is a more direct link with the seven lampstands in the opening vision of the Revelation (1.12 and 20) and the two faithful Churches (2.8–11 and 3.7–13), whose 'lamps are burning brightly', while the lamps of the less faithful Churches are only burning dimly.

11.5–6. And if any one would harm them . . . They have power . . . The details of the extraordinary powers given to the witnesses are symbolic. They serve to show that the faithful witnesses are equipped with everything that they need to carry out their task.

11.7. When they have finished their testimony. A clearer translation would be, 'When they have completed their testimony'. However much interference and opposition the faithful witnesses may meet, nothing will prevent the completion of their task.

The beast. The fact that the beast, which John did not see until a later vision, was already active here, shows clearly that John did not mean the Revelation to be a detailed history of the future (see notes on chapter 13).

11.8. The great city. The expression 'the great city' seems at first sight to mean Rome. But Jesus was crucified in Jerusalem. In the interpretation we must examine, whether John had any specific city in mind, or whether he used it as a term for the world of sinful mankind.

11.10. A torment. The gospel is a message of salvation, and therefore a joy to receive. But many people who do not want to accept the gospel regard the work of the faithful witnesses as an attack on their liberty.

11.11. A breath of life. The imagery in this verse is derived from Ezekiel 37, where the prophet tells how he saw in a vision a valley full of bones, which came to life at the word of God spoken by the prophet. Ezekiel's vision was a prophecy, not of the resurrection of individual people, but of the resurrection of the nation of Israel.

11.12. In the sight of their foes. This part of the vision is puzzling. It could mean that the testimony of the witnesses has opened the eyes of some of their enemies, so that these enemies now know that the faithful dead live with God. But it could also mean that John was looking forward to the

Last Judgement, when *all* peoples will see the triumph of the Church.
11.13. The rest were terrified and gave glory to God. Earlier visions had
shown that, when people are faced with the consequences of their sins,
this often has no effect on them. However terrifying the plagues described in chapter 9 were, people did not repent. In this vision, however,
people do give glory to God. The preaching of the gospel can bring
people to repentance. The word of God achieves what nothing else can
do by itself.

INTERPRETATION

Many scholars have found this chapter extremely puzzling, so much so,
that some have regarded it as an 'interlude' which interferes with the
main line of John's book, while others have thought that it must be a
piece not written by John, but added later by some editor. The chief
problem lies in the 'temple' and the 'city'. Which city did John have in
mind? Taken literally, vv. 1 and 2, mentioning the temple, the altar, the
court, and the holy city, seem to suggest Jerusalem, as does v. 8 with its
reference to the crucifixion of the Lord.

Some people have therefore thought that this chapter must be a
prophecy made by some unknown Jewish prophet during the siege of
Jerusalem which took place in AD 70. They assume that this prophet
foretold that the city and the Temple court would fall to the Romans,
but that the Temple itself would remain safe, and that God Himself
would eventually come to the rescue, so that the people besieged in the
Temple would win the war.

But it is difficult to see why such a prophecy should have been preserved after the Temple had been destroyed, when everyone knew that
the prophet had been mistaken. Moreover, why should such a prophecy
have been put into a book by a Christian author?

We must therefore turn to the two witnesses in v. 3. Who are they
meant to be? Are they perhaps Stephen and James, who were martyred
in Jerusalem, where the Lord was crucified (Acts 7; 12.2)? Or are they
Peter and Paul, who were probably martyred in Rome? But Jesus
certainly was not crucified there.

In fact, the details do not fit either the death of Stephen and James, or
that of Peter and Paul. Did people from all over the world really travel to
Jerusalem or to Rome to gaze at their dead bodies and gloat over their
death? In whatever way we interpret this chapter, vv. 8–11 must be taken
figuratively.

The picture of the two witnesses is probably derived from beliefs
about Enoch and Elijah, which were later applied to Moses and Elijah.
Sirach called Elijah 'a prophet like fire, whose word flames like a torch'
(Sirach/Ecclus. 48.1). Elijah does indeed fit the picture of the witnesses

very well. He had 'shut the sky' (1 Kings 17.1), so that no rain fell for three years and six months (Luke 4.25); he had called down fire from heaven (1 Kings 18.36–38 and 2 Kings 1.10–11); and he had gone straight to heaven (2 Kings 2.11). Yet a return of Enoch and Elijah, or of Moses and Elijah, does not fit this chapter very well.

Although John used symbolic language, his purpose was to enlighten his readers, not to confuse them. So there must be a clue to the identity of the witnesses, and indeed there is: 'They are the two olive trees and the two lampstands which stand before the Lord of the earth.' Two olive trees had been mentioned by Zechariah. To Zechariah they meant Joshua and Zerubbabel, the spiritual and secular leaders of the Jews who had returned from the exile (Zech. 4.11). But the important point is that these two men had been set apart to carry out God's purpose, and that they were faithful in carrying out their task.

As to the lampstands, we have seen that the lampstands in the vision described in Revelation 1 are the seven Churches, and chapters 2 and 3 showed that two of those Churches were faithful and without blemish. These were the two faithful witnesses. As the seven Churches represent the whole Church, it seems reasonable to regard the two lampstands, the two faithful witnesses, as a symbol for all those Christians who witness faithfully to the gospel.

So it becomes clear that this chapter is linked closely with the preceding vision. John was given the open book of God's word to swallow and digest, and was told to prophesy. But this order was not given to him alone. The word of God was given to the whole Church. It is the Church's task to swallow and digest the gospel, and to preach it, and this task is carried out by those who are faithful witnesses. Preaching in this sense is not only done from the pulpit, to the converted, but outside in the world. It is done by speaking the right word when the opportunity arises, and talking about Jesus whenever there is someone willing to listen. But faithful witnesses can also witness by the way in which they live.

Thus everything falls into place. The 'temple' of God is not a building, it is His people. Measuring is done in order to build and repair, and John is given a measuring rod, so that he and his fellow preachers can restore, that is to say, constantly reform and revive the Church.

Much of the world is in the hands of the ungodly. They 'trample' all over the 'holy city', that is to say, they exploit and spoil God's created world. They even trespass into the Temple court – the ungodly world, as we know only too well, invades the Church. But their time is limited, and the inner sanctuary will not be touched. There is in the Church a core of faithful people, in whom true life will always be found. This vision of the Temple being secure from the invasion of the enemy was not meant to encourage people to sort out those who are the 'true' members of the

Church, and those who are only 'hangers-on' (see Matt. 13.24–50). It was meant to encourage us not to be afraid that the world may overrun the Church (see Matt. 16.18; John 16.33).

But the work of the Church is not carried out within a group of faithful people. The two witnesses carry out their task in the city, that is to say, the Church works in the world. The vivid description of the powers of the witnesses is John's way of saying that no power on earth can effectively destroy the Church's ability to witness to its Lord. The Church's enemies can kill its witnesses, and gloat over their death and the Church's apparent feebleness. But the Church cannot be destroyed: 'the powers of death shall not prevail against it'. Whenever the Church appears to have been wiped out, it rises again. In the centuries since John wrote the Revelation, this scene has been re-enacted many times, with the Church's enemies gloating over its defeat, and yet it has risen again.

So this chapter focuses on three points:

1. the security of the Church's true life and the safety of the 'temple' which cannot be touched;

2. the Church's task to witness in a hostile world, which is nevertheless God's world, and therefore remains the object of His love and must be given the opportunity to repent;

3. the promise that the Church, though often seeming to be destroyed, yet will live.

STUDY SUGGESTIONS

WORDS

1. The word 'temple' can have a wider or a narrower meaning. What does each mean, and which of the two is meant in this chapter? In what ways is the same word used in other parts of the Bible?

CONTENT

2. What stood in the Temple building? What does this mean?
3. Which city did John have in mind?
4. Which temple did John have in mind?
5. What is the significance of the 1,260 days (v. 3)?
6. (a) From what or whom is the idea of the two witnesses likely to have been derived?
   (b) Whom do the two witnesses represent, in John's vision?
   (c) What is the significance of the powers given to the two witnesses?
7. What teaching is this vision meant to convey?

BIBLE

8. What was the function of two witnesses in Old Testament law?

'The Church', though often seeming to be destroyed, yet will live' (p. 104).

In the Vietnam war, American bombers aiming at a military target destroyed this church instead, killing many Christians who were sheltering inside. But the cross still stood as a symbol of faith and hope for those who escaped. What signs and symbols of hope for the Church can we see in the world today?

9. What did Jesus say about trying to separate 'true' Christians from those who are not really true Christians?

APPLICATION

10. What does v. 13b suggest about preaching and other ways of persuading people to give glory to God?
11. Do you think that God actually causes earthquakes and other natural disasters, as a means of making people repent and glorify Him? Give reasons for your answer.
12. In your experience, what are some of the ways in which 'the word of God' chiefly influences people and brings them to repentance? Is it through preaching? The witness of others? Bible-reading? Experience of disaster? (You may find it helpful to discuss this question with a group of friends or fellow-students.)

11.15–19
The Seventh Trumpet

SUMMARY

At the blowing of the seventh trumpet John is allowed another glimpse of heaven, where he witnesses the worship of God by the twenty-four elders, and sees the ark of God's covenant.

NOTES

11.15. The kingdom of the world has become the kingdom of our Lord and of his Christ, that is to say, God, through Christ, has resumed direct rule over His world. This is a vision of the end, but John was aware that in a very real sense the end has already begun. Many people may not yet see it, but God resumed the initiative, and took the government of His world directly into His own hands, when Jesus Christ came to proclaim the Kingdom of God. Though it would be true to say that God never lost the initiative, and that He had always remained in control of His creation, it is also true that the coming of Christ meant a decisive change in His government of the world.

11.18. The nations raged. These words are an allusion to Psalm 2, but they are more than that. John expected the members of the seven Churches to have that whole Psalm in mind. The Psalm describes in vivid words the conspiracy of the rulers of the world against the LORD and His anointed, the King of Israel. It tells how He who sits in the heavens laughs at the raging of the nations, and finally brings them to submission, and vindicates His son, His anointed. This Psalm was not meant to give an accurate assessment of the position of the kings of Israel among the much mightier nations surrounding them. It was a powerful reminder that, however much the nations might rage against God's people and their king, they were powerless against the living God of Israel. In New Testament times this Psalm was interpreted as referring to the Messiah, and that is how early Christians understood it (see Acts 4.23–28).

His wrath. Because 'wrath', meaning 'anger', is a word which is used for a very human emotion, some people feel that it cannot be properly used of God. God is love (see 1 John 4.13–18), and these people insist that love excludes wrath.

In actual fact there is a close connection between love and wrath. Parents know that they are much more hurt if their children do wrong than if other people for whom they do not care do wrong. Also, we are much more hurt by the faults of our friends than by those of strangers. Love makes us vulnerable, it makes us liable to get hurt badly, and 'wrath' is not only a natural reaction to being hurt, but is actually a sign of how much we are hurt.

Nevertheless, when Bible writers refer to God's wrath, they are not suggesting that God reacts in the way human beings do, but describing the practical ways in which God shows His displeasure, 'for the LORD reproves him whom he loves' (Prov. 3.12). Paul pointed out to the Romans that the wrath of God is revealed in the manner in which He leaves people to suffer the consequences of their sins (Rom. 1.18—3.20). Indeed, even where the Bible writers describe more positive ways in which God shows His wrath, this is usually closely connected with the outcome of the wrong that people have done. Thus, for example, the fall of Jerusalem to the Babylonians under Nebuchadnezzar was a sign of God's displeasure with the sins of His people, but at the same time it was the direct result of the dishonest policies of king Zedekiah and his counsellors.

The chief way, however, in which God shows His displeasure is through the preaching of His servants the prophets. For the purpose of His wrath is not to destroy people but to redeem them.

The time for the dead to be judged. John does not describe the Last Judgement until much later; but 'later' in the order in which the visions appear in the Revelation does not mean that they reveal things which will come later in time. This vision refers to the same time as chapters 20.11—22.5.

11.19. God's temple in heaven. According to 21.22 John saw no temple in heaven. But as the language is symbolic, there is no reason why the details should always be the same. John mentioned the temple here because he wanted to mention

the ark of his covenant, the symbol of God's presence and faithfulness.

INTERPRETATION

The seventh trumpet marks the end of the second series of visions, and gives John another glimpse of the End towards which the whole of God's creation is moving. Again, as in the vision of the seventh seal (8.1), John was not shown the winding up of history, only the end beyond it. The third woe, the winding up of the story of human folly, was left over for a later vision.

The words of this vision are few, but their meaning is very important. Although the kingdoms of the world are so powerful, they have no future while they remain as they are, that is to say, no eternal future. But they are moving towards a fundamental change, they are destined to become the Kingdom of our Lord. Of course, God is King now, but His royal government is hidden, though it is destined to become visible to all people and to make an end of the present unjust governments.

This great change will destroy all that is evil, but it will not destroy God's good creation. God does not destroy His own creation; on the contrary, He will destroy the destroyers of the earth, and vindicate His faithful servants.

John was shown in his vision that in heaven this change is already real even now. And on earth too the change has already begun, when Christ came. Jesus Himself had pointed out more than once that, small though His work might seem, and futile though it might look in the eyes of the world, His ministry would bear fruit and bring about God's victory (see especially some of His parables, Mark 4.8, 26–29, 30–32; Matt. 13.33).

The vision ends with John seeing the ark of God's covenant. The ark of the covenant had once stood in the Temple in Jerusalem, as a token of God's faithfulness and His presence among His people. It had disappeared many centuries before John wrote, having probably been stolen or destroyed on one of the occasions when Jerusalem was besieged or sacked. But John saw its heavenly counterpart, showing that God's faithfulness is eternal.

STUDY SUGGESTIONS

WORD

1. Keeping in mind that the word 'Christ' means 'anointed', that is to say, in most cases, a king, explain what is meant by 'his Christ' in

v. 15. It may be helpful, before you do this, to read Pss. 2 and 72; Luke 23.1–5; John 19.33–38; Acts 2.36.

CONTENT

2. What did the voices in heaven say, and what does it mean?
3. What did the twenty-four elders mean by 'begun to reign'?

BIBLE

4. What did the writer of Psalm 2 want to convey?

APPLICATION

5. Why was this vision important to John and his readers, and in what way should it be important to us?
6. For the Israelites 'The ark of the covenant had stood in the Temple ... as a token of God's faithfulness and His presence among His people' (p. 108). What, if anything, stands as a token of God's faithfulness and presence among Christians today? Do you think Christians *need* such a token? Give reasons for your answer.

12.1–17
The Woman and the Dragon

SUMMARY

12.1–4: John sees a woman, clothed with the sun, with the moon under her feet, and on her head a crown with twelve stars, about to give birth to a child; and a dragon, standing before the woman threatening to eat her child.

12.5–6: But when the child is born he is caught up to God and His throne, and the woman flees into the wilderness.

12.7–9: War in heaven. Michael and his angels throw the dragon down to earth.

12.10–12: The triumph song of heaven.

12.13–17: The dragon pursues the woman, but, being unable to attack her directly, he attacks the rest of her offspring.

NOTES

12.1. A great portent appeared in heaven. The picture language in this passage, derived from astrology, evidently comes from a myth (unknown to us), in which these events took place, not really in heaven but in the sky. The woman would have been the constellation *Virgo*, and the dragon would have been *Hydra* (not the constellation *Draco*, for *Draco* would have used fire, not water as the dragon does in v. 15; moreover, *Hydra* suits the picture better). In lands of the northern hemisphere *Virgo* is seen near the horizon, and *Hydra* as a long, narrow constellation, lying just above *Virgo*; and at times when *Hydra* is low in the sky, *Virgo* disappears below the horizon. Most ancient peoples believed that the movement of the stars affects people's lives on earth, as many still do today. But none of this is relevant to what John wanted to convey. We should note that he used the Greek word '*drakon*' which is the same as the Latin '*draco*' and our 'dragon'; he was not retelling the myth of Virgo and Hydra! John freely used pictures derived from astrology, but he does not seem to have taken astrology seriously, and merely used such pictures to colour his language.

A woman clothed with the sun, with the moon under her feet, and on her head a crown of twelve stars. Medieval artists loved to paint the virgin Mary like this. But in John's vision it is the People of God, as a community, which is shown in the likeness of the Queen of Heaven. Mary was, indeed, representative of the People of God, inasmuch as she received Him, gave birth to Him, and provided His earthly home. But this vision did not show John a life of Christ.

12.3. Red. In Babylonian tradition the chaos-monster Tiamat was believed to be red, as was the dragon Typhon in Egyptian myth.

Dragon. See Special Note D (p. 114).

With seven heads and ten horns, and seven diadems upon his heads. Ten is a simple round figure, meaning 'several'; the last of the four beasts which Daniel saw rising out of the sea had ten horns (Dan. 7.7). The seven heads were traditional; thus, for example, the monster Leviathan had seven heads. But maybe in this vision the number seven suggests that the dragon tries to imitate God, and to take God's place, seven being the number associated with God.

12.5. Her child was caught up to God. The story of Christ's life, passion, and death is not told here. John only says that the Christ was eventually brought safely home to God and His throne (v. 7). Needless to say, John and his first readers knew the story of the cross and the resurrection. In the purely physical sense the child was killed by the dragon, but John saw deeper than the surface of things, and he also knew the outcome.

One thousand two hundred and sixty days, that is to say, the same period in which the nations raged in the holy city and the two witnesses made their testimony (11.2–3). But it may also be a reminder of the forty-two years which the Israelites spent in the wilderness, fed by God with manna (forty-two months for forty-two years).

12.7. War arose in heaven. The defeat of the power of evil not only affects the earth. It is a cosmic event affecting the whole universe. Indeed it is more than a cosmic event, for it involves heaven, and heaven is not a place within the universe.

Michael and his angels. Michael was regarded as the chief of the archangels. The whole heavenly host is involved in the defeat of Satan. However, we must also take note of the following verses.

12.9. The devil and Satan. See Special Note D (p. 114).

12.11. They have conquered him. The Christians on earth, and particularly the martyrs, have also played their part in defeating Satan. 'For we are not contending against flesh and blood, but against the principalities, against the powers, against the world rulers of this present darkness, against the hosts of wickedness in the heavenly places' (Eph. 6.12). This battle is not in vain, for the victory is certain. But, important though the battle of the faithful against the power of evil is, neither their loyal fight for the Lord, nor the battle of Michael and his angels are decisive, for they cannot conquer Satan by their own strength alone, but only **by the blood of the Lamb and by the word of their testimony:** the final victory over the power of evil was only won by Christ on the Cross.

12.12. Woe to you, O earth and sea. The decisive victory has been won, but the devil is still able to inflict much pain.

12.16. The earth came to the help of the woman. The created world is God's world, and it is good. Nature is not on the side of evil, and those who abuse the earth and its resources often find that nature turns against them.

12.17. And he stood on the sand of the sea. Many early manuscripts read, 'I stood on the sand of the sea'. Whichever John actually wrote, this sentence is connected with chapter 13, and means, either that the devil was standing on the beach in order to bring about the events described in that chapter, or that John stood there and saw the vision of those events.

INTERPRETATION

This is the first vision of a third series. The parts of this series are not so clearly indicated as those of the two previous ones. It is possible to detect seven parts, but John does not count them. The reason may be that these visions refer much more directly to conditions when John and his first readers lived, and it is never easy to see the pattern of events in one's own time. It is true that the whole of the Revelation relates to what was happening in the world at that time, but here the connection is more direct.

This chapter uses pictures derived from astrology, but that is not really relevant to what John wants to convey. The first vision refers to the birth of the Messiah, but it is not the story of Jesus's birth, and the 'woman' is not the virgin Mary. Some features may remind us of the birth story as Matthew told it, but the symbolism of this vision points to something else. The woman represents the People of the Messiah. V. 1 seems to suggest that this means Israel, where Jesus was born, but v. 17 suggests the Church, as the woman's offspring are 'those who keep the commandments of God and bear testimony to Jesus'. However, John saw Israel and the Church as one (see note on 7.4).

The other chief figure in this vision is the dragon, 'that ancient serpent, who is called the Devil and Satan' (v. 9). The 'child', that is the Messiah, seems to play only a small part in this vision. All the light seems to fall on the woman and her enemy the dragon. Actually the victory of Christ occupies the central part of this chapter (vv. 7–12, the war in heaven and the triumph song), but John focuses attention particularly on the devil's hostility to the People of the Messiah, for that is what the faithful experience on earth.

In this third series John sees events on earth as a battle between God and the devil (see Special Note D, p. 114). The outcome of that battle was decided when the devil was thrown out of heaven. Verses 7–9 tell how John saw a war in heaven between Michael and his angels on the one side, and the devil and his servants on the other. Obviously the devil is no match for the host of heaven, and he is soon thrown down to earth. But the words of the triumph song (vv. 11–12) remind us that the vision of Michael fighting the dragon was symbolic, representing the real victory won by the blood of the Lamb and the preaching of the gospel. Jesus spoke of the same defeat of the devil when the seventy messengers returned from their first tour of preaching: 'I saw Satan falling like lightning from heaven' (Luke 10.18).

The hymn also reminds us of a terrible truth: the devil can make a certain claim on us. Our sins testify against us that we belong to him, and not to God. The devil can therefore accuse us, and is in a position to claim us for himself. But we can rejoice because by the life and death of Christ God has reclaimed us for Himself, so that the 'accuser' can no longer support his claim (see Col. 2.14).

This is a side of the New Testament teaching about justification that is often disregarded. Through our sins we have, as it were, enlisted in the service of the devil, and he can claim that we are his. But God made us His own by making Himself one of us. Jesus Christ, who is truly God, became a real man, and lived a perfect human life.

The fact that God made Himself one of us in Christ cancels out the devil's claim on us. God not only made us, which should already be a sufficient claim, see Ps. 100.3, but He has shared our life, He took the consequences of our sins upon Himself, and died with us and for us on the Cross. That is a claim which the devil can never make, and in God's judgement it cancels out any claim which the devil could make. And ultimately it is God's judgement that matters.

Christ has won the victory on our behalf. But His people share in His victory, and some of them, the martyrs, the conquerors of the letters to the seven Churches, have in turn shed their blood for Him.

God is beyond the devil's reach. Christ, after His resurrection, can no longer be touched directly. But He can still be hurt through His people, for whatever hurts us, hurts Him. The last verses of this chapter show the devil's hatred of the Church and his persecution of the faithful. John's language may seem strange to some, but many faithful Christians experience the reality of the devil's hatred.

STUDY SUGGESTIONS

CONTENT

1. Whom does the woman in this vision represent?
2. Who is meant by the 'red dragon'?
3. The Child is clearly the most important figure in this vision, but He receives little attention. What reasons can you see for this?
4. In what way was 'Michael's victory' actually achieved?
5. What is it that makes it possible for the devil to be an 'accuser'?
6. What reason does the voice have for saying, 'Woe to you, O earth and sea'?
7. What does it mean, that the dragon 'pursues the woman', and how does this affect Christ?
8. What does it mean, that 'the earth came to the help of the woman'?

BIBLE

9. What, if any, is the link between this vision and (a) Luke 10.18; (b) Matt. 18.18?

APPLICATION

10. (a) In what way is v. 10 relevant to us?
    (b) In what way is v. 11 relevant to us?
11. What are some of the ways in which Christians in your country chiefly 'experience the reality of the devil's hatred' today?

Special Note D
The Devil and his Works

Though Christians in some parts of the Church have developed a large body of teaching about the devil, the Bible does not teach us much about him. Even the Revelation, which is so much concerned with his works, does not say much about the devil himself. Yet John clearly expected his readers to know what he was talking about.

To get some understanding, however limited, of what is meant by 'the devil and his works', we should probably start from the idea of chaos. Most of the ancient peoples among whom the biblical faith took its form, believed that a power of chaos constantly threatened the created world. That belief was expressed in the mythical idea of a chaos monster, which the Babylonians called Tiamat.

Although it was expressed in the form of a myth, this belief in chaos was based on people's real experience of the world, and it embodies a genuine truth. Everything that is made has to be looked after and cared for, otherwise it will break down and eventually fall into ruin. To the Babylonians the obvious example was the great temple towers they used to build. These were made of sun-baked brick clad with kiln-baked tiles. As long as the covering of kiln-baked tiles was intact, the building was safe. But if only one tile was dislodged, the rain would come in and dissolve the mud-brick inside, and soon part of the building would collapse. Iraq is littered with the ruins of temple towers to which that has happened, for even in a land as dry as Iraq it rains sometimes, and in time these buildings fell into ruin. They only survived as long as they were properly maintained. The same is true of everything that is made. It must be looked after and cared for, or it will disintegrate. The Babylonians believed that this disintegration resulted from the activity of the monster Tiamat. In fact they believed that the creation of the universe had become possible only after their god Marduk had defeated Tiamat.

The ancient Israelites had similar beliefs, but these beliefs were not important in connection with their faith in the living God, and the biblical writers referred to them only very rarely. The Israelites certainly believed that God had to maintain His creation in good order, and so prevent it from falling into chaos; but they were chiefly concerned about the threat of chaos within society. For that was where the real danger lay: in the disintegration of society. And here God created order by His commandments. The order of the created world and the order of human society were regarded as very closely connected. We should note that according to the creation story in Genesis 1 God created the universe by ten commands, matching the ten commandments which He gave to order human society.

The power of evil is a negative power. It is not a created being, but the disintegration of the creation, which would happen if God did not continue to sustain the work of His hands.

Mere 'things' disintegrate when left to themselves. But human beings are given the freedom to choose whether or not to be left to themselves. They can choose to serve their Creator or to separate themselves from Him. That separation is not necessarily a purposeful choice; for most people it is not so much a matter of defying God as simply not listening to Him. The biblical story of Adam and Eve describes it, not as a proud rebellion, but as a fall. There is nothing grand about sin, it is something entirely negative.

Some people regard the devil and his angels simply as a personification of human sin, a manner of describing sin in the form of a person. Thus John Sweet writes in his Commentary on the Revelation that the devil 'represents man's free will, the capacity God has given for sin, and the terrible reality of its consequences'. There is some truth in this, but it is probably not the whole truth. There is a power of evil, a power of sin beyond human sin. The idea of the devil gives expression to this power of evil which is active in the world.

The idea of a devil, a determined opponent of God, comes from the ancient religion of Persia, in which Angra Mainyu, the Angry Spirit, was the almost equal opponent of Ahura Mazda, the Wise Lord. This idea was taken over by the Jews in the form of Satan, the chief power of evil and sin. But we must keep in mind that in the faith of Israel the power of evil is negative, a destroyer of God's work, but never His equal opponent.

In the Book of Job Satan acts as an accuser before God. The word *satan*, in fact, means 'accuser'. The Greek word *diabolos*, from which our word 'devil' is derived, means 'slanderer'. Part of the power of the devil comes from our guilt before God.

The devil has power over us chiefly because we give him that power. He represents, not so much our freedom of choice, but our abuse of the freedom which God has given us. We can see an example of this in the story of the fall in Genesis 3. There the temptation comes, not from a mythical monster but from a little, probably non-poisonous tree-snake, and it should have been quite easy for Adam and Eve to resist the temptation. But only a little later (Genesis 4.7) sin has become a monster 'couching at the door'. Evil has grown, and gained strength. The devil is like the vampire of legend: he lives by the strength he gets from his victims.

Because he is entirely dependent on his victims, the devil cannot create anything. He can only abuse the things that have already been created.

The creation is good, and all things exist to be used, but the devil wants us to abuse them. We can see that every day in the abuse people make of alcohol and drugs, in the terrible results of the abuse of atomic power, in the way in which sin perverts the joys of sexual relationships, in the deserts created by misuse of the soil, in fact, in all the good things that become tainted and ruined by the way in which we abuse and exploit them.

John, in the Revelation, used the symbolic language in which this power of evil had traditionally been described: the Dragon, the ancient Serpent, Satan, the Devil, and also the picture of a reservoir of evil in the bottomless pit. Many people today, to whom this sort of language is unfamiliar, tend to dismiss the idea of a devil altogether. But it would be unwise to disregard the reality of the power of evil. It is a borrowed power, preying on the power which sinners give it, but it is real. Its reality is shown in the works of evil, which John depicted so vividly, and which we ourselves see around us all the time.

One more point must be added. The power of the devil is not dependent only on the private sins of every individual person. We live in a community, and each of us is part of a larger whole: a family, a tribe, a country, the human race. For better or worse, we belong together. And we are all born into a world in which the devil already has great power over us. No one can escape him altogether. We may fight him in our own lives, and sometimes even achieve small victories over him. But no one is able *not* to sin. This is where the gospel of Jesus Christ comes in. He has come to save us from that terrible slavery of sin, and He has overcome the devil and saved us. Those who belong to Him can fight the devil with real hope, for they know that the victory has already been won.

STUDY SUGGESTIONS

WORDS

1. What is the meaning of the names 'Satan', 'the devil', and 'Apollyon', and why is it important for us to know the meanings?

CONTENT

2. What is the most important point to remember about the power of evil?
3. What is the connection between the idea of 'chaos' and the idea of a power of evil?
4. Why is it natural for people to get the idea of 'chaos'?
5. In what ways do people differ from mere 'things' in connection with the power of evil?
6. What gives the devil his power?

'Good things become tainted and ruined by the way we exploit and abuse them' (p. 116).

The widespread destruction of forests through ignorance, carelessness, or for profit, as here in Bolivia, is turning many areas into deserts, and changing the climate so that no crops will grow and the people starve. How can such exploitation of God's gifts be prevented?

7. 'The devil is just a symbol for human sin'. To what extent is this true? Do you think it is the whole truth?
8. 'Before the fall man was able to sin or not to sin; after the fall he was unable not to sin; through Christ he is again able not to sin'. Comment on this statement in connection with this Special Note.

BIBLE

9. What does a comparison between Genesis 3 and Genesis 4.1–16 teach us about the power of evil?
10. What function does Satan have in the Book of Job?
11. In which two ways does Revelation 12 describe Satan's defeat?

APPLICATION

12. 'In ancient times belief in the power of evil was expressed in the mythical idea of a chaos monster' (p. 114). In what mythical or symbolic form, if any, is the power of evil described in the traditional religion or folklore of your country?
13. 'The power of evil is not dependent only on private sins . . . each of us is part of a larger whole' (p. 116). Think of some of the larger groupings to which you belong. In which of those groups are you most aware of having to fight against the power of evil? Which of them gives you the greatest support and help in that fight? What conclusions, if any, can you draw from the answers you have given?

13.1–18
The Two Beasts

SUMMARY

13.1–4: John sees a monstrous beast rising out of the sea, to which the dragon gives his power and throne and great authority. The beast has a mortal wound, but the wound is healed, and the whole earth follows the beast with wonder, and worships it.

13.5–10: The beast blasphemes against God, makes war on the saints, and gains power over every tribe and people and tongue and nation.

13.11–18: A second beast rises out of the earth looking like a lamb but speaking like a dragon. It makes people worship the first beast, works great wonders, and causes all people who will not worship the first beast to be killed. It also marks out the followers of the first beast, so that all people who have not been so marked are robbed of their means of livelihood.

NOTES

13.1. A beast rising out of the sea. Some editions of the RSV give this part of chapter 13 the heading, 'War at sea'. But there is no reference to war, other than the warfare against the saints. The sea, surely, is another term for chaos, or the bottomless pit (see p. 62), that is, a world without God.
Ten horns, like the last of the four beasts in Daniel's vision (Dan. 7.7). In Daniel's vision this last beast represented the Greek Empire of Alexander, which after his death had disintegrated into a number of smaller but still quite powerful kingdoms. One of these was the Syrian kingdom, under one of whose kings faithful Jews suffered severe persecution. But John's vision refers to the Roman Empire.
Seven heads . . . and a blasphemous name upon its heads. Both the Syrian kings and the Roman Emperors had assumed 'divine' names, such as 'Saviour', 'Son of god', and 'Lord and god'.
13.3. Its mortal wound was healed. Soon after the Emperor Nero's death the story was told that he would return. In later years the Emperor Domitian was regarded by many as a second Nero, or as Nero returned to life, partly because there were some similarities between their reigns. Both had started very well, and it was only in their later years that they became vicious tyrants. This would seem to fit in well with John's numbers (starting from Augustus, Nero was the fifth emperor, the next two, Vespasian and Titus, would complete the seven, and Domitian would be 'an eighth but belongs to the seven', see also 17.10–11). But the mythical monster Leviathan was believed to have seven heads long before the time of the Roman Empire. John was certainly referring to the Emperor, and Nero was the prime example of vicious tyranny; but beside Nero John was not thinking of any specific ruler. The wound that was healed simply means that, after a tyrant has been killed, a new tyrant will come. Not only in Rome, but throughout the world and throughout history, the removal of one tyrant has often meant that another tyrant took his place. However, John may also have been hinting that both in its blasphemous names and in its 'resurrection' the beast tries to copy Christ, just as the dragon tries to copy God.
13.5. Forty-two months, see notes on 11.2, 3 and 12.5.
13.6. His dwelling, that is, those who dwell in heaven. This seems to suggest that the absolute state actually attacks God in His heaven. But John knew that God dwells with human beings (21.3), and that Christians are already *now* citizens of the City of God. They carry the passport of heaven (Phil. 1.27). So the persecution of the Christians is an attack on the heavenly city.
13.7. War on the saints means the carrying out of the threat mentioned in v. 6.
13.8. Written before the foundation of the world in the book of life of the

Lamb that was slain. The Lord has chosen who are to be His own. We recall the words in Jesus's farewell address to His disciples, 'You did not choose me, but I chose you' (John 15.16). But the book of life is not a closed list (see the interpretation of the passage on the Last Judgement, 20.11–15, pp. 162–164).

13.11. Arose out of the earth. The heading, 'War on land', found in some editions, is mistaken. The earth is mentioned in contrast with the sea (v. 1) to indicate that the two beasts claim authority over both land and sea. Both 19.20 and 20.1 confirm that this second beast is 'the false prophet as the slave of the beast' (JB).

13.16. Be marked on right hand or forehead. John's image is inspired by the custom in many religions of tattooing people as a sign that they belong to a particular god, the custom of tribal marking by means of scars, or the caste-marks customary in Hinduism today. But we must not confuse the origin of John's pictures with his intentions. The 'mark' means anything by which people could be identified, such as the tokens used in Rome for the people who were entitled to hand-outs of bread, or the identity cards widely used today.

13.18. This calls for wisdom. John did not mean that only clever people could figure out who could be meant by '666'. The wisdom required was the insight that 666 is only a *human* number which does not add up to the full sevens of God's design (see Special Note C, p. 69).

Six hundred and sixty six. In some languages letters are used also for numerals. John was a Jew, and so were many of the early Christians, and letters are used for numerals in both Hebrew and Aramaic. Moreover, Jews sometimes use the names of letters instead of numbers (thus, for example, in Amsterdam a *joed*, for *Yod* = Y = 10, means a ten guilder note). In their written form Semitic languages do not include vowels. So *Caesar Nero* would be spelt *QSR NRV*, or in the east, where he was called *Kaiser Neron: QSR NRVN*. The total value of the letters of *QSR NRVN* was 666 (Q = 60, S = 100, R = 200, N = 50, V = 6). In some manuscripts written in Italy, where the name was spelt without the final N, the figure given in Revelation 13.18 is 616, which seems to show that the number was regarded as referring to Nero. But it would be almost impossible to guess at the meaning of the number, unless people already knew that 'Nero' added up to 666 (and modern scholars would never have found it out, if they had not guessed that this number must mean Nero). However, the real significance lies not in the man who served as John's example of evil tyranny, but in the observation that it is a number of incompleteness.

INTERPRETATION

In this chapter John speaks quite specifically of the perils of his own time and its immediate future, illustrated by events from its recent past. Later readers, however, have been inclined to interpret this chapter as referring to *their* own time. This is natural, as similar conditions arise from time to time with depressing frequency.

There can be little doubt that the number 666 refers to Nero. Such references to people by a number were not unusual, but they could only be used if the connection between the number and the person was already known. We could think of many people whose names would add up to 666, and so could the first readers of the Revelation, but no one other than Nero would fit the picture.

Nero, however, was not a private person. He represents the power of the authoritarian state. He symbolized that power more clearly than any of the other Caesars, not only because the Church had suffered the first large-scale persecution during his reign, but also because many other people regarded him as the prime example of what could happen if too much power was placed in the hands of the wrong man.

Nero was also suitable for John's purpose because of the legend which was believed about him, namely that he was not really dead, but would return. John, however, used the idea of the deadly wound which was miraculously healed for another purpose. He wanted to convey that tyrants such as Nero have a nasty tendency to come back, not literally, but in the person of another tyrant.

Thus Nero, the first beast, stands for the totalitarian imperial state. The power of that state rested on brute force. Christians in Rome had already experienced this, and those outside the city, throughout the Roman Empire, would experience it sooner than they expected. John could not, of course, have foreseen how often such events would repeat themselves in other nations, and his vision did not tell him. But his picture of Nero's tyranny is strikingly similar to some of the totalitarian regimes which have followed, and to some of those we are seeing in the twentieth century.

Christians are not the only people to suffer, and modern tyrannies have been particularly violent in their hatred of Jews. Israel and the Church have this in common, that they present to the world the claims of the living God. Christians can renounce their faith and cease to be Christians, but a Jew remains a Jew, even if he is totally assimilated to the nation in which he dwells, and even if he renounces his Jewish faith.

Jews and Christians, as they present God's claims to the world, are hated by tyrants. The totalitarian state is not content with 'the things that belong to Caesar' (Mark 12.7); it demands the total devotion, obedience, and, indeed, worship, which are due to God alone. Under a totalitarian regime Jews and Christians must therefore expect persecution. Other people may be impressed by the power of the state, and be prepared to conform, but God's people owe allegiance to their heavenly

King, and have to live by the revealed will of the living God.

Other people may suffer as well. There are many people other than Jews and Christians who love their freedom, and are prepared to fight for that freedom. And even people who do not offer any resistance may suffer. The absolute state is the enemy of *all* truly human life. But God's people are the first obstacle to its demand for total obedience, and they are therefore its first victims.

Even the totalitarian state, however, cannot live by brute force alone. It needs an ideology, that is a set of ideas which people can be persuaded to follow and uphold. The second beast, the false prophet (19.20), provides that.

Tyrants like to pretend that they govern by the will of the people. The Roman Empire was a republic, and the Caesar was only a servant of the Popular Assembly. Julius Caesar, and later his adopted son Augustus, who reigned at the time of the birth of Christ, had come to power as the leader of the democratic party. Then as now, rulers liked to speak of 'democracy' and 'the will of the people'. One way of making sure of the support of the masses was by providing food and games: half the free citizens of Rome were dependent on public support, and keeping them fed and entertained was an excellent way to gain and to keep popularity.

But man does not live by bread alone, and the power of the Caesars needed some religious support. The status as gods, to which the Emperors increasingly laid claim, provided that support. On a more practical level they defended that absolute power on grounds of expedience; claiming that *imperium*, the power of the emperor, was the best way to secure the greatest good for the largest number of people. The two concepts, the divine right of the emperor, and the greatest good for the largest number of people, were very different ideas. But they were both proclaimed as noble ideals, and by treating them as interdependent, many people were persuaded to accept the totalitarian state with enthusiasm, and serve it with genuine loyalty.

An ideology is a powerful means of making people serve a cause with great enthusiasm, and of making them do things which they would not do otherwise. People will go to great lengths, and commit horrible crimes, if they can be made to believe that they are serving a high ideal. This is true even if the ideal is humanitarian; people find it surprisingly easy to love 'mankind' and to despise the real-life men and women they meet. As Charlie Brown (of the Peanuts cartoon) said, 'I love mankind, it's people I can't stand'. An idealist is a dangerous person, because if he feels it to be necessary, he will commit the most appalling outrages for his ideal. The most horrifying atrocities have been committed in the service of the best causes. John's vision shows the totalitarian state, but individual revolutionaries can be just as ruthless in their acts of terrorism.

This second beast works not only outside the Church but among Christians as well. History shows many examples of how the Church can become subservient to a tyrannical state, and support the state ideology. We have already mentioned (p. 55) that of the *Deutsche Christen*, the 'German Christians', as they called themselves, who supported the Nazi ideology. Most of them adhered strictly to the teaching set forth in the ancient documents of the Church, which, of course, did not mention the Nazi ideology (though it ought to have been obvious that this ideology contradicted the Christian faith). By God's grace there were also many faithful Christians in the German Church who were prepared to speak the truth, and to suffer for their Lord; and several suffered martyrdom. But the point that John wanted to emphasize by saying that the second beast looked like a lamb, is that false prophecy can seem to be wholly admirable, and can also be found within the Church. In the past, Christians have often allowed themselves to be swayed by nationalistic ideals which contradicted their Christian faith. It is sincerely to be hoped that young Churches will not make the same mistake.

The details of John's vision are symbolic. Thus the 'mark' on the right hand or the forehead is meant figuratively. Those who conform to the demands of the rulers are given means to identify themselves, so that they can claim the benefits due to them. But those who refuse to conform are isolated and robbed of their livelihood; they have their work taken away from them, and it is made difficult or impossible for them to obtain food.

John also describes how the apparent achievements of the state and its priests, and the marvels they produce, can impress the people, even the believers. His vision hints at some of the tricks used to make idols appear to be alive; but even without such tricks the marvels which Rome and its successors have produced are stupendous.

We must remember, however, that it is not only the state that can threaten the faithful. Pressure is often brought to bear upon Christians by the community in which they live, or by the achievements of the civilization of which they are part. The pressures of an ungodly society can be very heavy indeed, and state officials do not always have to do very much to keep the pressure up.

We must also remember that besides the two great beasts which John saw, the state and its ideology, there are also many smaller beasts, which are active in various organizations. States, political parties, liberation movements, religious groups, trades unions, pressure groups of many kinds, all have important roles to play. But they all run the risk of becoming the stamping-grounds of greater or smaller beasts.

Between them the two beasts have all the advantages. If necessary they can use brute force, and will not hesitate to torture and to kill, though very often their spectacular achievements are so impressive and effective that no force is needed. They seem bound to win.

But they do not win. In the end they come to nothing. All their effort, and all their achievement is in vain. Six hundred and sixty-six is their cipher, the number which points to human weakness and incompleteness, and they will never reach the 'seven' of God's perfect design. We are reminded of the Tower of Babel (Genesis 11): so much effort had been spent, and so much had been achieved, but God had to come right down from heaven before He could even see it. That, of course, is merely a manner of speaking: God sees and knows everything, but it is clear what the writer of Genesis wanted to convey. It is equally clear what the message of John's vision is. Here too, as in the story of Babel, we see the utmost that humans can achieve, but it remains unfinished. God has planned something entirely different, and He remains in control.

STUDY SUGGESTIONS

WORDS

1. Explain the words 'power', 'throne', and 'authority'.

CONTENT

2. (a) Who was the first beast like?
   (b) What does the first beast represent?
3. Explain the mortal wound.
4. What authority did the first beast claim?
5. Explain why Jews and Christians are nearly always the first victims of persecution.
6. What is the 'book of life'?
7. (a) Who was the second beast like in appearance?
   (b) What does the second beast represent?
   (c) How does the second beast work?
8. What is meant by the statement that 666 is 'the number of a man' (AV, JB), or 'a human number' (RSV)? Is it quite enough to say that the number represents 'a man's name' (NEB, GNB)? Give reasons for your answer.

BIBLE

9. In what ways does Revelation 13 chiefly resemble and differ from Romans 13.1–7.

APPLICATION

10. What task, and what authority, do governments actually have? (It may be helpful, before you answer this question, to read such

passages as 1 Kings 3.4–9; Ps. 72.1–7; Prov. 31.8–9; Jer. 23.4–6; Rom. 13.1–7.)
11. How would you describe the distinction between good government and tyranny?
12. Think of examples in the history of the Church and in the modern world, in which governments have claimed the authority which belongs to God alone. What was the result in each case?

14.1–5
The Church Triumphant

SUMMARY

John sees 'on Mount Zion' the Lamb and His followers, faithful and chaste, who sing a new song.

NOTES

14.1. On Mount Zion. John may have had in mind Psalm 2.6: 'I have set my king on Zion, my holy hill'. At any rate, he has used the name of the Temple mountain in Jerusalem. But in his vision he had seen, not an earthly mountain, but God's dwelling place in heaven (see note on 21.10).
On their foreheads. See note on 7.2.
14.3. No one could learn that song. The point is not that the words of the song are secret, but that the redeemed sing a song about a mystery which will remain beyond our understanding until we join the saints in heaven.
14.4. Chaste. The Greek word translated 'chaste' is *parthenos*, which means a virgin of marriageable age, but could also be used for a young man who had not touched any woman. It is perhaps just possible, but it is not likely, that John meant literally that the redeemed in heaven were all men who had not touched a woman, and women who had not been touched by a man. As we have seen, the 'firstfruits of the redeemed' were the Christian martyrs (7.9–17), who were certainly not all unmarried men and women (Peter, for example, was a married man).
First fruits. It was the custom in Israel, after the harvest, to offer the first corn, or fruits, to God, as a token that the whole harvest really belongs to God, and people live by what God gives them. Similarly, after the lambing season, the first lamb was offered to God. Here the meaning is slightly different. The 'first fruits' are, so to speak, a promise of what is to

125

come. The faithful witnesses, who have been put to death for their faith and now praise the Lord in heaven, are only the first of all those who will inherit eternal life. Christ came, not merely to redeem the Church, but to redeem the world.

INTERPRETATION

Before the end of this series of visions, John is allowed another glance at the first-fruits of the redeemed. Once more he and his readers are assured that, whatever may happen on earth, God's people are in safe hands.

John's statement that 'it is these who have not defiled themselves with women, for they are chaste' seems puzzling. Some interpreters think that John may have been alluding to the custom in ancient Israel for soldiers to abstain from sexual intercourse for as long as a campaign lasted; newly-weds were therefore excused all military duties (Deut. 20.7). The practice is illustrated clearly by Uriah's conduct in Jerusalem while his unit was in the field: he did not enter his house and did not even meet with his wife (2 Sam. 11.11). The statement that the martyrs had 'not defiled themselves with women' would then mean that they were 'soldiers of the Cross'.

But John is far more likely to have been alluding to the Old Testament writers' practice of referring to idolatry in terms of sexual vice, because it too was a form of infidelity. The comparison which Hosea made between his wife's infidelity and Israel's infidelity to the LORD, is a striking example. 'To play the harlot', or 'to go a whoring' after strange gods, were among the expressions by which Old Testament writers condemned the unfaithfulness of those Israelites who worshipped other gods beside the living God of Israel (see e.g. Exod. 34.15; Judges 2.17; Ps. 106.39; Ezek. 23.30; Hos. 9.1). The word *parthenos*, 'chaste', would then mean those faithful Christians who had *not* worshipped the Emperor or the Roman gods.

The purpose of the vision is clear: to give the assurance that, whatever may happen, God's victory is certain. The Lamb is victorious. His victory was gained on the cross, and those who belong to Him, who have 'his name and his Father's name written on their foreheads', are risking the same cross, but also share in His victory. They may suffer in this world, but from the point of view of eternity they are safe.

As before, life in heaven is described as being filled with song (see 4.8–11; 5.9–14; 7.12; 11.17). John tried in vain to describe what the sound was like: it was like the sound of many waters – no, it was more like the sound of thunder – but no, that was not right either, it was like the sound of harps . . . John just had to give up. How could he describe the music of heaven? It did not sound like anything that John had ever heard before, and it was also a *new* song, a song that no human beings can know until they join the redeemed in heaven. What had been revealed to John is so gloriously 'out of this world', that there is absolutely nothing to compare it with.

STUDY SUGGESTIONS

WORDS

1. In view of such passages as 2 Chr. 21.11–15; Ps. 73.27 (AV, JB); Jer. 2.20; Ezek. 16.15–17; Hos. 1.2, what do you think the word 'chaste' (RSV), or in other translations 'virgin' (AV) or 'pure' (NIV), means in v. 4?

CONTENT

2. Where was the 'Mount Zion' which John saw in his vision?
3. The GNB translates v. 3b: 'Of all mankind they are the only ones who have been redeemed'. Apart from the fact that this is *not* what John wrote, how does this wrong translation contradict the remainder of this passage?

BIBLE

4. What do the laws in Exodus 23 and 24 teach about first fruits?

APPLICATION

5. The words 'in their mouths no lie was found' probably refer to the fact that the martyrs had spoken the truth about Christ. But John's words seem to imply more. What more do they imply, and how does this affect us today?
6. John states repeatedly how he heard that life in heaven is filled with song. What, if anything, does that teach us about the way in which Christians ought to live on earth?

14.6–20
The Harvest of the Earth

SUMMARY

14.6–7: An angel, with an eternal gospel, calls people to 'fear God and give him glory'.

14.8: A second angel announces the fall of 'Babylon', that is to say, Rome.

14.9–11: A third angel warns of the terrible consequences of worshipping the beast.

14.12: John comments that 'here is a call for the endurance of the saints'.

14.13: A voice comments on the blessedness of those who die in the Lord, and the Spirit confirms this comment.

14.14: John witnesses the appearance of a human figure, who is ready to start the harvest.

14.15–16: The wheat harvest.

14.17–20: The wine harvest.

NOTES

14.6. An eternal gospel. The Greek word translated 'eternal' does not always mean 'everlasting'. Here John wants to say that this gospel, this good news, is important for this life and the next, for this world and the world to come.

Gospel. The Greek word *evangelion*, 'gospel', is usually translated 'good news'. But strictly speaking it means 'news well told', and it was used by the Greeks especially for news of a victory. Thus, for example, the Greek translators of the Old Testament used the verb *evangelisthai*, 'to bring the *evangelion*', for the message that Saul and Jonathan had been killed, which was good news to the Philistines, but bad news for the Israelites. But John could have understood the word only as meaning the gospel of God's grace, the victory which Christ had won on the Cross. In any case, 'an eternal gospel' could only mean that gospel of Jesus Christ.

14.7. The hour of his judgement has come. The judgement is brought about through people's response to the gospel.

14.8. Babylon the great. Ever since the story of the Tower of Babel had been known in Israel (Genesis 11), Babel, or Babylon, had served as a symbol of human civilization at its most splendid. But without God even the greatest human achievement is not good enough, and is under God's judgement. Here John is referring to the Roman Empire and its civilization, but the judgement applies equally to every civilization.

The wine of her impure passion. No doubt the first readers would hear in these words a reference to the immorality which was widespread in imperial Rome. John may also be hinting at the blood-thirstiness of the Romans, who gathered in vast crowds to watch public executions, or to see sword-fighters kill each other in the arena, rather like the pleasure which many people today get from watching gunfights and other violence in films. In the context of the Revelation, however, 'the wine of her impure passion' must have been referring to the persecution of the Christians.

14.10. The wine of God's wrath. The 'wine of impure passion' turns against those who indulge in it, and becomes the 'wine of God's wrath'. **Fire and sulphur,** as suffered by Sodom and Gomorrah (Gen. 19.24 – where 'brimstone', also used here in Revelation in earlier RSV editions, is another name for sulphur).

14.11. The smoke of their torment. The worshippers of the beast share in the fate of their sinful city.

14.12. Here is a call for the endurance of the saints. John warns against the temptation to join in the sins of the wicked city and the danger of sharing its fate, but also encourages his readers to 'endure', that is, to carry on faithfully with their Christian witness.

14.14. A white cloud. White is the colour used by John symbolically in connection with Christ. In the Old Testament clouds are a symbol for the presence of God. See p. 97.

14.15. The harvest of the earth is fully ripe. Jesus had used the idea of the harvest several times for the gathering of the faithful into God's eternal home (see Mark 4.8 and 29; John 4.35). In His conversation with the disciples after His talk with the Samaritan woman, Jesus emphasized that the fields are ready to be harvested even now (John 4.35). In the parable of the tares (Matt. 13.24–30) He stressed that the 'harvest' also means that the 'weeds' are separated from the 'wheat', in other words, that the 'harvest' also means judgement.

14.19. The great wine press of the wrath of God. A few Bible writers had used the picture of a wine press for the wrath of God, a notable example being Isaiah 63.3–6: 'I have trodden the wine press alone, and from the peoples no one was with me; I trod them in my anger and trampled them in my wrath; their lifeblood is sprinkled upon my garments, and I have stained all my raiment. For the day of vengeance was in my heart, and my year of redemption had come . . .' However, we should note that in this Isaiah passage God's redemption is present also. Christians would certainly have connected the wine with the blood of Christ. The picture thus has two sides. On the one hand it points clearly to the seriousness of

God's judgement, on the other hand it points equally clearly to the sacrifice of Christ on the cross, the blood of the New Covenant that was 'poured out for many for the forgiveness of sins' (Matt. 26.28).

INTERPRETATION

Again, at the end of another series of visions, we should expect a vision of the end, and, indeed, here for the first time John did receive a much clearer prophecy of the end. However, his vision did not show the end of *the* world, but the end of *John's* world, that is to say, of civilization as John knew it.

The first part of the vision emphasizes the terrible consequences of worshipping the beast. We may therefore be surprised to read that the first angel was sent to proclaim 'an eternal gospel'. 'An eternal gospel' can only mean the gospel of Jesus Christ, and that means salvation. We must remember this when we read the rest of this chapter.

God's judgement begins with the proclamation of the gospel, with the offer of the opportunity to repent. The Revelation stresses this again and again. This world is full of guilt and disaster; it is under God's judgement and His judgement must be taken seriously. But as long as human history lasts, the world is also under God's grace, and people still have time to repent.

The second angel announces the fall of Babylon, that is to say, of civilization. John would have seen in this God's judgement on Rome and its civilization, but the judgement applies to every civilization.

The third angel focuses on the consequences of worshipping the beast and its image. Some interpreters have accused John of 'gloating over the fate of the wicked' in this passage. But that seems to be a misunderstanding of his purpose. The Revelation was written to give comfort and encouragement to Christians who were soon to face persecution, and to warn those who did not see the troubles which lay ahead. John was encouraging them not only to remain faithful, but also to continue to preach the gospel. By showing them the consequences of worshipping the beast, he encouraged them to double their efforts to call their fellows to repentance. His readers were themselves first generation Christians. Many of them had once worshipped the beast but had repented, and now followed the Lamb. They must tell their fellows, as they themselves had been told, that the time was short and that the peril was great. John did, indeed, paint a horrific picture. But he was describing a vision that was meant to serve as a warning.

Such efforts to preach the gospel call for patience and endurance. The faithful will find it difficult to devote their time and energy to a task of which the results will be shown only in the next life, especially as this is a dangerous task, which may well lead to persecution and martyrdom. But their labour will not be in vain, and those who die in the Lord know that their deeds follow them.

The last four parts of the chapter show the appearing of the Judge, the harvest of the 'wheat', the appearing of another angel with a sickle, and the 'wine harvest'. The picture of a double harvest reflects the Jewish calendar. Grain and grapes were the two most important harvests in ancient Israel, and both ended with a religious festival. Between them the two harvests bring in the entire harvest of the earth, which, in John's vision, means the harvest of the entire world.

At first sight the 'harvest' seems to suggest the condemnation and savage punishment of the wicked. But such a use of the idea of the 'harvest' would be most unusual. When the Bible writers used 'harvest' symbolically, they usually referred to the salvation of God's people. And when Jesus said to His disciples, 'Pray therefore the Lord of the harvest to send out labourers into his harvest', He was clearly speaking of the preaching of the gospel to bring in His people (Matt. 9.38).

The wine harvest and the wine press point in the same direction. 'The wine press was trodden outside the city'. That is where executions took place, and in the New Testament it is particularly the place where Jesus was crucified (see Mark 15.20; John 19.17; Heb. 13.12). Wine was regarded as a precious gift, and at the Last Supper Jesus had connected the cup of wine directly with His blood (Mark 14.23–25). Here too the 'wine' must mean the blood of Christ and the martyrs. The blood which flowed from the 'wine press' was shed by 'Babylon'; it was the cruelty of the oppressors which produced the blood as high as a horse's bridle. This connects closely with v. 10, where those who worship the beast 'drink the wine of God's wrath': they drink it by shedding the blood of Christ and the martyrs.

The harvest is, indeed, the time of judgement. But the judgement is brought about by a parting of the ways. The preaching of the gospel is designed to bring about this parting of the ways (see Isa. 6.9–10; Mark 4.11–12). It created a division between those who followed the Lord and those who crucified Him, and the preaching of the Church still creates a division between the faithful and the unbelievers. Thus the gospel separates the tares from the wheat (Matt. 13.24–30), and separates the blood of the martyrs from the dross (see Isa. 1.24–26).

If this interpretation is correct – and more than any other interpretation it seems to follow what the text actually says – then the emphasis in vv. 9–11 on the terrible consequences of worshipping the beast and its image is meant to dissuade people from such folly. God's judgement must be taken seriously. God is not to be mocked, and those who refuse the offer of His grace cannot expect to escape His wrath. But the aim of the warning is not so much to threaten punishment as to offer salvation. Besides stressing the need for repentance while there is still time, this

'The harvest is the time of judgement . . . it separates the tares from the wheat . . . the blood of the martyrs from the dross' (p. 131) – as these Indonesian farmers harvesting their rice will separate the grain from the straw.

Besides warning of coming judgement, John's vision of the harvest gives promise that the sufferings of Christ, and of faithful Christians, will bear fruit. In what ways, if any, can we separate the tares from the wheat in our own lives?

chapter, through the metaphor of the harvest, gives the assurance that the sufferings of Christ and the martyrs will bear fruit for eternity.

STUDY SUGGESTIONS

WORDS

1. What does the word 'gospel' mean? How does this apply to this vision?

CONTENT

2. To whom was the gospel to be proclaimed?
3. What does 'Babylon' stand for in this passage?
4. What is the connection between 'the wine of her impure passion' and 'the wine of God's wrath'?
5. For what reason or for what purpose was the 'endurance of the saints' needed?
6. What does the picture of the 'harvest' suggest?
7. What did 'wine' mean to the first Christians?
8. Whose blood flowed from the 'wine press'?

BIBLE

9. In what way, and with what meaning, had Jesus used the idea of the 'harvest'?

APPLICATION

10. In what ways does the judgement over 'Babylon' relate to the world today?
11. The task which the angel in v. 6 had to carry out clearly implies that John also had a task to perform. What was John's task, and what task, if any, is demanded of us?
12. What encouragement does John's vision give us in carrying out our task?
13. In this passage the metaphor of the harvesting of fruit, grain, and grapes is used to describe the time of God's judgement, and the separation of the faithful from the ungodly, His wrath against the followers of the beast, and His gathering of the faithful who may now 'rest from their labours'. How effective do you think this metaphor is in conveying those ideas to people in cities and industrial areas today, who have no personal experience of the work of harvesting? What other metaphors and pictures might be effective in such situations?

15.1–8

The New Exodus

SUMMARY

15.1: John sees seven angels with the seven last plagues.

15.2–4: Before he is actually shown those plagues, he sees the faithful Christians who have come through the ordeal, whose Exodus from the world is completed. They sing the song of Moses and the song of the Lamb.

15.5–8: The seven angels are given seven bowls full of the wrath of God.

NOTES

15.1. Seven plagues. The salvation of the faithful is compared with the Exodus of the Israelites from Egypt. If taken literally these seven plagues are fewer than the ten mentioned in the Book of Exodus, but seven is the number of completeness. The Exodus from the realm of the beast is incomparably greater than the Exodus from Egypt, and the seven plagues are a complete number of disasters.

15.2. What appeared to be a sea of glass mingled with fire. The escape of the redeemed is compared with the crossing of the Sea of Reeds (Exod. 14), traditionally (though probably wrongly) identified with the Red Sea (the RSV translates 'Red Sea'). 'Mingled with fire', however, suggests more than just the red colour: it probably means a fiery ordeal, greater than that of the Israelites in Egypt.

Who had conquered the beast. In the eyes of the world the faithful Christians had been defeated, but in actual fact they had overcome the world.

15.3. The song of Moses, the servant of God, and the song of the Lamb. The words of the Song of Moses (Exod. 15.1–18) and the Song of Miriam (Exod. 15.21) are very different from those of the Song of the Lamb, and John was not suggesting that they were the same song. But both celebrate salvation from deadly danger. However, it is only fair to notice that Moses gloated over the fate of his drowned enemies, whilst the followers of the Lamb do not.

Just. It is 'just' for God to vindicate the innocent (see pp. 76, 145).

15.5. The temple of the tent of witness in heaven. The word 'tent' here shows that John saw the heavenly counterpart of the tabernacle, which had served the Israelites for a temple in the wilderness, rather than a counterpart of the Temple in Jerusalem. Moses's tabernacle contained the tablets with the Law, that is to say, God's revealed will.

15.8. Smoke from the glory of God. Throughout the Old Testament a cloud of mist or smoke was the sign of God's presence with His people (Exod. 21, and see Isa. 4.5).

No one could enter. No one was allowed to enter the tabernacle when it was filled with God's glory and the cloud remained upon it (Exod. 40.35), but in the heavenly temple people will be able to enter into the presence of God, once the seven plagues are ended.

INTERPRETATION

John sees another vision of seven angels, and again their work does not represent a new stage in the events that are to happen, but is a new expression of God's judgement on the events already recorded. Being expressions of God's judgement, their tasks point to the end, and John calls them 'the last plagues'.

These last plagues reminded John of the plagues of Egypt, and, indeed, their purpose is similar. Just as the plagues of Egypt preceded the deliverance of the Israelites from slavery, so these seven last plagues precede the final deliverance of God's people. In God's heaven the saints have already been delivered, and completed their Exodus from the power of the beast, and they sing their song of delivery, the song of the Lamb, joined by those who sing the song of Moses.

The bowls are given to the angels, not by God Himself, nor by the Lamb, but by one of the living creatures. This may be a hint that the creation itself 'waits with eager longing for the revelation of the sons of God . . . because the creation itself will be set free from its bondage to decay, and obtain the glorious liberty of the children of God' (Rom. 8.19, 21; see note on 4.6). But the bowls are full, not of the longings of the creatures, but of the wrath of God.

STUDY SUGGESTIONS

CONTENT

1. The Song of the Lamb is a hymn of praise. For what in particular do the saints praise God?
2. What promise does the Song of the Lamb contain?
3. What promise is suggested by the end of v. 8?

BIBLE

4. Of what did the sea of glass mingled with fire remind John?
5. (a) In what way(s) are the Song of Moses and the Song of the Lamb similar?
   (b) And in what way(s) do they differ?

6. What was the tent of witness, and what did it signify?

7. In what ways are the promises of vv. 4b and 8b important to us?
8. For what reasons was it important to John, and is it important to us, that John saw the tent of witness?

16.1–21
The Bowls of God's Wrath

SUMMARY

16.1–9: The first four bowls affect the natural world: the earth, the sea, the fresh water, and the sun.

16.10–21: The last three bowls affect the beast more directly, the fifth affecting his throne, the sixth bringing about an invasion of his kingdom by enemies, and the seventh bringing about the collapse and disintegration of 'Babylon'.

NOTES

16.2. On the earth, and foul and evil sores . . . This corresponds with the sixth plague of Egypt (Exod. 9.8–12). The earth is the place where people live; and this is the connection between the earth and the diseases mentioned. One problem for our understanding of this verse is that diseases strike the worshippers of the Lamb as well as the worshippers of the beast. True, some diseases are connected specifically with certain sins, but a godly life is no guarantee of good health. The question, 'Who has sinned, this man or his parents?' (John 9.2) is out of place here, and can be very cruel. But John sees that, even though there is no direct connection between individual sin and individual disease, there is a connection between sin and disease in the community.

16.3, 4. Blood. This corresponds with the first plague of Egypt (Exod. 7.14–25). The sins of the persecutors turn against themselves (see 14.8, 20; 17.6). The savage language of v. 6 was no doubt inspired by the horrors of the persecution under Nero.

16.8. Fire. There was no corresponding plague in Egypt.

16.9. They cursed the name of God. The 'acts of God' mentioned in vv. 2–8 did not lead to repentance.

16.10. The throne of the beast means the administration of the Empire. John foresaw civil strife. He may have been thinking of the strife of the years 68–69, after the death of Nero, when three emperors succeeded each other within a few months.

Darkness. This is like the ninth plague of Egypt. However, John probably meant 'darkness' in a symbolic sense, and may have been thinking of the contrast between the followers of the beast in their spiritual darkness, and the Christians, 'the people who walked in darkness' but 'have seen a great light' (Isa. 9.2).

16.12. The great river Euphrates. Beyond the Euphrates was the land of the Parthians. People who expect to find in the Revelation a detailed world history of the future are faced with an awkward question here. John saw that his world was heading for disaster in terms which would be intelligible to him. He was therefore shown the collapse of the Roman Empire in terms of the threat from the Parthians. In actual fact the Roman Empire was to last several more centuries, and eventually the western half was destroyed by Germanic tribes and the eastern half by the armies of Islam. That does not lessen the validity of what John saw and wrote, but it does mean that he did not receive or give a series of precise predictions.

16.13. The false prophet is the second beast (13.11–17). We must not make the mistake of thinking that this means a particular Church or denomination. John knew only one Church, and 'Churches' meant to him simply congregations of Christians in various towns, but all belonging to the one Church. John wanted his readers to beware of false prophecy in their own Church.

16.14. Demonic spirits. The ancient world believed in the existence of large numbers of evil spirits. Thus, for example, certain mental diseases were attributed to demons or evil spirits. But demons were also believed to be the cause of many other evils. Modern science refutes this idea completely. Nevertheless, behind this belief in demons and demonic spirits lies the very proper instinctive feeling that evil is unnatural, that it is not part of God's good creation, and that it is the work of the destroyer of God's creation (see Special Note D, pp. 114–118, and Interpretation of 9.11–19).

Kings of the whole world. Not only the Roman Empire, but every state that is based on violence, is satanic in origin.

16.15. Lo, I am coming. This verse interrupts John's description of his vision. Some scholars think it was added later by another writer. But it may also have been inserted by John himself to remind his readers that they must be prepared at all times.

Like a thief, see Matt. 24.43; 2 Pet. 3.10; and note on 3.3.

16.16. Armageddon, or, more properly, Harmageddon, is used here to mean the place of the decisive battle (rather as British people use the name 'Waterloo'). The name 'Armageddon' means, 'the Hill of Megiddo'. Megiddo had been the scene of two decisive battles in Israel's history, the battle in which Barak defeated the king of Hazor, and thus freed the northern tribes of Israel (Judges 4—5), and the battle in which King Josiah had been defeated and killed (2 Kings 23.29). The nearest mountain to Megiddo was Carmel, where Elijah had defeated the prophets of Baal (1 Kings 18).

16.19. Great Babylon. Though John seems to hint at the end of the present world, the words, 'great Babylon', remind us that John is speaking of the end of *his* world, the fall of the Roman Empire.

INTERPRETATION

Previous visions showed the things that happen in the world, and some of the inevitable results. They also made it clear what God's judgement must be. This vision deals more directly with God's judgement. But in spite of the expression 'the last plagues', this is not the Last Judgement at the end of time. This vision makes it quite clear what the Last Judgement must be, but John is still describing the judgement that is carried on in the present world.

The first four bowls show how sin has caused enmity between human beings and the natural world. This judgement is not threatened for a remote future but is carried out now, and it was already pronounced in Genesis 3.17–19: 'Cursed is the ground because of you; in toil you shall eat of it all the days of your life; thorns and thistles it shall bring forth to you . . .'. The story of the Garden of Eden has many sides. One side is that God had placed human beings in a world which was meant to be a garden, where they might 'freely eat of every tree of the garden', with one exception: 'of the tree of the knowledge of evil you shall not eat, for in the day that you eat of it you shall die', that is to say, the fruit of this tree was poisonous (Gen. 2.16–17). In spite of the warning, they did eat the fruit, in the vain hope of gaining supernatural knowledge (Gen. 3.5: this is probably what 'knowing good and evil' means), just as some people today take drugs in the vain hope that this will enrich their spiritual life. The punishment for their sin was closely linked to the sin: nature had been abused and was turned against the sinners. John's language is much more forceful, but it remains true that, because of sin, the natural environment, in which people ought to be at home, has in many ways turned against the human race.

The next two bowls affect human relationships. This part of John's vision shows how man turns against man, causing strife among the citizens of the Roman Empire and an invasion by foreign armies.

This leads inevitably to the pouring out of the seventh bowl, the final collapse of the Roman Empire and its civilization, in which both natural events and human actions play a part.

In John's vision the question of later empires and their destiny was not asked, and therefore not answered. Such questions would have been irrelevant to John and his first readers. The Revelation was meant to be a practical help for the readers in the situation in which they would soon find themselves. That situation was much too serious for them to ask questions with which later generations would have to deal.

Nevertheless, what John wrote is still relevant today. Though much in the world may change, much more remains essentially the same. Many people in later ages have lived in circumstances very much like those of John's first readers, and many people today live in very similar circumstances. We, today, may have to meet the attacks, not of the beasts which John saw, but of very similar beasts, led by the same 'dragon', that same 'ancient serpent'. And we can still find comfort and encouragement in the promises of that same God, who rules and judges now, as He did then.

There is one other thing. John's visions do not seem to have shown him much between the end of Rome and the end of the world (but see 20.1–6!). The persecuted Christians of the years following John's visions would not have looked much beyond the end of their troubles. Most people find it difficult to look much further than the end of their present troubles. People in lands under colonial rule long eagerly for their independence, and do not look much further. And those whose country is occupied by a foreign enemy, or policed by an oppressive political regime, look forward only to the day of their liberation and not beyond. This is not only natural, indeed it is necessary, for we must all deal with our immediate tasks first. 'Let the day's own trouble be sufficient for the day' (Matt. 6.34).

But God's judgement on Babylon presages the Last Judgement. However many Babylons there may still be to come, one will be the last. God will make an end. And the end will be good.

STUDY SUGGESTIONS

WORDS

1. When John heard the name 'Armageddon', what would he have thought of?

CONTENT

2. Explain vv. 2–8 in terms of the hostility of nature.
3. What was significant about 'blood to drink'?
4. What is meant by the 'throne of the beast', and what does the 'darkness' mean?
5. If John's vision prophesied the fall of the Roman Empire, how does this vision affect later Empires?

6. What is the connection if any between the end of the Roman Empire and its civilization, and the end of the world?

BIBLE

7. What is the connection between the story of Paradise and the Fall, and the first four bowls?

APPLICATION

8. Many people today regard the belief in demonic spirits as mistaken. What is your opinion? If it is mistaken, what truth, if any, does it yet convey?
9. Does the 'false prophet' mean a 'false Church'? If not, what does the 'false prophet' signify, and in what way is this important to us?
10. What makes it so important for us to recognize that John's visions deal with the problems of his first readers?
11. Not only in the past, but in our own days too, many 'Empires' have come to an end. Give as many examples as you can of the endings of such present-day 'Empires', and say what connections, if any, you can see between what caused them to fall and the causes of the fall of the Roman Empire.

17.1–18
The Scarlet Woman

SUMMARY

17.1–2: One of the seven angels with the bowls invites John to come and see 'the great harlot who is seated upon many waters'.

17.3–6: John sees a woman seated on a scarlet beast. The beast is described in the same terms as the first beast of chapter 13. The woman is beautifully dressed, but holds in her hand a golden cup, 'full of abominations and the impurities of her fornication'; her name is given as 'Babylon the great, mother of harlots and of earth's abominations'; and John sees that she is drunk with the blood of saints and martyrs.

17.7–18: The angel interprets the vision.

NOTES

17.1. Harlot. As religious infidelity was often called 'fornication', (see interpretation of 14.1–5), idolatrous communities were sometimes called 'harlots', such as, for example, Nineveh (Nahum 3.4), Israel

(Ezek. 16.35; Hos. 2), Jerusalem (Isa. 1.21), and here Rome.

Seated upon many waters. Rome was master of the 'Great Sea' (the Mediterranean), which the Romans proudly called *Mare nostrum*, 'our sea'; But John interprets the 'many waters' as the many nations subject to Rome (v. 15).

17.3 The wilderness was regarded as the dwelling place of demons (Luke 11.24) and of temptation (Mark 1.12–13).

17.4. Purple and scarlet. We may be tempted to see in these brilliant colours a contrast with the Bride of the Lamb clothed in white (19.8). The scarlet woman is indeed contrasted with the pure Bride of Christ, but the first thing John wanted to emphasize was the *splendour* of the woman's outfit: she was dressed in imperial purple.

Golden cup. The outside of the cup is beautiful and precious, but inside are abominations and impurities.

17.6. Drunk with the blood of the saints and the blood of the martyrs of Jesus. John was reminding his readers of the persecution under Nero, but at the same time warning them that similar events were to come.

17.8. Was, and is not, and is to ascend. The wounded head (13.14) has not yet returned to life. John was writing at a time when the Church seemed safe, but the beast would raise its ugly head again, and persecution would return in all its ferocity.

17.10. They are also seven kings . . . Starting from Augustus, and disregarding the very short reigns of Galba, Otho, and Vitellius, Vespasian and Titus would be the sixth and seventh Emperors, and Domitian, whom some people regarded as a second Nero ('one of the seven') would be the eighth (see Special Note C, p. 69, and Appendix, p. 188). But John was probably not counting the actual number of Emperors. He saw that the beast would come back, the beast being, not so much the historical Nero, as the tyrannical power which Nero represented.

17.12. Ten kings. Some interpreters have suggested that the ten kings represent barbaric nations outside the Roman Empire; but that seems unlikely, for John describes them as 'horns of the beast', and says that they are 'of one mind and give over their power and authority to the beast'. They may represent vassal kings dependent on Rome, or governors of provinces, or the nations making up the Roman Empire.

17.13. The Lamb will conquer them. Elsewhere in the Revelation the Lamb has already conquered. But it is clear that here John wanted to convey that any attack on the Lamb is in vain.

17.17. To carry out his purpose. In spite of their attempts to frustrate His plans, God's enemies can in fact only manage to fulfil them.

INTERPRETATION

In the visions described in chapters 17 and 18 John was given a closer look at the collapse of his world. As in chapter 13, there are specific references to conditions, attitudes, and events of his own days. If the devil and his works ever changed fundamentally, or if God ever forsook His love or gave up His determination to save, we could lay these chapters aside as being irrelevant for us today. The situation in which John and his readers would soon find themselves, and the trials which they had to face, are indeed things of the past. But the conditions in which later generations have lived, and the trials which they have faced, have been basically very similar; and they still are.

The scarlet woman represents the city of Rome. Even the simplest reader in the Roman Empire knew that Rome was the city of the 'seven mountains' (v. 9), and even if someone missed that point, v. 18 would have made it clear. We must emphasize that this means the *city* of Rome, not the Church of Rome. In John's days there was only one Church, and 'the Church of Rome' meant the Christian Church in that city, that is to say, a Church which had suffered more severe persecution than any other, a Church which could be regarded as an example to many others.

The beast, here as in chapter 13, is the absolute power of the Emperor. We can make an intelligent guess about which Emperor may be meant by the 'beast that was and is not' (see note), but then we miss the point. John was shown that the vicious persecution, which the Church had suffered once in the past, would return.

The ten kings of v. 12 cannot be identified precisely, but it is clear that they represent nations in league with, or subject to Rome. But there is no true loyalty between them and the city that rules them, and they will take part in bringing about its downfall (v. 16). The beast, the woman, and her friends, are united in their hatred of God's people, but they do not love each other either.

At first sight the picture of the scarlet woman is quite attractive, until John realizes that this gorgeous creature is dressed in her finery in order to seduce, and that she is drunk with the blood of saints and martyrs. Allowing for the symbolic language, she presents a marvellously apt picture of first century Rome, and also of many cities in the world today.

The woman and her friends make war on the Lamb. But as the Lamb was raised from the dead, and is out of their reach, His people suffer under their attacks. But the Lamb is victorious, for He is Lord of lords and King of kings, and those who belong to Him are called and chosen and faithful. Those whom He has called will not fall away, and will not be lost, for He keeps those whom He has chosen.

STUDY SUGGESTIONS

WORDS

1. Apart from their literal meaning, what do the words 'harlot' and 'fornication' often mean in the Bible?

CONTENT

2. What is the significance of the 'wilderness' in v. 3?
3. What does the 'scarlet woman' represent?
4. Explain why the scarlet woman cannot be the Church of Rome.
5. 'This calls for a mind of wisdom' (v. 9). Does John mean that the readers must be clever enough to guess which Emperors he means? If not, what sort of wisdom is needed?
6. Who are actually attacked in the war on the Lamb?

APPLICATION

7. At first sight the scarlet woman looks quite attractive. Comment on the attractions of any great city, and on the dangers and evils people experience there.
8. John used the words 'harlot' and 'fornication' in a metaphoric sense. What if anything does the *literal* meaning of the words also suggest about ancient Rome and about the modern world?

18.1—19.5
Lament over the Fall of Babylon

SUMMARY

18.1–3: An angel announces the fall of Babylon.
18.4–8: Another voice from heaven calls people to come out of Babylon, and pronounces judgement on its sins.
18.9–19: Kings, merchants, and sailors watch from afar, and bewail the fate of the city.
18.20–24: Saints, apostles, and prophets, and heaven itself, are called to rejoice over the fall of Babylon. But a mighty angel expresses the sorrow of heaven, though the judgement on the wicked city was just.
19.1–5: The vindication of the righteous.

NOTES

18.3. The wealth of her wantonness. John used a rare Greek word, of which the precise meaning is not certain, but which probably refers to arrogance rather than wantonness; so we should probably translate this as 'the power of her arrogance', or 'her bloated wealth' (NEB).

18.4. Come out of her, my people. This call for people to come out of Babylon had a double purpose. On the one hand John was urging the Christians not to join in the sins of the pagan world; on the other hand he was urging the unbelievers to repent.

18.6. Repay her double was a conventional phrase for proper punishment.

18.7. Played the wanton. As in v. 3, this is probably a mistranslation; we should probably read 'flaunted her power'.

A queen I sit. The lament over Babylon is very similar to Ezekiel's lament over Tyre (Ezek. 28.1–19) and especially to the Second Isaiah's prophecy about the historic Babylon: 'You said, "I shall be mistress for ever," . . . Now therefore hear this, you lover of pleasures, who sit securely, who say in your heart, "I am, and there is no one besides me; I shall not sit as a widow or know the loss of children": These two things shall come to you in a moment, in one day; the loss of children and widowhood shall come upon you in full measure . . . there is no one to save you' (Isa. 47.7–15).

18.9. The kings of the earth. The fact that there are people who stand far off (v. 10) reminds us that John was not shown the end of *the* world but of *his* world, the end of the Roman Empire.

Were wanton with her, see notes on vv. 3 and 7.

18.11. Since no one buys their cargo any more. The merchants are interested in the loss of their profits, and care little for the people of the city.

18.13. Slaves, that is, human souls. The Greek word *somata*, here translated as 'slaves', actually means 'bodies', but this was a common term for slaves. The phrase could also be translated as 'slaves *and* human souls', but that would not make sense. The point of the phrase is that the merchants listed the various sorts of merchandise in order of decreasing value, beginning with precious gold and ending with cheap slaves, worth less, in commercial terms, than cattle. Slaves were regarded as 'bodies', or mere 'things'. But to God they are 'human souls', worth more than the whole world. In ancient times people took slavery for granted, and the Bible contains no explicit protest against slavery. The Old Testament laws, however, contain strict measures to ensure the rights of slaves, and make it quite clear that slaves are human beings, not different from other people. The New Testament contains Paul's Letter to Philemon, in which Paul does not attack the institution of slavery, but does tell Philemon that he must regard Onesimus 'no longer as a slave but more than a slave, as a beloved brother' (Philem. 16). The Bible thus implies a criticism of slavery, though this is not made explicit, except here in this verse. For these few words, 'that is, human souls', are a clear indictment

144

of the institution of slavery, and of worldly values generally.

18.20. Judgement for you against her. The English of the RSV is a very free translation of the Greek, but reflects very clearly the principles underlying justice in the Old Testament. A good example is Judah's judgement on Tamar: 'She is more righteous than I' really means, 'I find for her against myself' (Gen. 38.26). The primary object of Old Testament justice is to vindicate the innocent.

19.1. Hallelujah. The great multitude in heaven takes up the praise of Psalms 113—118 with their repeated 'Hallelujah', 'Praise the LORD'.

Salvation and glory and power. Note how salvation is mentioned first. The word 'salvation' implies more than merely 'being saved' from the power of evil and from death. 'Salvation' also means safety and security, and above all wholeness and health. Those whom Christ saves are restored to perfect health of body, soul, and mind. The gospel is the marvellous news that God's almighty power works for the salvation of His people.

His judgements are true and just, unlike the judgements of earthly tribunals, which even in the most just societies are sometimes mistaken, and in a tyrannical state are prejudiced and *un*just. The Christians had suffered much from false accusations in the past, and would do so again in the future, and under the tyranny of the Caesars they could expect no just verdict in this world. But God's judgement would vindicate them.

INTERPRETATION

This lament over Babylon falls into four parts: (1) an announcement of the fall of Babylon, and a call to 'come out' of the city (vv. 1–8); (2) a lament by people who witness the fall of Babylon (vv. 9–19); (3) a call to rejoice over the fall of the city, answered by a lament by heaven itself; and (4) the vindication of the righteous.

In the first part John hears two voices. The first voice simply states that the city has fallen, and describes its desolation after its fall. When civilization collapses, the forces of chaos take over (see Special Note D, p. 114). John, for all his criticism of civilization, did not have a romantic view of nature. Both the natural world and civilization are infected by evil, and neither of them are now as God wants them to be. The natural world must be looked after properly. Paradise was a garden, not a jungle or a desert.

The other voice begins with a last call to repentance. Even at the very moment of collapse it is not too late for people to repent. The judgement is necessary, and the voice makes quite clear the reason why it is necessary, and the fact that its consequences are terrible for an unrepentant world. But the prophecy of the judgement is meant as a warning to sinners, as a last call to turn to God.

In the second part John witnesses the lament of the people who mourn the fall of the city. He clearly shared their sadness. The sight of the ruin of Babylon/Rome hurt him. John was not an ascetic who despised the good life, nor was he a barbarian without civilization, nor did he fail to appreciate beauty. He knew that Rome's civilization carried the seeds of its own destruction, and was doomed, but it gave him no pleasure to see the vision of its doom.

The words, 'Rejoice over her, O heaven, O saints and apostles and prophets, for God has given judgement for you against her', are not part of the sailors' lament, as the RSV seems to suggest. The angel of v. 1 is reminding John that, in spite of his love for the city, he must recognize the righteousness of God's judgement, and be glad of the vindication of the people who have suffered for the gospel; at the same time calling to those in heaven to rejoice at God's just judgement. This verse thus leads to the third part.

But in the third part the voice expresses the sadness of heaven itself at the need for judgement. All those things mentioned in vv. 22–23, which will be found in the city no more, are good things, gifts of God, which people should have used and enjoyed. How sad that people should lose them through their own folly! These verses express a real love for the city and genuine grief for the waste of so many good things. John saw that the ruin of Babylon must come because of people's sins. Yet there was so much in Rome that was of real value. The city was full of the good things of the earth, full of God's gifts. Heaven itself laments the fact that these gifts had not been used for the purpose for which God gave them, and had not been enjoyed innocently.

But in Babylon/Rome was also found the blood of prophets and saints, and of all who had been slain on earth. Thus in the fourth part the lament changes into a hymn of praise, and the sadness over the ruin of civilization gives way to the praise of God for His righteous judgement and His vindication of the saints.

STUDY SUGGESTIONS

CONTENT

1. Which sins are mentioned particularly in v. 7?
2. What purpose does the list in vv. 12–13 serve?
3. What does the lament of heaven in vv. 21–24 show?

BIBLE

4. (a) In what ways does the attitude of the merchants in Rev. 18.13 differ from the laws in Exod. 21.1–11?
   (b) In what ways were the attitudes of Abraham (Gen. 15.3), and

Paul (Philem. 15–16), different from those of most people of their days?

(c) What conclusions should Christians have drawn from the last words of v. 13 long before they actually did so?

5. Where does the word 'Hallelujah' come from, and what does it mean?

APPLICATION

6. What relevance does the expression 'slaves, that is, human souls' have for such matters as the caste system in India and the continuing plight of the 'scheduled castes', apartheid in South Africa, tribal conflict in other African states, racial discrimination in other countries? What problems of this sort, if any, do people experience in your own country?

7. Do vv. 22–24 remind you of any cities you know? If so, give some details.

19.6–10
Invitation to the Wedding Feast of the Lamb

SUMMARY

19.6–8: John hears the voice of a great multitude announcing the joys of the wedding feast of the Lamb.

19.9: The angel mentioned in 17.1 tells John to write: 'Blessed are those who are invited to the wedding feast of the Lamb'.

19.10: John falls down to worship the angel, but is told that he must worship God.

NOTES

19.6. The sound of many waters . . . and mighty thunderpeals: John finds it impossible to describe the sound accurately (see p. 126).

19.7. Rejoice and exult and give him glory. Giving glory to God is our proper response to God, but it is also our greatest joy. We say that it is our duty to worship and to serve God, but in the New Testament 'duty' is mentioned only once (Luke 17.10). Serving God and worshipping Him is a great privilege; and it is such a joy that the idea of 'duty' becomes unimportant.

19.9. The angel is not actually mentioned in the Greek text, but can be inferred from 17.1.

19.10. I fell down to worship him. John follows a natural inclination to worship the bringer of the gospel. But neither he nor we must worship the messenger, whether that messenger is a human being or an angel. We must worship God alone.

The spirit of prophecy was an expression used by the rabbis for the Holy Spirit. 'The testimony of Jesus', that is to say, the preaching of the gospel of Jesus Christ, is the work of the Holy Spirit.

INTERPRETATION

Once more John has been brought to the threshold of the end. The end of civilization as he knew it was not the end of the world, but it pointed forward to that end. It showed the limit of what humans can do, the limit both of their achievements and of their sins. In that way it was a real end. History would still continue, but it was a sure sign that all civilization is ultimately doomed.

As we saw before, people do not find it easy, if they live under a cruel and despotic regime, to look much further than the end of that regime (see p. 139). John's visions did not demand that he or his readers should look any further than was necessary, so he was shown very little between the end of Rome and the end of time. Thus the lament over Babylon leads straight into a vision of the world to come, which is here presented as the Wedding Feast of the Lamb.

This vision brings together a number of motifs from various parts of the Bible. In many Bible passages the joys of heaven are pictured as a banquet to which the faithful have been invited (as in Luke 14.15–24). Similarly this vision shows the bliss of heaven as a great feast to which the faithful have been invited.

Another motif is the union of God and His people, depicted as a marriage, as in the prophecies of Hosea and the Song of Solomon. The song of Solomon may originally have been a collection of secular love songs, but it became part of the Scripture because the love it depicts was regarded as a mirror of the love of God for His people. In the New Testament the same figure is used for Christ and His people (as in Eph. 5.31–33). Here the marriage feast of the Lamb is the union of Christ with His Bride the Church.

If we take these motifs too literally, we may object that the 'Bride' seems to be made up of the 'guests', which is absurd. But the absurdity lies in our failure to understand the meaning of the symbolism. The marriage feast of the Lamb means that He is being united with His people in the most intimate manner. On earth no union is more intimate than that between a husband and wife joined in genuine love. Not all

'The invitation to the marriage feast of the Lamb is *now*' (p. 150).

The union with Christ is available when faithful Christians meet for Communion at the Lord's Supper – like this congregation in Nigeria. In what other ways can we respond to that invitation?

marriages are like that, for sin has caused terrible havoc in the relationship between the sexes. But God intends that the relationship between husband and wife should reflect His own love. The marriage of the Lamb is the perfect union of Christ and His people.

In the vision the Bride is clothed with 'fine linen', that is 'the righteous deeds of the saints'. This may seem strange, as we were told earlier, on the one hand that white garments were *given to* the martyrs (3.5), on the other hand that the saints had themselves *made* their robes white in the blood of the Lamb (7.14). So, we were told first that the saints were dressed in white because of what Christ had done, and now that they are dressed in fine linen, bright and pure, that is to say, white, because of their own righteous deeds. But one effect of being redeemed by Christ is that we are set free to live the sort of life for which God created us. Redemption produces righteous deeds.

This vision does more than merely inform us of God's plans. The announcement of the wedding feast of the Lamb is an invitation, not only to the saints in heaven, but also to us who live on earth. In today's language it might have been put on a printed invitation card: 'The Lord God the Almighty requests the pleasure of the readers' company at the Marriage Feast of the Lamb. RSVP'. The last four letters are important: they mean, 'Reply, if you please' (from the French *Répondez s'il vous plaît*).

The invitation to the marriage feast of the Lamb demands an answer *now*. The call to respond by choosing to repent becomes more and more urgent in the last chapters of the Revelation. God's future is already present in heaven, but to some extent it is also already present on earth. The union with Christ, which will be made perfect in the end, is already available now, when the faithful meet for worship and have communion with Christ.

STUDY SUGGESTIONS

WORDS

1. Besides the literal meaning, what does 'marriage feast' often mean in the Bible?
2. Who is the Bride of Christ?

CONTENT

3. What does John say about the 'fine linen' in which the 'Bride' is clothed, and how does this compare with things he has written earlier? Explain how his various statements link up.
4. What do the words 'rejoice and exult' in v. 7 suggest?
5. What error did John commit, and how did the angel correct him?

6. What is meant by the statement that 'the testimony of Jesus is the spirit of prophecy'?

7. In the parable of the excuses (Luke 14.15–24) Jesus tells the story of some people who, when invited to a great banquet, began to make excuses. They actually intended to be present at the banquet, but they wanted to be asked again before they would say 'yes'. What happened to them, and how does this link with John's vision?

APPLICATION

8. Was this vision of the marriage feast of the Lamb only a prophecy of things to come, or was it something more? And if it was more, how does this affect us?
9. What is the connection between the marriage feast of the Lamb and the Eucharist or Lord's Supper?

19.11–21
The Rider on the White Horse

SUMMARY

19.11–16: John sees a rider on a white horse, who judges and makes war in righteousness. His name is called 'Faithful and True' and 'The Word of God'. With the sword of his mouth he smites the nations.
19.17–21: John sees the devastation following the defeat of the beast, and witnesses how the beast and the false prophet are captured and destroyed.

NOTES

19.11. In righteousness he judges. God is the righteous Judge (see, for example, Pss. 9.8; 67.4; 98.9; Isa. 11.4; Jer. 11.20), and all that is true of God is true of Christ.
And makes war on the beast and his followers, including those within the Church.
19.12. Like a flame of fire, see 1.14.
A name inscribed which no one knows but himself. The secret name hints at a mystery as yet unknown (see 2.17, and by way of contrast 17.5).
19.13. A robe dipped in blood. The blood which Christ shed on the Cross. But the blood of Christ, which is the salvation of God's people, is also a

blot on the people who have shed it. John is referring not so much to those who commanded and carried out the crucifixion, as to the beast and those who worship it.

The Word of God. The Prologue to the Gospel according to John calls Jesus the *Word* (of God). That Gospel was probably written in Ephesus, and may have been written before John wrote the Revelation; John and his readers may already have known the phrase 'the Word of God' as referring to Jesus.

19.14. The armies of heaven are not angels, but the 144,000 who follow the Lamb wherever He goes (see 14.1–5).

19.15. He will tread the wine press. The Greek text puts a strong emphasis on *'He'*: not those who crucified Him, but He who was crucified is the Victor. See John 19.30: the word *tetelestai*, translated 'It is finished' (RSV), does not mean 'It is all over', but 'It is accomplished' (JB), in other words, 'I have completed the work I came to do'.

The wine press of the fury of the wrath of God the Almighty. Those who have shed the blood of Christ and the martyrs become the victims of their own sins. The wrath of God shows His care both for the culprits and for the victims. He cares so much even for the beast and its followers, that He will not leave them empty-handed, and returns to them the blood that they have shed. In simpler language, the judgement of God is such, that the consequences of evil deeds will in the end return to those who cause them.

19.17. The birds that fly in midheaven. The picture of vultures preying on the victims of war must be understood metaphorically.

19.20. The false prophet is the second beast of chapter 13.

Were thrown alive into the lake of fire to be destroyed.

19.21. And the rest were slain. In John's vision they did not share the fate of the two beasts, but are left dead to wait for the Last Judgement.

INTERPRETATION

John had already seen a rider on a white horse in an earlier vision (6.2). So the question arises: are these two horsemen connected? As we saw, most interpreters regard the four horsemen of chapter 6 as closely related, all four bringing disaster, and if this is correct, then there is no connection between the earlier horseman and the rider on the white horse in chapter 19. But we noted that the white horseman of chapter 6, though awe-inspiring, was not described as being threatening. It seemed that he was connected with Christ, and represented the presence in the world of God's determination, right from the start, to carry out His plans (pp. 74, 75).

If that interpretation was correct, then there must be a close connection between the two white horsemen. But they are described in different terms, and, moreover, the picture of the horseman in chapter 6 was vague and mysterious, whilst the rider in chapter 19 is identified clearly as the 'Word of God'. Thus, whilst the horseman of chapter 6 represented God's *hidden* purpose right from the very beginning, the rider on this white horse represents God's *revealed* will.

That 'Word of God' is Christ. The sharp sword issuing from His mouth was already mentioned in the vision of Christ that opened the Revelation (1.16), and suits the present passage beautifully. The sword is a weapon of war, and also an instrument of justice, but it is not held in His hand but issues from His mouth. Christ moves victoriously through the world by the preaching of the gospel. The preaching of His word brings about a division between those who do accept Him and those who do not, gathers the faithful under His royal government, and gains the victory against all opposition.

But there is another side to His victory. The robe dipped in blood is not stained with the blood of His enemies but with His own precious blood. His victory was won on the cross, and the wine-press of the fury of the wrath of God the Almighty was His sacrifice on the cross (see p. 131).

The names by which Christ is known, Faithful and True, the Word of God, the King of kings and Lord of lords, speak for themselves. But He also has a name which no one knows but Himself, a deeper mystery which will be revealed to those who follow Him most closely (2.17), but is not part of what John is to reveal to the Church.

The word of God had been proclaimed by the prophets over many centuries, it had been made flesh in Jesus Christ, and it had been preached in the Church. It had been there all the time. But John is shown this Rider, the Word of God, at this stage, after the fall of Rome/Babylon, as a reminder that the course of the gospel is not finished or come to its end with the ending of John's world. The fall of Rome, or of any civilization, is not by itself the victory of Christ. These things must happen, but the flames of the burning cities, Babylon or Persepolis, Rome or Berlin, do not bring about the reign of Christ. The Kingdom of God is brought about by the sword of His mouth.

However, His victory will be complete, and His enemies will flee. The picture of the battlefield, with the birds of prey gorging themselves on the flesh of the slain, is horrifyingly realistic, and people have been inclined to take it literally. But we must make a choice: either we take it literally, and make nonsense of Christ battling with the sword of His mouth, or we take seriously the assertion that the Rider on the white horse conquers with the sword of His mouth. It must be the latter, and the scene of the battlefield must be figurative.

Though the citadel of the beast has fallen, he continues to wage war against the Word of God and those who serve it, the armies of heaven.

But the outcome of the war can be in no doubt, and the doom of the beast and its followers is certain. Christ may do battle only with His word, and the gospel may seem to have no defence in a world of violence; but His victory is certain, and the defeat of the enemies of the gospel is as devastating as the defeat suffered by the losers on any battlefield.

STUDY SUGGESTIONS

WORDS

1. The term 'the Word of God' is used by the Bible writers in three different ways. Examples are:
   (a) Gen. 15.1; Isa. 2.1; 38.4; Jer. 1.4; Hos. 1.1; 2 Peter 3.5;
   (b) John 1.1–14; Rev. 19.11–16;
   (c) Exod. 9.20; Isa. 1.10; 16.13; Jer. 2.4; 17.20; Ezek. 20.47; Dan. 9.2; Acts 4.31; 6.7; 11.1.
   What are those three different ways?

CONTENT

2. Explain how this vision in 19.11–21 links up (or perhaps does not link up) with John's vision described in chapter 6.
3. What did John mean by 'the army of heaven'?
4. What is the significance of the sword issuing from the Rider's mouth?
5. In what way is the 'wine press of the fury of the wrath of God the Almighty' connected with the vision in chapter 14.17–20?
6. What does the vision of the battlefield mean?

BIBLE

7. Read John 1.1–18. What light does that passage throw on the vision of the Rider on the White Horse.

APPLICATION

8. What does it mean to us that the vision of the Rider on the White Horse comes after the visions of the fall of Babylon?
9. 'Christ may do battle only with His word' (p. 154). What is the full meaning of this statement, and what are its implications for us today? What are some of the ways in which Christ – and His followers – can 'do battle with His word' in the world? And what are the methods which His followers must *not* use?

20.1–6
A Thousand Years of Peace

SUMMARY

20.1–3: The devil is bound for a thousand years.
20.4–6: The saints reign with Christ a thousand years.

NOTES

20.1. The key of the bottomless pit. The bottomless pit, that reservoir of evil, is not one of God's creations (see Special Note D, p. 116, and what is said there about the 'chaos'), but God can give His angel the key to close it.

20.2. That ancient serpent is the serpent which tempted Eve in the Garden of Eden (Gen. 3). But there is a difference. The serpent in the Garden was a tiny thing. The devil feeds on the power which the sinners give him, and human sin has made him strong.

Bound him. Satan is bound but not dead.

A thousand years simply means a very long time (see Special Note C, p. 70), or as we should say, 'hundreds of years'.

20.3. That he should deceive the nations no more. During the 'thousand years' the devil is bound, and unable to deceive. He has been unmasked, and people are able to know him for what he is. (But v. 8 shows that he still has his followers.)

20.4. Those to whom judgement was committed. The martyrs, who had been sentenced to death by unjust judges, now themselves become the judges.

Those who had been beheaded . . . and who had not worshipped the beast or its image. The RSV translators seem to suggest that John meant only the martyrs. But what John actually wrote (in Greek) means: 'all who had been beheaded for having witnessed for Jesus and for having preached God's word, and those who refused to worship the beast or his statue' (JB). In other words, John saw not only those who had actually become martyrs, but also other faithful Christians who had died in the Lord.

They came to life again, and reigned with Christ. Many readers have thought that this means that Christ and the saints were to come back to earth for these 'thousand years'. But John does not say that either the risen dead or the risen Christ walked on earth.

20.5. The first resurrection. The general resurrection of the dead will follow later, but the faithful witnesses already live with Christ, and share in His reign.

20.6. The second death, that is to say, final exclusion from life with God, see note on 20.14.

Priests. See note on 1.5.

INTERPRETATION

The hopes aroused by apocalyptic writers were almost infinitely varied. One of those hopes was the expectation of a Messianic Kingdom. This was not the expectation of the end of the present world. The Messiah was expected to reign on earth, and his reign would be an era of peace and righteousness; it would be in every way a godly and therefore beneficent reign, not only for the faithful, but for all people, Jews and gentiles, believers and unbelievers alike. But it would be a reign on earth, over people who would be very much the same as they had always been, sinners, but under the firm control of a just government.

Many people believed that such a reign could only be brought about by war, and many Jews looked forward to the coming of a warrior-messiah. Thus Jesus had to contend with the expectations of people who wanted Him to be such a warrior-messiah. This may be the reason why He did not call Himself the Messiah (though He did not contradict Peter, when Peter called Him the Christ, the Messiah, Mark 8.27–30).

This expectation of the Messiah was very different from the hope of a new heaven and a new earth, the expectation of some world-shaking event in which the universe as we know it would vanish, and a new creation would take its place.

John's vision took up the expectation of a Messianic Kingdom, but at the same time corrected it. This vision certainly did not confirm the fantastic expectations which some people cherished, and which are still popular with some Christians.

This vision of the 'Millennium', the 'Thousand Years', has been interpreted mainly in three ways.

1. In the first place there are those who believe that John prophesied that Jesus and the risen saints would come back to earth, and govern for a thousand years. Some have even tried to discover, with the help of some of the numbers in Daniel and the Revelation, when exactly the Millennium is to begin. The great differences in the dates thus calculated (the years 1000, 1534, 1834, 1843, 1874, 1914, 1925 are just a few of the many different dates suggested), should warn us that there must be something wrong with these calculations. On the other hand, this belief in the coming Millennium is an attempt to take the message of the Bible seriously. Unfortunately we must ask: Have those people who expect the

Millennium really read this passage of the Revelation carefully enough?

2. A second line of interpretation regards the 'Thousand Years' reign of Christ' as a symbol for the Church. As we shall see, this comes nearer to the actual content of this vision. But it must be asked, did the Church ever 'reign' in the sense in which this was apparently envisaged in this vision?

It seems therefore that we have to interpret this vision in a different way. But we cannot do this, until we have looked at it a little more closely.

This vision foresees a rule of Christ within the restrictions of the present world. The devil is bound, but he is not dead; his freedom is restricted, but only for a time, and (though John does not say so) only up to a point. The situation shown is one in which the power of evil is restricted but not completely overcome. The Church is at peace, and Christ and his people exercise considerable power. The Word of God can still be resisted, but it cannot be silenced, and even the secular rulers must reckon with it.

Meanwhile the martyrs have come to life, and reign with Christ. We must not read more in this than John actually wrote. He did not write that they had come back to earth. They have been raised from the dead, and are alive with God, as we have already seen more than once. They reign with Christ, who exercises power on earth, but in the vision neither Christ nor the saints actually walk on earth.

We must not take the thousand years literally, any more than the other numbers in the Revelation; the phrase simply means, 'a long time'.

3. The vision thus promises that there will be a time when the persecution will have ended, when the Church will live in peace, and when all aspects of life will be affected by the will of Christ. The Revelation was written for people who would find it a great comfort to know that their ordeal would end even before the creation of a new heaven and a new earth. But it is meaningful for later generations too. Those who suffer persecution will find it a great comfort to know that the time of their ordeal is limited, and that it will be followed by a time of peace.

There have, in fact, been periods in history when the Church was at peace. There have even been times when the name of Christ was publicly honoured, when nations made serious attempts to influence people to live according to His will. Such a reign of Christ was never perfect, it never extended to the whole earth, and it did not last. But while it lasted it was real.

However, if people live in such a time, they must remember that Satan is not dead, that he is bound, perhaps for a long time, maybe for 'a thousand years', but that he is waiting 'in the pit' to come back. Meanwhile, they may rejoice while such times last.

'The outcome of the war can be in no doubt . . . Christ's victory is certain . . . there will be a time when persecution is ended, when the Church will live in peace' (pp. 155, 157).

Townspeople of Jinja joyfully greet the troops coming to free them from oppression. What is the chief difference between the peace that follows military or political victory, and the victory John was talking about?

STUDY SUGGESTIONS

CONTENT

1. What did some apocalyptic writers mean by the expectation of the Messiah, and how did this lead to the hope for a warrior-messiah?
2. Did Jesus call Himself the Messiah, and if not, can you see a good reason for this?
3. What did the vision in 20.1–6 show John about the saints?
4. What does it mean, that Satan was 'bound'?
5. What does 'a thousand years' mean in John's language?
6. This vision has been interpreted chiefly in three different ways. What are they, and which do you think is the right way? Give reasons why you reject the two other ways.

BIBLE

7. How did Jesus react when Peter called Him the Messiah (see Mark 8.27–38; Matt. 16.13–28).

APPLICATION

8. What are the practical implications of this vision? What opportunities does the Church have when it lives in such conditions as John describes? And how can Christians use those opportunities?

20.7–10
Satan's Final Defeat

SUMMARY

Satan is let loose from his prison, and gathers his followers from the ends of the earth for a final attack on the 'beloved city', but he is defeated by fire from heaven, and condemned to the lake of fire and sulphur.

NOTES

20.8. To deceive. Deception is Satan's strong weapon. He is a great liar (John 8.44), and when he is at liberty he is able to seem attractive (see Cor. 11.14).

The nations which are at the four corners of the earth: the years of peace (vv. 1–6) were not world-wide; even then Satan had his followers.

Gog and Magog were originally the names of real tribes. According to Genesis 10.2, Magog was the name of a tribe of the Steppes (in what is now southern Russia). But in Ezekiel, and in Jewish tradition, the names had come to be used as symbols for the resilience of evil (see Ezek. 28.2–3, 14–18; 39.1–15).

20.9. The camp of the saints and the beloved city. The RSV translation misses the point that the camp of the saints *is* the Beloved City. It is better to translate: 'the camp of the saints, which is the city that God loves' (JB) or 'the camp of God's people, the city he loves' (NIV). The New Jerusalem, the Beloved City, is forever coming down out of heaven from God, and is even now established on earth. The Church is the New Jerusalem, though still imperfect. See note and interpretation for 21.2).

20.10. Lake of fire and sulphur. Fire and sulphur were known to destroy all impurity and contamination. Like the word 'consumed' in v. 9, the picture suggests that the creation will be cleansed from the devil and his works, and that there will be nothing left of them.

INTERPRETATION

The power of evil is resilient: it will not be kept down. It may be restrained for a time, even for a long time, but so long as it is not destroyed, it will come back, and find willing supporters. Thus John sees in this vision how, after the 'thousand years' the devil 'is loosed' again.

Gog and Magog, here as in the book of Ezekiel, represent the resilience of evil: just as it seems that God's work is completed, they unexpectedly appear. At the very moment when it seems that all troubles are over, they rally round the devil, and stage a horrifying world-wide revolt ('at the four corners of the earth'). But Satan's final revolt leads to his final defeat.

So far the Revelation had been concerned with things that were to happen soon after John wrote, and which in fact did happen. It is true that ever since that time they have happened again and again; but, as Jesus said, 'This must take place, but the end is not yet' (Mark 13.7). Now, however, John sees the beginning of the end, the extinction of all evil.

No matter how long it will take, no matter how resilient the power of evil may be, no matter how often the devil may get loose, there is to be an end to it all. The lake of fire and sulphur signifies thorough cleansing from all impurity and contamination. The 'torment' of the devil, the beast, and the false prophet 'day and night for ever and ever' means their total removal, and results in their non-existence: they will be gone forever.

STUDY SUGGESTIONS

CONTENT

1. What do Gog and Magog represent?
2. What do the nations at the four corners of the earth show?
3. What did John mean by 'the Beloved City'?
4. What was the function of fire and sulphur, and what do they represent in John's vision?
5. V. 10 describes the punishment of the devil, the beast, and the false prophet. What does John's picture actually mean?

BIBLE

6. How does this vision link up with Jesus's prophecy of the end in Mark 13?

APPLICATION

7. What warning and what hope does this vision contain?
8. 'Things that were to happen soon after John wrote . . . have happened again and again since that time' (p. 160). Give some examples of such things from the history of the Church through the centuries, and, if you can, from what has been happening in our own time.

20.11–15
The Last Judgement

SUMMARY

John sees a great white throne and Him who sits upon it. Earth and sky flee away from His presence, and all people, raised from the dead, stand before the throne. Judgement is given according to two sets of books, one being the record of all that people have done, and the other the 'book of life'. Death and Hades are thrown into the lake of fire, as are those whose names are not in the book of life.

NOTES

20.11. Earth and sky fled away. The old order disappears.
20.12. The dead, great and small. The saints are alive with God even now, but John had a vision of the general resurrection, the resurrection of all the dead.
Books were opened. These books are records of people's actions.

Another book . . . which is the book of life. This is the roll or list of the citizens of the City of God. Note that this is *one* book: there is *no* book of death.

20.13. The sea gave up the dead in it, Death and Hades gave up the dead in them, and the dead were judged . . . This verse repeats what John had said in v. 12. John here followed the pattern of Hebrew poetry, in which the same statement is made twice in different words.

20.14. Death and Hades were thrown into the lake of fire. 'The last enemy to be destroyed is death' (1 Cor. 15.28). This is the death of death itself. **The second death,** that is to say, exclusion from the life of the world to come, exclusion from life with God. John does not mention any torment, as he did in v. 10, and even there the torment seems to consist of the non-existence of the devil, the beast, and the false prophet.

INTERPRETATION

In the end all must stand before God. As in chapter 4, John does not attempt to describe Him, but makes it quite clear that no other reality can have any substance before God. Those who know the Old Testament will be familiar with the idea that sky and earth are subject to decay, but John's vision suggests more: earth and sky have been the scene of sin, and they 'flee away'.

There is also a more personal side to this. As people stand before God, on the threshold of eternity, their temporal life lies behind them.

The scene of the books reflects a truth which must always remain a paradox, that is to say, it seems to contain a contradiction that cannot be solved. John first sees the books which contain the record of people's deeds, but then he also sees the book of life. The first set of books confirms a truth, which we find expressed in many parts of the Bible, namely that our actions here on earth have consequences which we cannot hope to escape, and that God will judge us according to what we have done or not done. Jesus's words in Matthew 25.41–46 are particularly eloquent on this subject. But the second book is the book of life. The names contained in this book were written there before the foundation of the world (13.8; 17.8). This is the book of God's grace, of God's undeserved goodness and kindness. People's names were entered in this book, not because of any good that they had done (they had not done any, for they were not yet born!), but simply because God chose to enter their names even before the world was created.

We can solve the paradox to some extent (but only in part) by pointing out that the record of people's lives is bound to show their bad deeds as well as their good ones. Judging by the records, all people would have to be condemned. But God, in His goodness, has written the names of the redeemed in the book of life, that is to say, He is willing to forgive.

Our deeds deserve eternal death, but God's grace gives us eternal life. The medieval poet Jacopone da Todi expressed this admirably in his *Dies Irae*, 'Day of Wrath' (which used to be part of the Latin Mass for the dead). After the opening of the books, which show clearly how guilty he is, the sinner asks, 'What shall I, miserable I, then say . . .?' – and finds the only possible answer: 'King of tremendous majesty, Who saves the redeemed freely, save me, Fountain of mercy!'

The Calvinist poet Willem de Merode expressed a similar sentiment in his poem *Voorbereiding*, 'Preparation (for the Lord's Supper)'. He was not writing about the Last Judgement, but because the Eucharist is a foretaste of the messianic banquet, preparation for the Lord's Supper brings the faithful face to face with the Judge. In De Merode's words, 'they felt as if their hearts were books held in God's mighty hand', and they found that there was nothing good in them. But then, as God was ready to give His verdict, 'their voice found courage to break the silence: "O Lord Jesus, have mercy upon us." And the trembling heart they found within, was without blemish, without sin.'

John's vision showed the same truth: the record of our deeds is super-seded by the book of life, the book of God's grace. This does not mean that the records of people's lives are simply laid aside: in John's vision all were judged by what they had done. The decisions which people make in this present life, the godly deeds which they do or do not do, the sins which they commit or do not commit, also their faith or unbelief, all these things are meaningful, and have their consequences, in heaven as well as on earth.

But God judges according to the book of life. He is not bound by any rules. If that were the case, if He was bound always to punish the guilty, acquit the innocent, and reward the deserving, all in exact proportion to what they deserved, then there would be no need of a Last Judgement. A recording angel could deal with it all quite adequately. But to believe that would be to believe in a God who was not really free, a God who could not exercise the freedom of His grace. Moreover, no one could then claim to be innocent before God, or to deserve a reward from Him. The prospect of a Judgement without God's grace does not bear thinking of: we have all sinned, so it would damn us all.

On the other hand, the presence in this vision of both the records of people's deeds and the book of life, reminds us that God's choice was made by a living God. There is no doubt that the book of life, written before the foundation of the world, is the book of God's grace, and therefore of God's eternal election. The doctrine of election, that is to say, the teaching that our eternal destiny depends not on us but only on God's decision, stresses rightly the absolute priority, pre-eminence, and sovereignty of God's grace. But if God's choice was an automatic pro-cess, then there would not have to be a Last Judgement at all: everything could then be worked out by a computer. When we see how we owe our eternal life to God's grace, we should reverently adore God's incomprehensible goodness. We must not try to examine how exactly God makes His decisions.

God is the living God. He is free to decide as He chooses, and holds the judgement firmly in His own hand. His judgement must therefore be presented in the form of a paradox, emphasizing on the one hand the seriousness of our decisions and actions, whilst stressing on the other hand the freedom of God's decision, and the certainty that whatever He decides at the Last Judgement completes the carrying out of His plan laid before the foundation of the world, before the creation of the universe. And His plans are good: they are written in the book of life, not in a book of death!

This vision presents these truths better than any reasoned argument could ever do. The two books show that our earthly lives are important and meaningful. They show that our decisions and actions, our obedience or disobedience, our repentance or refusal to repent, our faith or unbelief, have eternal significance, and are taken into account at the Last Judgement. But the books also show that ultimately our eternal destiny is determined by God's choice, by God's grace, by God's amazing goodness.

So, whichever turns world history may take, and whichever way our own road may turn, we shall all end up standing before God. This qualifies the importance and significance of our present lives. To be sure, this life is important, and God is its Judge. Life is a serious business, but it is qualified and judged by God. Our decisions and actions are serious matters, but their seriousness is qualified by God's grace.

STUDY SUGGESTIONS

CONTENT

1. John saw in his vision that 'books were opened. Also another book was opened, which is the book of life' (20.12). Explain the significance of the two books.
2. In this vision God is the Judge, but in 19.11 John wrote that Jesus is called 'Faithful and True, and in righteousness he judges'. Does this mean that one passage is right, and the other wrong? If not, what does it mean?

BIBLE

3. How do (a) Jesus's words in Matthew 25, and (b) Paul's words in Romans 11.32–36, link up with this vision?

APPLICATION

4. Some Christians believe that our eternal destiny depends chiefly on our own actions, or on our own faith. Comment on this in the light of John's vision.
5. Some Christians believe that our present lives and our eternal destiny are both pre-ordained by God, and that nothing that we do makes any difference. Comment on this in the light of John's vision.
6. Some people who believe firmly that our eternal destiny depends solely on God's choice, add as an afterthought, 'But we are not mere "things".' Comment on this in the light of John's vision.
7. Some Christians have said, 'When I say that I believe that my salvation depends solely on God's choice, I do not mean to say that I understand God's ways, but only that I have not deserved God's love.' What would you say to that, in view of John's vision?

21.1–8
A New Heaven and a New Earth

SUMMARY

21.1–2: John sees a new heaven and a new earth, and the New Jerusalem, which is coming down out of heaven from God.
21.3–4: He hears a voice from the throne announcing that God's dwelling is with human beings, and that He will end all sorrow and pain.
21.5–8: Then He who is seated on the throne speaks, and tells John that He is making all things new. This is a firm promise to the faithful, but also a warning to those who persist in their sins.

NOTES

21.1. New. The Greek word, *kainos*, does not mean 'another', but 'a new kind'. A person who, after having been very tired, has taken some refreshment and a rest, may well say that he feels like 'a new man', meaning, not that he is no longer the person he was before, but that he feels renewed. Similarly, but in a much deeper sense, a person who has become a Christian, is 'a new man', or a 'new woman'. He or she is, of course, still the same individual, but has been completely renewed; he or she 'has been born anew' (see John 3.3–8). The same is true here: John sees a completely renewed heaven and earth, for God makes all things new (v. 5).
Heaven ... earth. 'Heaven and earth' is the normal biblical expression

for the universe. So we do not need to ask if God's heaven needed renewal.

21.2. City. The Greek word, *polis*, means people rather than buildings. Also, as early Greek cities had been small, and the citizens of a city were usually well known to each other, *polis* suggests a community. In John's days some cities were already very large, but the idea of a city being a community still survived.

Coming down. The Greek text suggests, not that John saw the City coming down, but that he saw a city whose nature it was to be continually coming down (see also note on 21.10).

Dwelling. John used the Greek word *skene*, which means a 'tent'. The Greek translation of the Old Testament used this word particularly for the tabernacle, which housed the Ark of the Covenant, and which had been the sign of God's presence among His people while they dwelt in the desert (Lev. 36–38).

21.3. And they shall be his people. The best Greek manuscripts read, 'and they shall be His peoples'. In the Old Testament we frequently read how God promises that Israel will be His people. That is a firm promise. But here the promise is extended to *all* peoples, Jews and gentiles as well.

21.5. He who sat upon the throne said. This was the first vision in the Revelation in which God Himself actually spoke. In the present world, and right up to the final fulfilment of God's plans, God speaks through messengers, but at the last He will be close enough to speak directly.

21.8. As for the cowardly . . . John and his readers were warned not to take God's goodness for granted. The 'cowardly' means those who compromise with the world, either for fear of persecution, or for fear of being despised or laughed at. The warning is meant as a call to repentance. Those who call themselves Christians, but indulge in the sins mentioned, are called to change their ways.

INTERPRETATION

John sees a new heaven and a new earth, for the first heaven and the first earth have passed away. Yet the existing universe has not been discarded as old rubbish: for God makes all things new. The new heaven and the new earth are the re-creation of God's original plan. God did not make a mistake when He first created the heavens and the earth, and He intends to carry out all that He proposed to do from the beginning.

We have seen that in Jewish thought the sea traditionally stands for the threat of chaos and destruction (see p. 61). The new heaven and earth will no longer be exposed to that threat. In John's vision of the throne of heaven (in chapter 4) the threat was held in check, but it was still real; here the threat has been removed entirely.

The New Jerusalem is coming down out of heaven from God. John mentions this twice, not as if he saw the City come down twice, but because he saw that City, whose nature it is to be continually coming down out of heaven from God.

When John refers to a 'city' he does not simply mean the bricks and mortar, but the people. The City of God is the *People* of God. In v. 9 John calls it 'the Bride, the wife of the Lamb', that is to say, the fellowship of the redeemed (see also 19.7–8).

John's vision thus points in two directions. The City of God is the *future* for which the universe is heading. The new heaven and the new earth with the New Jerusalem is the future of the present world. But the City of God is also a reality *now*. It is coming down out of heaven from God even now, while the present world lasts. God's people, who live on earth now, are already citizens of the New Jerusalem.

John was not the first person to realize that Christians are already citizens of the heavenly city. Paul had called the Christians children of the Jerusalem that is above (Gal. 4.26), and stated that they carry the passport of heaven (Phil. 3.20: 'our commonwealth is in heaven', or, as the NIV translates more accurately: 'our citizenship is in heaven'). The Church is more than merely a religious institution. It is the communion of saints, the community of the faithful, the fellowship of all God's people in heaven and on earth. The homeland of that community is in heaven, from where it is coming down from God all the time.

Thus the dwelling of God is with men and women. He is in the midst of His people, even now. John's vision of the new heaven and earth with a new Jerusalem not only promised a glorious future towards which the universe is moving, but also assured his readers that even now God's 'scene', God's dwelling, God's presence, is amongst human beings, and that even now we are surrounded by God's steadfast and sustaining love.

Paul had carried this idea further when he wrote that the Jerusalem which is above is our mother (Gal. 4.26). Similarly John's vision of the woman and the dragon (12) had depicted the faithful as children of the 'woman' who symbolized the people of the Messiah. Throughout the Bible God is described as a loving Father, but the picture of a mother emphasizes the tenderness of His love. The Bible writers rarely use this figure of the mother in connection with God. In the religions of the people surrounding ancient Israel mother-goddesses symbolized the fertile earth, and that was a picture which the faithful in Israel could not use for the living God. So they used the picture of the Father. Only in such rare cases as Isaiah 49.15 is God's love compared with that of a mother: 'Can a woman forget her sucking child, that she should have no compassion on the son of her womb? Even they may forget, yet I (God) will not forget you'.

This vision clearly showed the tenderness of God's love: 'He will wipe

'When John refers to the 'city' he means not only the bricks and mortar, but the people . . .
The City of God is the future for which the universe is heading . . . it is also a reality now'
(p. 167).

Those who plan new cities or special townships (like modern Nairobi, or the Independent
Zionist Church's 'holy city' of Moria), see them as both symbols and foundations of their
future. But sometimes they are more concerned about the splendour of the buildings than
the happiness of the inhabitants. When this happens, what is likely to happen to the city
itself?

away every tear from their eyes' (v. 4). The words probably allude to Isaiah 25.8: 'He will swallow up death for ever, and the LORD God will wipe away every tear from all eyes', but they also remind us of Isaiah 66.13, where God promises: 'As one whom his mother comforts, so I will comfort you; you shall be comforted in Jerusalem'.

We often find it difficult to believe that all this is already here. The Church on earth is the place where God has fellowship with sinners, and often it is only too obvious that its members *are* sinners. Also, the Church on earth is organized as a human institution, and sometimes we get so overwhelmed by meetings, committees, and office-bearers, that we cannot even see the people who are God's Church. John had the great privilege of seeing the Church completed: his vision showed him the Bride of Christ in her glory (vv. 2 and 9). At present the eternal City of God is concealed in the Church. At present we find it difficult to see the presence of God among His people, and to appreciate His tender love for His people. But nothing is hidden that will not be revealed in God's good time.

STUDY SUGGESTIONS

WORDS

1. What did the word *polis*, 'city', suggest to Greek readers?
2. What is the precise meaning of the word translated 'new' in v. 1, and what does this tell us about the 'new heaven and the new earth'?
3. What did John mean by the 'dwelling' of God among human beings?

CONTENT

4. What did John mean when he wrote that he saw 'New Jerusalem, coming down'?
5. Comment on the promise that God will wipe away every tear.
6. What was the purpose of v. 8?

BIBLE

7. Explain John's use of the word 'son' in v. 7, as compared with John 1.18; 3.16; 8.33; Rom. 8.29; Gal. 4.7.
8. The Bible writers called God 'Father'. Give one of the reasons why they did not use the word 'mother'.
9. Compare these two translations of Genesis 1.27: 'God created man in his own image, in the image of God he created them; male and female he created them' (RSV); 'So God created human beings, making them to be like himself. He created them male and female' (GNB). Which of the two translations do you think is the clearer,

and why? What does this verse tell us about God, and about the relationship between men and women?

10. In what way do Paul's words in Gal. 4.26 and Phil. 3.28 help us to understand John's vision?

APPLICATION

11. Does the vision of the New Jerusalem, coming down out of heaven from God, teach us to sit down and wait? If not, what does it teach us?

12. 'We find it difficult to see the presence of God among His people' (p. 169). What are some of the ways in which we *can* see Him?

21.9–21
The City of God

SUMMARY

John is shown a vision of the City of God, which he describes in terms of a sort of supernatural architecture.

NOTES

21.9. The Bride, the wife of the Lamb. The angel uses the same language as in the vision in 19.6–8. This should remind us that this vision of the City of God uses the picture of buildings to describe the *people* of God.
21.10. A great, high mountain. A 'high mountain' was a traditional way of describing God's dwelling place. In Canaanite religion people believed that the gods actually lived on the mountain tops, just as people still believe in many religions today. The Israelites did not actually believe that God dwelt on a mountain, but they still used 'mountains' as a symbol for God's dwelling place. In some Old Testament passages the 'mountain of God' is one that cannot be found on any map, but in others it means the mountain on which the Temple in Jerusalem was built (see Pss. 48.1; 74.2; Isa. 2.2; but also 1 Kings 8.27).
The holy City Jerusalem, coming down out of heaven from God. The fact that John refers twice (here and in v. 2) to the Holy City 'coming down' does not mean that he saw the City come down on two separate occasions. John was merely repeating that he saw that City which is forever coming down, for it is God's gift to His people and also the meeting place between heaven and earth. In his vision he saw it in its heavenly

glory, as it will be at the last, but this City of God is already a reality in the Church as it is on earth.

21.11. Having the glory of God. The glory of God filled the Temple (1 Kings 8.11; Ps. 24), but the City of God is *all* temple (see v. 22).

21.12. Twelve angels. The description of the City of God (the *people* of God!) is meant to be symbolic, but it is yet pictured very precisely, with guards at the gates.

Names of the twelve tribes. The city gates give the name of the City: God's people is not something different from Israel, though it contains much more than the natural Israel, for people have come in from all the nations (see 7.9–17; 14.1–5; also Gen. 13.3).

21.13. Names of the twelve apostles. The City is founded on the gospel preached by the apostles (see Matt. 16.18).

21.15. Measuring rod. Measuring is done to preserve, as in 11.1, where John was told to measure the shrine, but not the court, for that was given over to the gentiles. Here the whole City is to be measured: no nation is excluded. The measuring means that the City of God is to be preserved. The Church is under God's protection, and in the world to come it will be secure.

21.16. The city lies foursquare, that is to say, its length is the same as its breadth. The same arrangement is found in the organization of the tribes in Numbers 3, and in Ezekiel's vision of the City and the Temple (Ezek. 41.13; 48.20). But John's City is a cube, its height also being the same, like the Holy Place in Solomon's Temple (1 Kings 6.20): the New Jerusalem is the new Holy Place. In all the cases mentioned the square and the cube mean order and perfection.

21.17. A man's measure, that is, an angel's. This seems a puzzling expression, and various attempts have been made to explain it. The most simple explanation seems to be that John, when writing this down, saw in his mind the angel doing the measuring.

21.18. Jasper is probably diamond (see note on 4.3).

Pure gold, clear as glass. This sounds contradictory, but 'clear as glass' is probably a phrase to highlight the purity of the gold.

21.19. Every jewel, that is to say, every kind of jewel, as a bride adorned for her husband. The names of the twelve jewels have been connected variously with the precious stones on the High Priest's breastplate (Exod. 28.16–21, but the names given to those stones differ from the names John gives), or with the stones associated with the twelve signs of the Zodiac. But John was probably simply thinking of the beauty of the Bride's adornment, so different from the false jewels of the scarlet woman (see 17.4).

INTERPRETATION

John saw the New Jerusalem in a vision which consists of two very different parts. In this first part John describes the City in terms of a sort of supernatural buildings, quite different from the second part (21.22—22.5). If we take the two pictures of the Holy City literally, they would be full of contradictions, but John never meant us to take them literally. Thus the picture of the New Jerusalem as a huge cube (v. 16) is meant to suggest divine perfection; we must not regard it as an accurate description.

John is carried to a high mountain (v. 10), not so that he could look down on the city, but because that is where it is located. The 'high mountain' in John's vision is meant to show that in the future prepared for us by God there will be no distinction between the 'Mountain of God' and the dwelling place of his people, between the sacred and the secular, so that there will be no separation between God and His people. The 'high City' of God is also the dwelling place of His people.

The twelve gates and the twelve foundation stones, with the names of the twelve tribes of Israel and the twelve apostles, are clearly meant as a reminder of God's promises to Israel, and of the testimony of the apostles. God alone grants entry to the City, and Christ alone is the foundation on which the City of God rests. But John makes it clear that Israel as the bearer of the promises, and the apostles as the bearers of the gospel, are vital parts of God's plan.

It is important at this point for us to remember that the City of God as John saw it is the perfect completion of the Church which is on earth now. We cannot be the true Church, if we do not build our lives on the testimony of Israel and the Apostles, which we have in the Scriptures of the Old and the New Testaments. It is true that the Bible writers were fallible human beings, but it is also true that it has pleased God to build His Church on the testimony of Israel and the Apostles.

The measurements of the City are symbolic. The information supplied by the RSV footnote, that twelve thousand stadia is about fifteen hundred miles, is correct but irrelevant, and obscures the purpose of John's figures. John saw a City of perfect proportions.

Similarly, there is little point in trying to find out which precious stones John had in mind. The different stones may have had some symbolic meaning for some of John's readers, just as they have for some people today, but John was probably not interested in this. His chief intention was simply to give an impression of surpassing unearthly beauty.

The fact that John gives such clear and seemingly precise architectural and mathematical details should not lead us to forget that John was not writing about buildings but about people. He made this clear at once at the beginning of this section: the angel was showing him the Bride, the wife of the Lamb, that is to say, the Church in heavenly glory. The 'Church' in the New Testament, never means a building, it always means the *people* of God, either a local congregation, or the Church in the whole world.

STUDY SUGGESTIONS

CONTENT

1. How did the angel make it clear that John was being shown the future of God's people?
2. What did the 'high mountain' mean, and in what respect was it important for John to see that the City was on the mountain?
3. What did John mean by the statement that the City 'had the glory of God'?
4. What was the significance of the names of the tribes of Israel and of the twelve apostles?
5. What did John mean when he said that the City was lying 'four-square', and that it formed a cube?
6. What is the significance of the jewels mentioned?

APPLICATION

7. In what way are the names of the twelve tribes of Israel and of the twelve apostles significant for the life of the Church today?
8. What does the perfection of the City of God as John saw it mean for the Church as it is today?

21.22—22.5
The Paradise of God

SUMMARY

21.22–23: The City of God needs neither temple nor sun nor moon, for God Himself is its temple and its light.

21.24–27: The nations walk in the light of the city, and bring in their glory and honour.

22.1–2: The New Jerusalem is now seen as that same Paradise which God created in the beginning as a home for human beings, with the river of the water of life, and the tree of life.

22.3–5: The Lord God and the Lamb are in the midst of Their servants.

NOTES

21.22. I saw no temple. A temple is a holy *place*, which need not be a building. Most Canaanite shrines were simply open air places of worship, usually on hilltops, where the gods were supposed to live, and throughout the world there are many holy places without any buildings. John wanted to convey that in the Holy City, as he saw it in his vision, there was no need for any place set apart especially for worship, because the whole City was filled with God's presence.

21.23. Its lamp was the Lamb. Compare the words in the prologue to the Gospel according to John: 'the true light that enlightens every man was coming into the world' (John 1.9).

21.24. By its light shall the nations walk . . . John was quoting from Isaiah 60, but he was quoting freely, and made some very important changes. The fulfilment of the prophecy of Isaiah 60 is far more wonderful than the prophet foresaw, and God's mercy encompasses all the nations. It may seem strange that there are still nations outside the eternal City, but God's mercy is much wider than the Church.

21.25. There shall be no night there. According to Genesis 1.3–4 God created the light, and separated the light from the darkness. The writer did not say that God had created the darkness. Darkness is, in fact, not something on its own, but the absence of light. There will be no darkness in the City of God.

21.27. Nothing unclean shall enter it. John was not suggesting that there would still be anything unclean in the new creation, but simply that there would be nothing unclean in the Holy City.

22.1. The river of the water of life. Compare the river of Paradise, Genesis 2.10. John painted a picture of clean, fresh, life-giving water. To him, as to us, the story of Paradise was an ancient story. But both the Greeks and the Romans valued clean water in their cities, and John knew what water meant in a hot climate (and not only in a hot climate!).

22.2. The tree of life. The word translated 'tree' usually means 'a piece of timber', rarely a living tree. Some interpreters think that John was hinting at the Cross of Christ, for which the same word is used in Galatians 3.13 and 1 Peter 2.24. But it seems more likely that John was simply quoting from the Greek version of the Old Testament, where the same word is used in Genesis 2.9.

Fruit. Many nations believed, and some still believe, that there is a food of the gods, which enables them to enjoy eternal life, and also a food of life that might, perhaps, give human beings eternal life, if only they could get it. John certainly did not want to suggest that God needed any food, but he did want to make it clear that in the City of God there will be everything that people need.

For the healing of the nations. The 'tree of the knowledge of good and evil' had been poisonous, and led to all the ills of the world. (Gen. 2.17; 3.1–19). The tree of life brings healing.

INTERPRETATION

John's vision now changes. The change comes gradually, and vv. 22–27 of chapter 21 can be linked either with 21.9–21 or with 22.1–5. However, as the first part of the vision is concerned primarily with the Church, while the last part is concerned with the world, it seems better to study these middle verses, which are also concerned with the world, together with the last part.

In the last part John sees the New Jerusalem as a city in an oasis. The picture reminds us of the Paradise story in Genesis 2, and indeed, it had been part of God's promises in the Old Testament that in the end Paradise would be restored. Ezekiel 47 is a clear example of such a promise of the Holy Land as a new Paradise. But both Ezekiel and John saw something that was more than a garden. The New Jerusalem will be a *polis*, a *city*, that is to say, a community (see note on 21.2). The two parts of John's vision convey, each in its own way, the perfection of God's new creation, and together present a picture that is as complete as John could make it.

John sees no temple in the city. That may seem to contradict what he had seen in earlier visions (see 3.22; 7.15; 11.19). But the New Jerusalem needs no sacred place set apart for worship, for it is all filled with the presence of God and the Lamb.

We should not be surprised that the city needs no light from the sun, let alone from a lamp, for God himself is its light. But many people are puzzled by the statement that 'the nations walk by its light, and bring their glory into the city' (21.24–25), wondering if there really could be any other people beside the citizens of the Holy City. Some interpreters explain this away by saying that John was not thinking of the implications when he quoted from Isaiah 60.3.

But we have already noted that John was never careless. His mentioning the nations serves a double purpose. On the one hand he was writing about the future of that same Church which was at work in the world at that time, and is still at work in the world today, and much of what he wrote related to both the future and the present. Thus the vision reminded him and his readers that the Church is open to all the nations.

On the other hand, this is a vision of the future, the eternal future, and the coming in of the nations and their rulers is a reminder that the mercy of God is much wider than many people think. God's plan includes the salvation, not only of the Church, but of the world. John was not suggesting 'that all people will be saved in the end', in fact, he was not teaching any doctrine at all. He had simply been shown in his vision that God's grace is wider than the Church. Whilst he was reminded of the seriousness of God's judgement (there is no room for those who continue to flout God's will, 21.27), he was left in no doubt of God's determination to save. Here is another paradox of the gospel: the paradox of the narrowness of the gate of life (Matt. 7.13–14; Luke 13.24) and the wideness of God's mercy (Rom. 11.32).

Just as many people find it difficult to think that God judges both by the records of our lives and by the book of life (see interpretation of 20.11–15), so they also find it difficult, or even impossible, to believe in both the narrowness of the gate to life and the wideness of God's mercy. Some Christians stress the narrowness, and exclude the wideness. The story is told of Radbod, the last great chieftain of the Friesians (but it could have been told about many other would-be converts), how he became convinced of the truth of the Christian faith, and wanted to be baptized. But at the last moment he asked the missionary who was to baptize him, 'What has happened to my father and my mother, who were not Christians?' The missionary answered, 'They are now in hell', and Radbod said, 'Then I will not be baptized, for I want to be with my parents.' Perhaps Radbod had understood the love of God better than the missionary, for no one can love God, if he does not love the people around him (see 1 John 4.7–12). In any case, the missionary could not possibly know what God's judgement was on any particular person. But he could have known that God's mercy is much greater than we could possibly think.

On the other hand there are many people who would like to know what will be the eternal destiny of good unbelievers and good people who follow other religions than the Christian faith. John would probably have thought that an impertinent question. We are not to know in advance what God's judgement will be. But we can be certain that His verdict will not only be just, but that it will be in accordance with His infinite mercy. We can leave the judgement safely in His hands. John's vision showed that there will be eternal life for more people than we could ever hope.

The tree of life is pictured as a luxuriant growth. Actually the words of 22.2 suggest a whole orchard rather than a single tree, a new, gloriously rich and variegated Paradise, on both sides of the river of the water of life. Its beauty is suggested rather than depicted, and the emphasis is on its purpose: the tree of life provides healing of the ills of the past, and nourishment for the life eternal.

The 'river of the water of life' and the 'tree of life' were familiar ideas in the traditional and symbolic language of Israel, and of many other nations in various parts of the world. Drink and food are essential to sustain life, and people quite naturally thought that food and drink would be needed for eternal life. John's vision of the water of life and the tree of life follows this traditional language, in order to convey that the City of God has everything that is needed for eternal life. In the present world there are millions of people suffering through lack of clean water, or lack of any water at all; there are also countless people who never get enough to eat, and time and again people die from hunger. In the City of God there will be enough for everyone.

The picture John gives us of the Paradise of God can only be a pale reflection of what it is really like, or of what John actually saw. But it is realistic enough to show that God's future is *real*. John did not have the words to describe the City of God adequately, and neither have we. All human language is limited to words which express our own limited experience in this present life on earth. So no one can express properly 'what no eye has seen, nor ear heard, nor the heart of man conceived, what God has prepared for those who love Him' (1 Cor. 2.9). So, if we want to speak about Paradise and eternity at all, it is best to do so in terms of what we know. That is what John has done. Only in that way could he make it clear that the eternal life is not a dream, but a reality which is more substantial than the present world.

Artists often understand this more clearly than scholars. The Flemish artist Van Eyck's painting *The Adoration of the Lamb* in the Cathedral Church of Saint Bavo in Gent, for example, comes close to the spirit of this vision, though it is actually an illustration of Revelation 7.2–10. The landscape with the trees which the artist knew both from his own country and from his travels, the flowers of the Flemish countryside, all painted with loving care and in minute detail, the towers both of cities he knew and those made up from his imagination, but built to last, all this adds up to a real world, like the world he knew. But it is a world that is made perfect, and dedicated to the adoration of the Lamb. Van Eyck painted God's future as real. Other painters may have been better at expressing something of the mystery of God's future, but if we want to picture in our mind what God has in store for us, it is best to picture it like the best of the world we know, like the finest trees and flowers and buildings which we know, but *better*. Clever people may call this naive, but it is the best way to realize that God's future is real.

John knew that God's future is beyond our knowledge and our imagination, but his vision had also shown him that what God has prepared for us is real and solid, something that can be seen and touched and smelled, something to be enjoyed. He knew that it will be a very substantial joy 'to glorify God and to enjoy Him for ever'.

This promise is for the future, but not only for the future. The City of God is always coming down from God: that is its nature. God is always

'In this world millions of people suffer through lack of water . . . or die from hunger . . . the City of God has everything needed for eternal life' (p. 177).

Even where water is fairly plentiful, millions of families have the daily burden of carrying it home from a river or lake – like this little girl somewhere in South-east Asia. What are the 'things' you yourself think are 'needed' for eternal life?

the God who is coming. His dwelling is always with men and women. Even now we are His people, and even now this is the greatest joy.

STUDY SUGGESTIONS

CONTENT

1. In which two ways does this second part of the vision differ from the first?
2. What does it mean, that there is no temple in the City?
3. Which two purposes does the mention of the nations serve?
4. What is the significance of the river of the water of life?
5. What is the significance of the tree of life?
6. What is the true significance of this realistic picture?

BIBLE

7. Compare the description of the New Jerusalem in this part of John's vision with the description of Paradise in Genesis 2. What does this comparison teach us?

APPLICATION

8. What important contribution can this part of John's vision make to our preaching of the gospel?

22.6–21
Conclusion

SUMMARY

22.6: A testimony to the trustworthiness of the Revelation.

22.7a: Christ's promise that He is coming speedily.

22.7b: How fortunate are those who receive the promise of this book and take it to heart!

22.8–9: John repeats his mistake of wanting to worship the angel who showed him the Revelation, and again he is told to worship God.

22.10–12: A warning that the time is short.

22.14–15: How fortunate are those who 'wash their robes' and are allowed to enter the City of God! But John adds a warning to those who do not want to 'wash their robes'.

22.16: Another assurance that Jesus Himself sent His messenger to give John the Revelation.

22.17: A final invitation to come, and take 'the water of life', which is offered freely.

22.18–19: A warning not to tamper with this book.

22.20: A final assurance by Jesus that He is coming speedily, and a prayer for His coming.

22.21: The blessing.

NOTES

22.6. And he said to me. 'He' must mean the angel who had shown John the Revelation, see note on 1.1.

The Lord, the God of the spirits of the prophets. God himself had sent the angel to John, the same God who had inspired the prophets.

22.7. And behold, I am coming soon. These are words of Jesus. The punctuation in the RSV suggests that the angel spoke these words, but if so, the angel would be passing on Jesus's promise.

22.8. I fell down to worship at the feet of the angel. It is not clear whether John repeated his earlier mistake (see 19.10), or whether he thought it necessary to repeat what he had written before, or whether a later copyist inserted the repetition.

22.10. Do not seal up the words, that is to say, Do write this Revelation down, and pass it on. John must not regard the visions as a wonderful religious experience for his own benefit. The faithful must be assured, and the unfaithful must be warned, that the world is moving towards the end appointed by God.

The time is near. Before they know where they are, the Christians will face persecution, and they will need the comfort of this book.

22.1. Let the evildoer still do evil . . . The Christians must not expect an immediate end to the troubles of the world, and while the righteousness of the faithful and the holiness of the saints continue, so will the wrongs of the evildoers.

22.12. To repay every one for what he has done. A reminder that, though our salvation depends entirely on God's grace, we must not take His grace for granted.

22.13. The beginning and the end. The end is not an event but a person. The Christian hope is not that certain events will take place at the end of time, but that Jesus will come, that same Jesus whom we know so well.

22.15. Outside. We may well ask if there will be any 'outside' in the world to come. But John simply meant that those mentioned will not be 'inside'. They will not be in the heavenly City.

Dogs. It may seem strange to some people who like dogs, that 'dogs' should have been used as a term of abuse. They would approve of Luther's assuring his little boy that there will be lots of dogs in heaven. But such considerations are beside the point. In Near Eastern cities people were familiar with the sight of packs of scavenging dogs, very much as they still are in many cities in India and elsewhere today; and 'dogs' had become a term for all that was unclean. Even John's Greek readers, who regarded their own dogs as faithful friends, were familiar with that term, and would be thinking, not of the animals, but of ungodly people.

22.16. I Jesus have sent my angel to you. 'You' is plural (which is clear in John's Greek, but cannot be shown in the English translation). This means that the Revelation is meant not only for John but for the whole Church.

22.17. The Spirit and the Bride say, 'Come'. The Spirit, who speaks through the prophets, and the Church, pray for Jesus to come.

And let him who is thirsty come . . . This is an invitation from Jesus.

22.18. I warn every one . . . Books were copied by hand, and copyists often added comments of their own, or left out words which they thought were unsuitable. A good example is the story of the woman taken in adultery (John 7.53—8.11), which was known in the Church, but had not been written down in any of the gospels. A copyist added it to the Gospel according to John (and, we may add, it is fortunate that he did, for it tells us something about Jesus that we ought to know). John here warns copyists, not to add anything of their own, nor to leave anything out.

INTERPRETATION

John has come to the end of the Revelation. His book was meant for a wider readership, but it was written in the form of a letter to seven Churches in Asia, and John concludes with the sort of last remarks which people put at the end of their letters.

He thus assures his readers that he did not write the Revelation by his own authority. It was Jesus who gave him this Revelation, and urged him to write the book, even though He did use an angel to show it all to John.

John also uses the opportunity to repeat the invitation to the wedding feast of the Lamb (see 19.1–6), here given as an invitation to come and take the water of life, which God freely offers to His people, and also to warn against the peril of refusing the invitation.

Two points need some special comment. Many readers feel that John's warning, that in passing on his message to others we should not add to his words, nor leave any out, is not very helpful. Some people even think that it makes John *less*, not more, trustworthy. But John was well aware of the habit of some copyists to add comments of their own, or to leave some things out. People in the ancient world did not think that this mattered very much. But when people were dealing with Holy

Scripture, it was a different matter. So the Jewish scribes were very careful, when they made copies of the Scripture. Once they were sure that a book was Holy Scripture, they took great care, not to alter, or to add, or to leave out, a single word. Now John had received a Revelation directly from Christ. So he wanted to make sure that nothing was altered, or added, or left out.

Something further must also be said about the promise of the Lord's coming. This promise caused much confusion in the early Church, and has done so ever since. For example, it seems that Paul at one time hoped he might live to see the day of the Lord's coming, but he learned to live with the realization that this was not to be (it is interesting to see, in 2 Cor. 4.7—5.10, how he learned to resign himself to this). Luke found it necessary to remind his readers that Jesus had said that no one knew the day of the Lord's coming (Acts 1.7); and the writer of 2 Peter took considerable trouble to explain that the delay of the second coming did not mean that the Lord would not keep His promise (2 Peter 3.3–13).

The structure of the Revelation showed that the end of the present world was not as near as some people expected, and that the end of John's world would not be the end of the world as a whole. We must therefore see the promise that Jesus is coming speedily in the light of the repeated assertion that there will be delay.

Seen in this light, the promise serves a double purpose.

1. It is given in the present tense: 'I am coming' (vv. 7, 12, 20), which means, not merely that Jesus will come, but that He is actually on His way. Also, the word which the RSV translates 'soon' means 'fast', 'speedily'; it refers to speed rather than a short time. Jesus is hurrying towards His people, and any delay is not due to any wish of His to keep us waiting. This assurance that He is on His way was on the one hand a warning to people who had made themselves comfortable in the present world, like the Churches in Sardis and Laodicea. And on the other hand it was a word of comfort to people who were waiting eagerly for their Lord.

2. But this promise is also a reminder that Christ is always 'He who comes'. Christ is the coming of God among us. We have got into the habit of speaking of His 'first coming', his advent, when He was born in Bethlehem, and His 'second coming', his *parousia*, when He comes at the end of time. But actually the two words, the Greek *parousia* and the Latin *adventus*, mean exactly the same: 'coming', and the New Testament writers do not use such terms as 'first' and 'second' coming. In fact these terms hide the truth that Jesus is He who comes. He came among us when He was born in Bethlehem; He will come on the Last Day. But He also came when He was raised from the dead and appeared to His disciples; and He also comes among us now, particularly when we meet at His table. The word *maranatha*, 'Come Lord', was part of the earliest

known eucharistic liturgy (Didache 10.6); and today some Churches still use those same words, 'Come Lord Jesus', in their Communion services to welcome Christ among His people (though most Churches use the *Benedictus*, 'Blessed is He who comes in the name of the Lord').

Christ is He who comes. He is on His way to come speedily. Therefore, we can be confident and should be patient. And if we do not have the patience to wait till the end – we probably shall not be on this earth that long anyway – He is ready to come now. He comes speedily, wherever people meet in His name (see Matt. 18.20). No one has to travel far to meet Him.

STUDY SUGGESTIONS

WORDS

1. What is the precise meaning of the word translated 'soon'?
2. Explain what is meant by the assertion that Jesus 'is coming'.

CONTENT

3. What do Christians expect at the end of time?
4. What is the purpose of vv. 6 and 16?
5. What is the purpose of the word 'Come' in v. 17?
6. What is the purpose of the warning in v. 18?

BIBLE

7. In what ways do Jesus's words in Mark 13.32 and Acts 1.7 link up with the message of the Revelation?
8. In what ways do Jesus's words in Mark 13 and Matthew 25 (other than the words in Mark 13.32) link up with the message of the Revelation, especially chapters 20—22? (If you can, point to particular verses in the Mark and Matthew chapters which carry the same message as particular verses in the Revelation chapters.)

APPLICATION

9. Comment on the connection between vv. 17 and 20 and the Christian life in general and the Eucharist in particular.
10. In what other ways, if any, besides those listed in Matt. 25.35–40, do you think we can 'see' and 'minister to' Jesus in the world today?

Postscript

Having come to the end of the Revelation, we have found that it is not, after all, such an obscure book. There are difficult passages in it, and a few details about which even the experts are not quite sure, but it is not too difficult to see what John wanted to convey. Now that we have some idea of the circumstances, the problems, and the needs of the people for whom John wrote, his message has become clear.

Also, we have discovered how relevant this book is to us, who live so much later. We may find it surprising that a book which was written so long ago, and which was planned so precisely for the needs of particular people at that time, should also meet our needs today. But it is chiefly through understanding the differences as well as the similarities between the situation of people then and our own situation, that we can hear the Revelation speaking to us.

As long as the stars in the right hand of Christ remain to us a strange symbol for the angels of the Churches (1.16, 20), we shall never get the point of that vision. Once we know that they were a familiar symbol, representing the powers which were believed to govern the world, the picture becomes clearer. But to grasp the real meaning we must learn that we are *not* dealing with outdated and unfamiliar beliefs.

For one thing, there are still millions of people who believe as firmly in the power of the stars to affect our lives as people did twenty centuries ago. And even more important, the seven stars symbolize realities which really do have great power. The 'gods' which many people worship in this modern age have different names, and some of them, though not all, are different gods. But people do worship them, and these gods are powerful. We should remember that, whatever a person worships, and whatever he allows to rule his life, is his god, 'For where your treasure is, there will your heart be also' (Matt. 6.21). We should consider, not only what the ancient gods were called and what their temples looked like, but how they affected the whole of life, how they dominated the town hall and the market place, the sportsfield and the theatre, the dinner table and the doctor's surgery, the marriage bed and the brothel, the means of communication and people's livelihood. Then we shall see how closely they resemble the powers that govern life today. And this in turn will help us to recognize the importance of John's vision of the Lord, who has them in His hand, and makes them serve His purpose, in spite of their hostility.

Similarly it is important that we should see how the beast described in Revelation 13 refers specifically to the Roman Empire, for only then can we see its relevance to us. There will never be another Empire quite like Rome. Whatever people may say, history does not repeat itself. Nero was unique, and we should be thankful for that. Yet all totalitarian regimes have certain family characteristics. They are all different, yet in a deeper sense they are all the same. They may have different ideologies, but the difference is only on the surface. Having a picture of the tyrant whom John actually had in mind helps us to see the family likeness in other, greater or smaller, beasts, whether they are called Adolf Hitler or Joseph Stalin, or Pol Pot or Idi Amin, or whatever their name may be.

If we look to the terrors of chapter 9 for an accurate description of future events, we shall fail to see what kind of events John had in mind. But once we realize that John saw terrors which actually existed, and do exist, not in the natural world but in the sick minds of men and women, then we shall see the dangers which are present in some of the pseudo-religions of his days and of our own time, and in such dangerous practices as drug-taking.

If we misunderstand the vision in which John saw, after the fall of Babylon/Rome, a period of peace during which Christ and the saints were to reign on earth, and interpret this vision purely as a prediction of future events, then we miss the challenge contained in the words, 'and they reigned'. When the Church is at peace and even in a position to influence events on earth, then it is the task of Christians to try and ensure that the will of Christ is done. Christians will not always agree about the best means to achieve that. But there should be no disagreement among Christians that, whenever the Church has the opportunity to do so, its members should be in the forefront of those people who work for justice and freedom.

In the past the Church claimed proudly, and rightly, that it was the task of governments to render obedience to Christ in their policies and in their actions. That claim was made, not only by powerful Churches, but also by very small minority groups. They were upholding, not the power of the Church, but the authority of Christ the King. Today most Churches are quite content if the authorities recognize the freedom of people's conscience, and ask for nothing more, They may join in with the cry for 'human rights' and 'civil liberties', and rightly so, but they forget how empty such slogans are, if they are divorced from the will of God. God alone really cares for people. He is the One who vindicates people's rights and champions their freedom. Only obedience to His will can make the world a fit place for human beings to live in.

Thus one of the first things the Revelation did then, and can do now, is to help people to see the dangers ahead of them, as well as the opportunities. The dangers and evils of the twentieth century are different from those of the first, but there is a family likeness, so we should be able to see them, and to be on our guard.

We must also be prepared to suffer. The power of evil is real, and it is really evil. We are following a crucified Lord, and, since faithfulness to the gospel implies suffering, we must be prepared to take up our cross.

But God is in command. Again and again John told his readers of a vision of the redeemed, and so reminded them of their own redemption. Whatever their fate in the days that lay ahead, they were in God's hand, and their future was secure. This too is as true today as it was two thousand years ago.

Judging by the way in which some Christians act, one would think that they follow a God who is in retreat. We say that we believe in God, the Father, the Almighty, but some of us act as if we do not believe any such thing. There have always been people like that, and there were some among the first readers of the Revelation. They needed to learn, as we need to learn again, that God is not in retreat. If you fear that God has had His time, you are wrong. It is the devil who has no future. That is why he is in such a hurry. Christ, on the other hand, has all the time in the world, and all eternity as well. He can afford to be patient. He has already gained the victory. His disciples are not fighting for a lost cause. They are following Him who has already won.

The Revelation also reminds us *who* this is who has gained the victory. The Victor is He who loves us, and has redeemed us by His own blood. The destiny of the world and of our own lives is not determined by mere chance or by a dark fate, nor is it subject to some despotic and capricious god or power. It is in the hand of this Jesus whom we know, who has shared our life with us, who has carried our burdens, even the burden of our sins, and who died for us on the Cross. This Jesus has the whole world in His hand.

So be confident and patient. And remember, as John reminded us, if we have not the patience to wait till the end, He is ready to come now, wherever people meet in His name.

Appendix
The First Roman Emperors

48–44 BC: Julius Caesar (*Caius Iulius Caesar*), a brilliant general, and a firm but tolerant and humane ruler. He came to power after a vicious civil war, as the leader of the 'democratic' party, and was given the power of a dictator for a limited time only. It was he who granted the Jews exemption from the obligation to worship the state gods, a privilege which was extremely important to the Jews, and which a century later also made it possible for Christians to preach the gospel freely. He was assassinated in 44 BC.

30 BC–AD 14: Augustus (*Caius Iulius Caesar Octavianus Augustus*), Julius Caesar's adopted son, came to power after another civil war. He was granted powers similar to those given to his adopted father, and they were renewed regularly until his death. By this time Rome, though still nominally a republic, had in fact become an autocratic monarchy.

29 BC: Divine honours were paid to Augustus for the first time in Pergamum; the custom soon spread.

7/4 BC: The birth of Christ.

AD 14–17: Tiberius (*Tiberius Claudius Nero*), suspicious and cruel, but nevertheless a reasonably good ruler. He caused much suffering to individuals in Rome, but in the provinces there was not much mismanagement. John 19.12 gives a hint of his suspicious character.

27/30: The crucifixion and resurrection of Jesus.

31/33: Martyrdom of Stephen; conversion of Paul.

37–41: Caligula (*Caius Caesar Augustus Germanicus*), vicious and cruel, probably insane. His mad government, however, mainly affected Rome. He was assassinated before he could do much harm in the provinces.

39: Caligula set himself up as a god.

41: He ordered a cult statue of himself to be set up in the temple at Jerusalem but because of his death the order was not carried out.

41–45: Claudius (*Tiberius Claudius Drusus Nero Germanicus*), an eccentric but good ruler. He put the finances of the Empire on a sound basis, and reorganized the administration. During his reign some disturbance took place among Jews in Rome, probably between Christian and non-Christian Jews. Some of them were banished from Rome, which may have put the Church there under some strain. Claudius's friendship with Herod Agrippa I, the ruler of Judea, gave the latter the opportunity to persecute the Church in Jerusalem.

44: Martyrdom of James the son of Zebedee in Jerusalem.

54–68: Nero (*Lucius Domitius Ahenobarbus Nero Claudius Drusus Germanicus*) started his reign well, but came under the influence of bad advisers, and became mentally deranged. His misrule caused great hardship throughout the Empire.

61: Revolt of Boudicca in Britain.

62: Parthian invasion of the Empire. Armenia came under Parthian influence. Food was scarce, and there was considerable inflation.

64: A large part of Rome was destroyed by fire. Nero was suspected of arson, but found a scapegoat in the Roman Christians. This led to a terrible persecution, in which many Christians were put to death; Peter and Paul were probably among the victims.

65: Laodicea was destroyed by an earthquake.

67: The Jews in Palestine rose in revolt; Vespasian was sent to quell the revolt.

68–69: Galba, Otho and **Vitellius** each reigned for a few months.

69–79: Vespasian (*Titus Flavius Vespasianus*) created order in the chaos created by Nero's mismanagement.

70: Vespasian's son Titus took and destroyed Jerusalem. Large numbers of Jews were crucified. Jews outside Palestine were left in peace, but the tax which every Jew had to pay to the Temple was transferred to the temple of Jupiter in Rome.

71–73: Large numbers of Jewish captives were sold into slavery.

73: The fall of Masada ended the Jewish War.

79–81: Titus (*Titus Flavius Vespasianus*, like his father).

79: An eruption of Vesuvius destroyed Pompei and other cities.

80: Opening of the Flavian Amphitheatre ('Coliseum'), where later many Christian martyrs were killed in the arena.

81–96: Domitian (*Titus Flavius Domitianus*), Vespasian's second son, was at first an effective and successful ruler, but, like Nero, became more and more despotic.

82: Large fires in Rome.

88: The Empire was attacked by tribes from the Steppes.

89: Domitian demanded to be addressed as 'Lord and god'.

92: Several people were put to death for refusing to pay divine honours to Domitian, among them some prominent citizens, probably also some Jews, and perhaps some Christians.

96–98: Nerva (*Marcus Cocceius Nerva*), a wise, tolerant, and effective ruler. During his short reign he changed the government of the Empire, and the rules of succession, and enabled it to survive several more centuries.

98–117: Trajan (*Marcus Ulpius Traianus*), a very successful ruler, and by his own standards a just and tolerant man. Yet it was he who started the systematic suppression of the Christian faith.

108: Martyrdom of Ignatius of Antioch.

112: Correspondence between Trajan and Pliny about how to deal with Christians.

114: Successful campaign against the Parthians.

117–138: Hadrian (*Publius Aelius Hadrianus*).

132–135: Jewish revolt under Simon Bar-Kochba.

135: The Jews were banned from Palestine. Jerusalem was rebuilt as a Roman city, and renamed Aelia Capitolina. Actually some Jewish communities in Palestine did manage to remain, but officially Jews remained banned from Palestine until the country was conquered by the Arabs in 638.

Key to Study Suggestions

Introduction

1. See p. 8, paras 2, 3.
2. See p. 2.
3. See p. 3, para. 6.
4. See p. 5, paras 3, 4.
5. See p. 7, paras 1–3.
6. See p. 10, paras 2, 5.
7. See p. 8, paras 3, 4.
8. See p. 8, paras 4, 5.
9. See p. 8, para. 6.
10. Paul meant to say that the gospel shows what God's righteousness is like (different from human righteousness), and that to us the righteousness of God means the justification of the sinner.
13. See p. 9, paras 4–6.
14. See pp. 10, 11.

1.1–8

1. See p. 16, note on 'Priests'.
2. See p. 17, note on 'The Almighty'.
3. See p. 17, para. 1 of the interpretation.
4. See p. 17, last para.
5. See p. 18, para. 4.
6. See p. 18, para. 7.
7. See p. 19, para. 2.
8. Pss 72.18–19; 106.48; 135.21; Matt. 6.13; Luke 2.14; Rom. 11.32–36; 16.27 are all doxologies (some interpreters would also include Ps. 29.1,2).
9. See p. 18, para. 2, lines 7–11.
10. Various Churches would give different answers to this question, and students should find out, not only what the views of their own Churches are, but also those of other Churches in the area where they live. But see page 16, note on 'Priests', lines 11–14.

Special Note A: Angels

Gen. 21.15–21: The angel speaks on God's behalf (note v.17).

Gen. 22.1–13: The angel speaks for the LORD.

Judges 6.11–18: The angel carries a message from God.

Ps.103.20: Angels surround God in heaven, where they listen to His words and carry out His will; their task as messengers is not mentioned.

Matt. 26.53: Angels are ready to carry out God's will.

Luke 1.11: The angel Gabriel is God's messenger.

Luke 1.26: Here too he carries a message from God.

Acts 11.11–18: Again the angel is God's messenger.

Acts 12.6–11: The angel carries out God's plan.

1.9–20

1. See p. 24, note on 1.13.
2. See p. 25, note on 'Death and Hades'.
3. The mystery of the seven stars is that they are not what they seem to be: they seem to be a threat to the Church (for they are the 'gods' of this world), but in the hand of Christ they must serve the good of the Church.
4. See pp. 22, 23, notes on 1.11.
5. See 1.12.
6. See p. 25, last para., and also pp. 26, 27.
7. See p. 27, paras 4, 5.
8. See p. 27, last para.
9. Isaiah 6 and Ezekiel 1 describe visions of God. This is a vision of Christ. It is true that John speaks about Christ in the same terms as he does about God the Father, but he emphasizes that He who appeared to him was the One who died and was raised from the dead. Note, however, that John's vision shared with Ezekiel's the human form, not mentioned in Isaiah's; and that both John and Isaiah saw Him who appeared to them in the midst of His people (among the lampstands, and in the Temple), whereas Ezekiel's vision remained remote.

2.1–7

1. See p. 29, note on 2.2.
2. See p. 31, paras 7, 8.
3. See p. 30, note on 'The paradise of God'.
4. See p. 31, paras 1–3.
5. See p. 31, paras 4, 5.
6. The 'patient endurance' in 2.2.

2.8–11

1. Here and in Jas. 1.12 the test or testing means a trial of faith, which will show whether or not a person is loyal to his Lord; in 1 John 4.i. the testing means an examination of the teaching of 'inspired' preachers, in order to find out whether or not their teaching agrees with the gospel.
2. See p. 33, notes on 2.9.
3. By the hands of the authorities.
4. Romans 9–11 can help us to remember that God has not forsaken His people Israel.
5. See p. 36, paras 2, 3.

2.12–17

1. See p. 38, note on 2.13.
2. The sword identifies Christ as the Judge, who will pass sentence on those who mislead others by their teaching.
3. See p. 40, para. 4.
4. (a) In practical terms there seems to be little difference, but in Rom. 14 the emphasis lies on 'accepting one another', on the understanding that the conduct of the 'strong' is the better way; in 1 Cor. 8 and 13

Paul is much more concerned with the risks involved in sharing in non-Christian religious customs.

(b) Jesus was not actually speaking about this question at all, but Luke may well have thought on the same lines as Paul.

2.18–29

1. See p. 42, note on 'prophetess'; also p. 8, paras 4, 5.
2. In spite of 'Jezebel''s teaching, this is a sound Church.
3. See pp. 42, 44, numbered paras 1–3.
4. See p. 42, first para. of the interpretation.
5. See p. 42, note on 2.26.
6. The historic Jezebel had led her husband, and through him God's people, astray.

3.1–6

1. See p. 46, note on 'The book of life'.
2. See pp. 46, 47, first para. of introduction, and p. 47, two last paras.
3. See p. 46, note on 3.2.
4. See p. 46, note on 3.3.
5. See p. 46, note on 3.5.
6. Jesus acknowledges those who are His own; but those who only pretend to be His disciples He does not want to know.

3.7–13

1. See p. 49, notes on 3.7 and 3.8.
2. See p. 50, para. 2. of the interpretation.
3. They have believed the words of Jesus, remembered them, acted on them, and remained faithful.
4. See 2.2, 7, 13.
5. See p. 34, note on 'The crown of life'.
6. See pp. 49, 50, note on 'The new Jerusalem . . .'.
7. The 'pillars' in Gal. 1.9 are means of support, those here are lasting monuments.
8. They are all about doors which only God can open.

3.14–22

1. See pp. 51, 52, note on 3.14.
2. See p. 51, summary of 3.15–17.
3. See p. 53, para. 1.
4. The words, 'It is finished', or rather, 'It is accomplished' (NEB, JB), express the certainty that by His death on the cross Jesus had overcome all obstacles and accomplished His task.

4.1–11

1. See p. 61, para. 2.
2. See p. 61, para. 1.
3. See p. 58, note on 'An open door'.
4. See p. 61, para. 3.
5. See p. 46, note on 'White garments'.

6. See p. 62, para. 2.
7. See p. 62, para. 3.
8. See p. 59, notes on 'Four living creatures'.
9. See p. 62, para. 5.
10. The very considerable differences show that John was not simply building up pictures from things which he had read. Some may see here an indication that John actually saw the visions which he described.
11. See p. 62, para. 3, last lines.
12. See p. 62, para. 4.

5.1–14
1. See p. 64, note on 'A Lamb', and p. 65, notes on 'Blood'.
2. See p. 66, para. 3 of the interpretation.
3. See pp. 63, 64, note on 'A scroll', and p. 66, para. 2 of the interpretation.
4. See p. 66, para. 4 of the interpretation.
5. See p. 67, paras 1–3.
6. See p. 67, para. 2.
7. See p. 64, note on 'As though it had been slain', and p. 67, para. 2.
8. See p. 68, para. 1.
9. See 5.13.
10. David had been Israel's most successful king, he was also a man after God's own heart (1 Sam. 13.14), and was regarded as the prototype of the Messiah.
11. 'Like a lamb that is led to the slaughter, so he opened not his mouth', and 'the LORD has laid on him the iniquity of us all'.
12. See p. 67, para. 2.

Special Note C: Numbers in the Revelation
2. ONE: see p. 69, para. 2.
   TWO: see p. 69, para. 3.
   THREE: see p. 69, para. 4.
   SIX: see p. 69, para. 7.
   SEVEN: see p. 69, para. 6.
   TWELVE: see p. 70, para. 2.
3. See p. 70, paras 3, 4.

6.1–8
1. See pp. 71, 72, notes on 6.2, 6.4, 6.5, and 6.7.
2. See p. 71, note on 6.1.
3. See p. 71, note on 6.2; p. 73, para. 5.
4. See p. 73.
5. See p. 73, last para.
6. The chief difference is that the horsemen of the Revelation serve a purpose which is entirely different from that of the chariots in Zechariah's vision.

6.9–11
1. See p. 76, note on 'Souls'.
2. See p. 76, note on 6.9.

3. Vindication of the innocent means that justice is done to the innocent.
4. Justice is done to the innocent rather than to the guilty (there is no mention of any punishment for the guilty woman).
5. It gave them the prospect of vindication after their own trials.

6.12–17
1. See p. 79, para. 2 of the interpretation.
2. Few natural phenomena are as frightening as a volcanic eruption.
3. See p. 78, note on 6.15.
4. See Genesis 3.17–19.

7.1–17
1. 'Israel' could mean the Israelite nation, or the people of God. See p. 81, notes on 7.4.
2. See pp. 82, 83, note on 7.17.
3. See p. 80, summary of 7.1–3, and note on 'The four winds of the earth'.
4. See pp. 80, 81, note on 7.2.
5. See p. 83, last para.
6. See p. 84, para. 3, lines 3–5.
7. See p. 84, para. 2.
8. He is both the victim of their sins and their King.
9. See p. 81, note on 7.4, para. 1.
10. See p. 82, note on 7.16.
12. See p. 84, para. 3.

8.1
1. See p. 69, para. 6; and p. 86, para. 1 of the interpretation.
2. See p. 86, para. 1 of the interpretation.
3. See p. 87, two last lines.

8.2–13
1. See p. 89, note on 8.11.
2. See p. 90, paras 2, 3.
3. See p. 89, second note on 8.11.
4. See p. 90, para. 5.
5. They led up the deliverance of God's people.
6. See p. 90, para. 3.
7. See p. 90, para. 3, last two lines.

9.1–21
1. See p. 92, note on 9.1, first para.
2. (a) See p. 93, note on 9.4.
   (b) See p. 95, para. 4.
   (c) See p. 94, lines 3–10.
3. See p. 93, note on 'What looked like crowns of gold'.
4. See p. 94, paras 2, 3 of the interpretation.
5. See p. 94, lines 1–10.

10.1–11
1. The command to prophesy is an order, not only generally to preach the gospel, but also specifically to make known the visions of the Revelation.
2. See p. 97, note on 10.1
3. See p. 98, para. 2 of the interpretation.
4. (a) See p. 98, para. 3 of the interpretation.
   (b) See p. 99, para. 2.
7. See p. 99, para. 3.

11.1–14
1. The word 'temple' can mean either the actual shrine, the 'house of the god', or the whole temple precinct, including the courts and various outbuildings; but the Greek word used by John can only mean the house of god, or, here, the House of God. See also p. 100, note on 'The temple', and p. 103, para. 5.
2. See p. 100, note on 'The temple'; also p. 88, note on 8.3.
3. See p. 102, paras 1 and 5 of the interpretation, p. 103, paras 5, 6, and p. 104, para. 2.
4. See p. 102, para. 2. of the interpretation, and p. 103, para. 5.
5. See pp. 100, 101, note on 11.3
6. (a) See p. 102, last para.
   (b) See p. 103, paras 2–4.
   (c) See p. 101, note on 11.5, 6.
7. See p. 104, para. 3.
8. See p. 69, para. 3.
9. See p. 103, last para., and p. 104, para. 1.
10. See p. 102, note on 11.13.

11.15–19
1. The Christ is the legitimate King, appointed by god, to whom absolute obedience is due; see p. 106, note on 11.15.
2. See p. 108, paras 2, 3 of the interpretation.
3. See p. 108, para. 4.
4. See pp. 106, 107, note on 11.18.
5. It gave John and his readers real hope and, indeed, certainty.

12.1–17
1. See p. 112, para. 1.
2. See p. 112, para. 2.
3. See p. 112, para. 2.
4. See p. 112, para. 3.
5. See p. 112, paras 4, 5.
6. See p. 113, para. 2.
7. See p. 113, para. 2.
8. See p. 111, note on 12.16.
9. (a) Luke 10.18 links the defeat of Satan with the preaching of the gospel.
   (b) Matt. 18.18 links eternal life with the preaching of the gospel.

Special Note D: The Devil and his Works
1. See p. 94, para. 2 of the interpretation; p. 115, para. 6.
2. See p. 115, para. 2.
3. See p. 114, para. 2; p. 115, paras 2, 3.
4. See p. 114, para. 3.
5. See p. 115, para. 3.
6. See p. 115, para. 7.
8. See p. 115, para. 4.
9. See p. 115, para. 7; p. 116, para. 3.
10. See p. 115, para. 6.
11. See p. 112, para. 3.

13.1–18
1. *Authority* is the right to enforce obedience; *power* is the ability to enforce obedience; a *throne* is a symbol of power.
   (But the 'authority' in v. 2 was an assumed authority, and not a right.)
2. (a) He was like his master the dragon.
   (b) See p.121, para. 5.
3. See p. 119, note on 13.3.
4. See p. 121, last para.
5. See p. 121, para. 6.
6. See p. 120, note on 'Lamb that was slain'; p. 46, note on 'The book of life'.
7. (a) He was like a lamb, suggesting *the* Lamb.
   (b) See p. 122, para. 3.
   (c) See p. 122, paras 4–6; p. 123, para. 1.
8. See p. 124.
9. Romans 13 gives instruction about the duty of Christians in view of the God-given task of government; Revelation 13 warns of the dangers of corrupt government and tyranny.

14.1–5
1. See p. 126, paras 2, 3 of the interpretation.
2. See p. 125, note on 14.1.
3. The words '*first* fruits' suggest that there are more to follow.
4. See pp. 125, 126, note on 'First fruits'.

14.6–20
1. See p. 128, note on 'Gospel'.
2. See v. 6.
3. See pp. 128, 129, note on 14.8.
4. See p. 129, notes on 'The wine of her impure passion', and 'The wine of God's wrath'.
5. See p. 130, last para.
6. See p. 131, paras 3, 5.
7. See p. 131, para. 4.
8. See p. 131, para. 4.
9. See p. 129, note on 14.15.

15.1–8

1. 'Just and true are thy ways'; 'Thy judgements have been revealed'.
2. 'All nations shall come and worship thee'.
3. See p. 135, note on 15.8, last two lines.
4. See p. 135, note on 'No one could enter', last two lines.
5. See p. 134, note on 15.3.
6. See p. 134, note on 15.5.

16.1–21

1. See pp. 137, 138, note on 16.16.
2. See p. 138, para. 2 of the interpretation.
3. See p. 131, para. 4.
4. See p. 136, last two lines.
5. See p. 139, para. 2.
6. See p. 139, para. 4.
7. See p. 138, para. 2 of the interpretation.
8. See p. 137, note on 16.14.
9. See p. 123, para. 1, and p. 137, note on 16.13.

17.1–18

1. See p. 126, para. 3 of the interpretation; p. 140, note on 17.1.
2. See p. 140, note on 17.3.
3. See p. 142, para. 2.
4. See p. 142, para. 2, lines 4–8.
5. See p. 120, note on 'Six hundred and sixty-six', p. 142, para. 3.
6. See p. 142, last para.

18.1—19.5

1. Arrogance and pride are the chief sins mentioned, but the arrogance led to the persecution of God's people.
2. See p. 144, note on 18.13.
3. See p. 146, para. 3.
4. (a) and (b) The merchants in Revelation 13, and people in the ancient world generally regarded slaves as things; the laws in Exodus 21.1–11 demand that slaves be regarded as human beings, and Abraham and Paul did regard them so.
   (c) Slavery should have been outlawed long before it was.
5. See p. 145, note on 19.1.

19.6–10

1. See p. 148, para. 3 of the interpretation.
2. See p. 148, para. 4 of the interpretation.
3. See p. 150, para. 2.
4. See p. 147, note on 19.7.
5. See p. 148, note on 19.10.
6. See p. 148, note on 'The spirit of prophecy'.
7. By not answering the invitation when it came, they lost the opportunity to be present.
9. See p. 151, para. 4.

19.11–21

1. (a) God speaking directly.
   (b) The Word made flesh in Jesus Christ.
   (c) The word of God spoken by prophets, apostles and preachers.
2. See p. 152, interpretation, and p. 153, para. 1.
3. See p. 153, last line.
4. See p. 153, para. 2.
5. See p. 152, note on 'The wine press of the fury...'
6. See p. 153, para. 6.
7. See p. 153, para. 2.

20.1–6

1. See p. 156, paras 1, 2 of the interpretation.
2. See p. 156, para. 2 of the interpretation.
3. See p. 155, note on 'They came to life...'; p. 157, para. 5.
4. See p. 157, last para.
5. See p. 155, note on 'A thousand years'.
6. See pp. 156, 157, numbered paras 1, 2, and 3.

20.7–10

1. See p. 160, para. 2 of the interpretation.
2. See p. 159, note on 'The nations...'
3. See p. 160, note on 20.9.
4. See p. 160, note on 20.10.
5. See p. 160, last para.
6. There are considerable differences, but both emphasize that tribulations will be recurring right until the end.

20.11–15

1. See p. 163, paras 3–5.
2. See p. 25, note on 1.18.
3. Jesus's words were meant as a warning, and emphasized the importance of what we do, or do not do, in this life. Paul, on the other hand, emphasized the freedom of God's grace.
4. See p. 163, para. 4; p. 164, para. 2.
5. See p. 163, last para.; p. 164, para. 2.

21.1–8

1. See p. 166, note on 21.2.
2. See p. 165, note on 21.1.
3. See p. 167, para. 5.
4. See p. 167, para. 1.
5. See p. 169, para. 1.
6. See p. 166, note on 21.8.
7. John 8.33 explains the relationship between the only Son, and His brothers: His brothers have been set free and adopted.
8. See p. 167, para. 6.
10. See p. 167, para. 4.

21.9–21

1. See p. 173, para. 1.
2. See p. 172, para. 2.
3. See p. 171, note on 21.11.
4. See p. 172, paras 3, 4.
5. See p. 172, para. 1.
6. See p. 172, para. 6.
7. See p. 172, para. 4.

21.22—22.5

1. The City, first referred to as situated on a high mountain, and described in terms of geometry, is now described as a city in an oasis; see also p. 175, para. 1 of the interpretation.
2. See p. 175, para. 3 of the interpretation.
3. See p. 175, paras 4–6 of the interpretation; p. 176, para. 1.
4. See p. 174, note on 22.1.
5. See p. 176, para. 4; p. 177, para. 1.
6. See p. 177, paras 2, 4.

22.6–21

1. See p. 182, para. 5; p. 183, para. 2.
2. See p. 182, para. 6.
3. See p. 180, note on 22.13.
4. These verses assert the trustworthiness of the Revelation.
5. See p. 181, para. 3 of the interpretation.
6. See p. 181, last para.; p. 182, para. 1.
7. See p. 182, para. 2.

Index

Besides the names of people and places, this index lists all the major references to themes and ideas appearing in the Revelation or discussed in the Guide. Bold type indicates the pages where a subject is discussed in detail.